AutoCAD 2020
Beginners Guide
(7th Edition)

CADFolks

Dedication

To all technical and non-technical audience

Special Thanks to

Employees of CADFolks

Family & Friends

Training and Consulting services by CADFolks

Proper training is one of the most important factors in determining your success. With qualified trainers, we provide training for a variety of applications. Not only do our trainers have industry experience, but they continue to use the software we support in real-world applications. Whether manufacturing, architecture or engineering, our instructors' top credentials, deep industry knowledge and enthusiasm will help you work better and smarter. With our experienced trainers, we can provide online training (in colleges and organizations). The advantages of training with CADFolks are:

• We have industry experts as instructors
• Small classes and personalized attention
• Free technical help upto one year after training (for the same software)
• Flexible time schedule
• Free industry standard course workbook, sample files, and exercises
• Valuable Tips & Tricks

We also provide consulting services in CAD/CAM/CAE domains. We offer companies a comprehensive, tailored range of services facilitating their business and allowing them to launch into new markets rapidly and safely. We have our office in New Delhi from where we cater to the Engineering Design requirements of our global customers. A dynamic team of our experienced engineers and consultants provide the following services.

• CAD/CAM/CAE Services
• Design & Engineering Services
• All type of Mechanical/Automobile/Design Industries - Project consultancy services
• Architecture and building design
• Ready-to-use Software solutions for the Engineering and Manufacturing Industry

For Technical Support, contact us at:
cadfolks@gmail.com, **training@cadfolks.com**
(Resource files are available only on request)

Table of Contents

Title Page
Table of Contents
Preface

Chapter 3: Drawing Aids in AutoCAD — 71

Chapter 4: Editing Tools in AutoCAD — 95

Chapter 5: Multi View Drawings in AutoCAD   139

Chapter 6: Dimensions and Annotations in AutoCAD   161

Chapter 13: Solid Editing Tools & Generating 2D Views   373

Index

Preface

CAD is an abbreviation for Computer-Aided Design. It is the process used to design and draft components on your computer. This process includes creating designs and drawings of the product or system. AutoCAD is a CAD software package developed and marketed by Autodesk Inc. It can be used to create two-dimensional (2D) and three-dimensional (3D) models of products. These models can be transferred to other computer programs for further analysis and testing. In addition, you can convert these computer models into numerical data. This numerical data can be used in manufacturing equipment such as machining centers, lathes, mills, or rapid prototyping machines to manufacture the product.

AutoCAD is one of the first CAD software packages. It was introduced in the year 1982. Since that time, it has become the industry leader among all CAD products. It is the most widely used CAD software. The commands and concepts introduced by AutoCAD are utilized by other systems. As a student, learning AutoCAD provides you with a greater advantage as compared to any other CAD software.

Scope of this Book

The *AutoCAD 2020 Beginners Guide* book provides a learn-by-doing approach for users to learn AutoCAD. It is written for students and engineers who are interested to learn AutoCAD 2020 for creating designs and drawing of components or anyone who communicates through technical drawings as part of their work. The topics covered in this book are as follows:

- Chapter 1, "Introduction to AutoCAD 2020", gives an introduction to AutoCAD. The user interface and terminology are discussed in this chapter.

- Chapter 2, "Drawing Basics in AutoCAD", explores the basic drawing tools in AutoCAD. You will create simple drawings using the drawing tools.

- Chapter 3, "Drawing Aids in AutoCAD", explores the drawing settings that will assist you in creating drawings.

- Chapter 4, "Editing Tools in AutoCAD", covers the tools required to modify drawing objects or create new objects using the existing ones.

- Chapter 5, "Multi View Drawings in AutoCAD", teaches you to create multi view drawings standard projection techniques.

- Chapter 6, "Dimensions and Annotations in AutoCAD", teaches you to apply dimensions and annotations to a drawing.

- Chapter 7, "Parametric Tools in AutoCAD", teaches you to create parametric drawings. Parametric drawings are created by using the logical operations and parameters that control the shape and size of a drawing.

- Chapter 8, "Section Views in AutoCAD", teaches you to create section views of a component. A section view is the inside view of a component when it is sliced.

- Chapter 9, "Blocks, Attributes and Xrefs in AutoCAD", teaches you to create Blocks, Attributes and Xrefs. Blocks are group of objects in a drawing that can be reused. Attributes are notes, or values related to an object. Xrefs are drawing files attached to another drawing.

- Chapter 10, "Layouts and Annotative Objects in AutoCAD", teaches you create layouts and annotative objects. Layouts are the digital counterparts of physical drawing sheets. Annotative objects are dimensions, notes and so on which their sizes with respect to drawing scale.

- Chapter 11, "Templates and Plotting in AutoCAD", teaches you create drawing templates and plot drawings.

- Chapter 12, "3D Modeling Basics in AutoCAD", explores the basic tools to create 3D models.

- Chapter 13, "Solid Editing & Generating 2D Views", covers the tools required to edit solid models and create new objects by using the existing ones.

Chapter 1: Introduction to AutoCAD 2020

In this chapter, you will learn about:

- **AutoCAD user interface**
- **Customizing user interface**
- **Important AutoCAD commands**

Introduction

AutoCAD is legendary software in the world of Computer Aided Designing (CAD). It has completed 36 years by the 2018. If you are a new user of this software, then the time you spend on learning this software will be a wise investment. If you have used previous versions of AutoCAD, you will be able to learn the new enhancements. I welcome you to learn AutoCAD using this book as it provides step-by-step examples to learn various commands and techniques.

System Requirements

The following are system requirements for running AutoCAD smoothly on your system.

- ❖ **Operating System**: Microsoft Windows 7 SP1, Windows 8.1, Windows 10 (64 bit only)
- ❖ **Processor:**
  - ➢ **Basic:** 2.5 to 2.9 GHz
  - ➢ **Recommended:** 3+ GHz processor
- ❖ **RAM:**
  - ➢ 8 GB (16 GB recommended)
- ❖ **Display Resolution**:
  - ➢ **Conventional Displays** - 1920 x 1080 with True Color
  - ➢ **High Resolution & 4K Displays** - Resolutions up to 3840 x 2160 supported on Windows 10, 64-bit systems (with capable display card)
- ❖ **Disc Space:** 6 GB of free space for installation
- ❖ **Browser :** Google Chrome
- ❖ .NET Framework Version 4.7 or later

Starting AutoCAD 2020

To start **AutoCAD 2020**, double-click the **AutoCAD 2020** icon on your Desktop. Alternatively, click **Start > AutoCAD 2020 > AutoCAD 2020**, as shown.

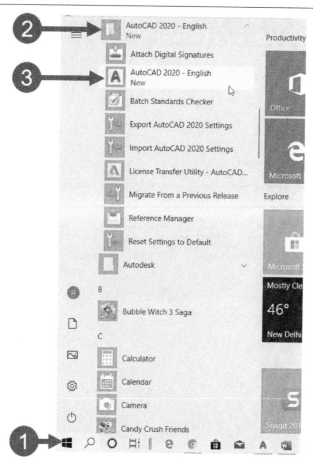

AutoCAD User Interface

When you double-click the AutoCAD 2020 icon on the desktop, the initial screen of AutoCAD 2020 will get displayed, as shown.

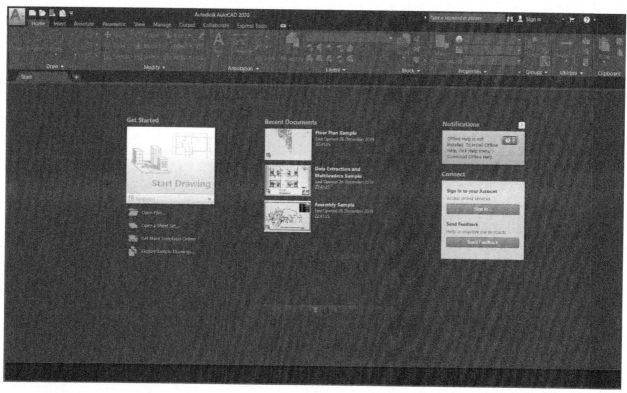

Click on the **Start Drawing** under **Get Started** area of the initial screen to open a drawing file. The drawing file consists of a drawing window, ribbon, menu bar, toolbars, command line, and other screen components, depending on the workspace that you have selected. Note that for the better visibility, we have changed its color which will be discussed further in this chapter.

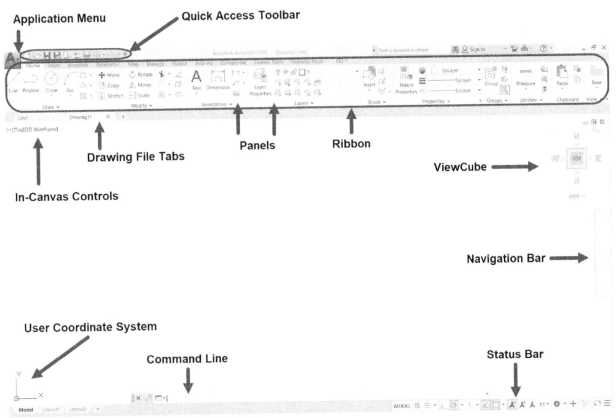

Note: In the above figure, we have changed display colors for the better visibility. The procedure of changing of colors in AutoCAD is discussed next in this chapter.

Changing the Color Scheme in AutoCAD

AutoCAD 2020 is available in two different color schemes: **Dark** and **Light**. You can change the color scheme by using the **Options** dialog box. Click the right mouse button and select **Options** from the shortcut menu. On the **Options** dialog box, click the Display tab and select an option from the Color Scheme drop-down.

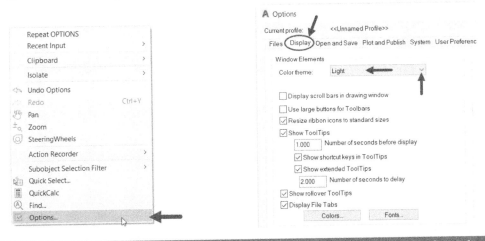

Tip: You can also display the **Options** dialog box after clicking on the **Option** button from the **Application Menu**, as shown below.

Workspaces in AutoCAD

There are three workspaces available in AutoCAD: **Drafting & Annotation**, **3D Basics**, and **3D Modeling**. By default, the **Drafting & Annotation** workspace is activated. You can create 2D drawings in this workspace. You can also activate other workspaces by using the **Workspace** drop-down on the top-left corner or the **Workspace Switching** menu on the lower-right corner of the window.

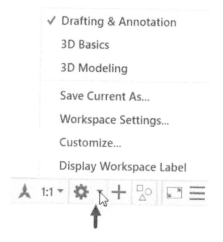

Drafting & Annotation Workspace

This workspace has all the tools to create a 2D drawing. It has a ribbon located at the top of the screen. The ribbon is arranged in a hierarchy of tabs, panels, and tools. Panels such as **Draw**, **Modify**, and **Layers** consist of tools which are grouped based on their usage. Panels in turn are grouped into various tabs. For example, the panels such as **Draw**, **Modify**, are **Layers** are located in the **Home** tab.

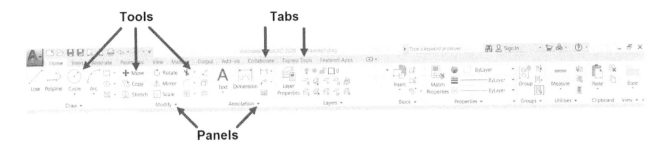

3D Basics and 3D Modeling Workspaces

These workspaces are used to create 3D models. You will learn more about these workspaces in Chapter 12. The other components of the user Interface are discussed next.

Application Menu

The **Application Menu** appears when you click on the icon located at the top left corner of the window. The **Application Menu** consists of a list of self-explanatory menus. You can see a list of recently opened documents or a list of currently opened documents by clicking the **Recent Documents** and **Open Documents** buttons, respectively. The Search Bar is used to search for any command. You can type any keyword in the search bar and find a list of commands related to it.

Quick Access Toolbar

This is located at the top left corner of the window. It consists of commonly used commands such as **New**, **Save**, **Open**, **Save As**, and so on.

File tabs

Files tabs are located below the ribbon. You can switch between different drawing files by using the file tabs. Also, you can easily open a new file by using the + button.

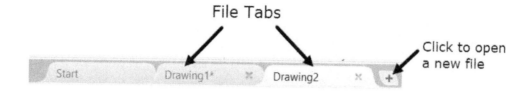

Drawing Window

Drawing window is the blank space located below the file tabs. You can draw objects and create 3D graphics in the drawing window. The top left corner of the drawing window has **In-Canvas Controls**. Using these controls, you can set the orientation and display style of the model.

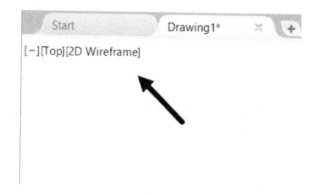

ViewCube

The ViewCube allows you to navigate in the 3D Modeling and 2D drafting environments. Using the ViewCube, you can set the orientation of the model. For example, you can select the top face of the ViewCube to set the orientation to Top. You can click the corner points to set the view to Isometric.

Navigation Bar

The Navigation Bar contains navigation tools such as **Steering wheel**, **Pan**, **Zoom**, **Orbit**, and **ShowMotion**.

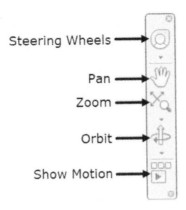

Command line

The command line is located below the drawing window. It is very easy to execute a command using the command line. You can just type the first letter of a command and it lists all the commands starting with that letter. This makes you to invoke commands very easily and increases your productivity.

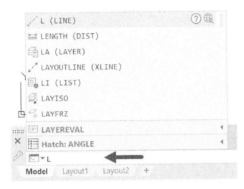

Also, the command line displays the current state of the drawing. It displays various prompts while working with any command. These prompts are series of steps needed to successfully execute a command. For example, when you invoke the **LINE** command, the command line displays a prompt, "Specify the first point". You need to click in the drawing window to specify the first point of the line. After specifying the first point, the prompt, "Specify next point or [Undo]:" appears. Now, you need to specify the next point of the line. It is recommended that you should always have a look at the command line to know the next step while executing a command.

Status Bar

Status Bar is located at the bottom of the AutoCAD window. It contains many buttons which help you to create a drawing very easily. You can turn ON or OFF these buttons just by clicking on them. Some buttons are hidden by default. To display the missing buttons on the status bar, click on the **Customization** button available at the bottom right corner and select the options from the menu. The buttons available on the status bar are briefly discussed in the following section.

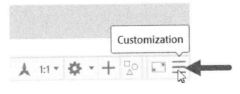

Button	Description
Drawing Coordinates 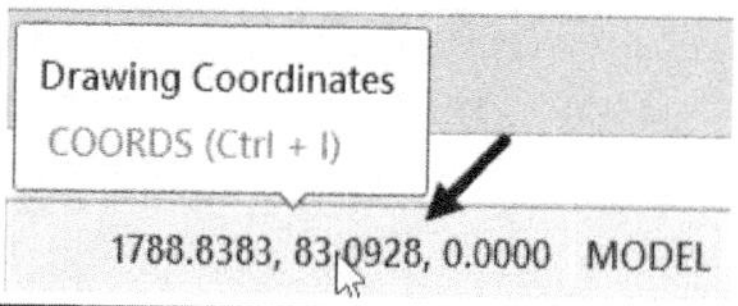 Drawing Coordinates COORDS (Ctrl + I) 1788.8383, 83.0928, 0.0000 MODEL	By default, this button is hidden. You can make it visible by using the **Customization** menu. It displays the drawing coordinates when you move the pointer in the graphics window. You can turn OFF this button by clicking on it.
Grid Display (F7)	It is used to turn the Grid display ON or OFF. You can set the spacing between the grid lines by right clicking on this button and selecting the **Settings** option. You can use grid lines along with the Snap Mode to draw objects easily and accurately.
Snap Mode (F9) s	The Snap mode forces the cursor to align only with the Grid points. When you turn ON this button, the cursor will be able to select only the Grid points.
Infer Constraints	This button is used to automatically create constraints when you draw objects in the drawing window. Constraints are logical operations which control the shape of a drawing. You can turn it ON or OFF by clicking on it. 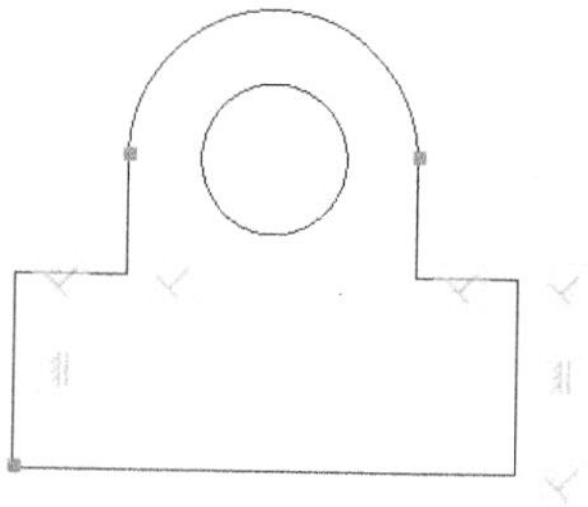
Ortho Mode (F8)	It is used to turn the Ortho Mode ON or OFF. When the Ortho Mode is ON, only horizontal or vertical lines can be drawn.
Polar Tracking (F10)	This button is used to turn ON or OFF the Polar Tracking. When the Polar Tracking is turned ON, you can draw lines easily at regular angular increments, such as **5**, **10**, **15**, **18**, **23**, **30**, **45**, or **90** degrees. You will notice that a trace line is displayed when the cursor is at a particular angular increment. You can set the angular increment by right-clicking on this button and selecting the required angle.

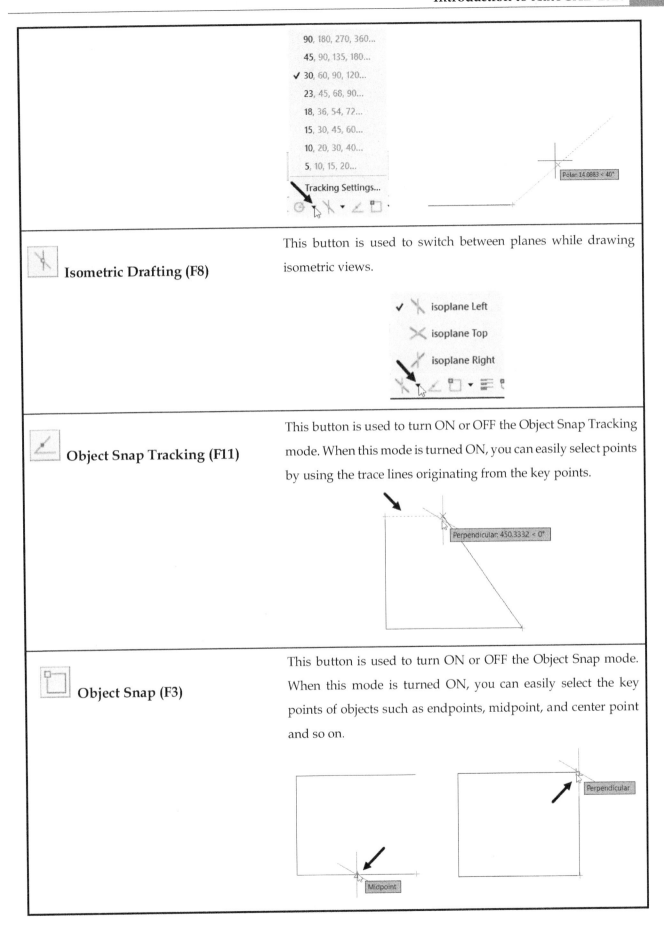

	Isometric Drafting (F8)	This button is used to switch between planes while drawing isometric views.
	Object Snap Tracking (F11)	This button is used to turn ON or OFF the Object Snap Tracking mode. When this mode is turned ON, you can easily select points by using the trace lines originating from the key points.
	Object Snap (F3)	This button is used to turn ON or OFF the Object Snap mode. When this mode is turned ON, you can easily select the key points of objects such as endpoints, midpoint, and center point and so on.

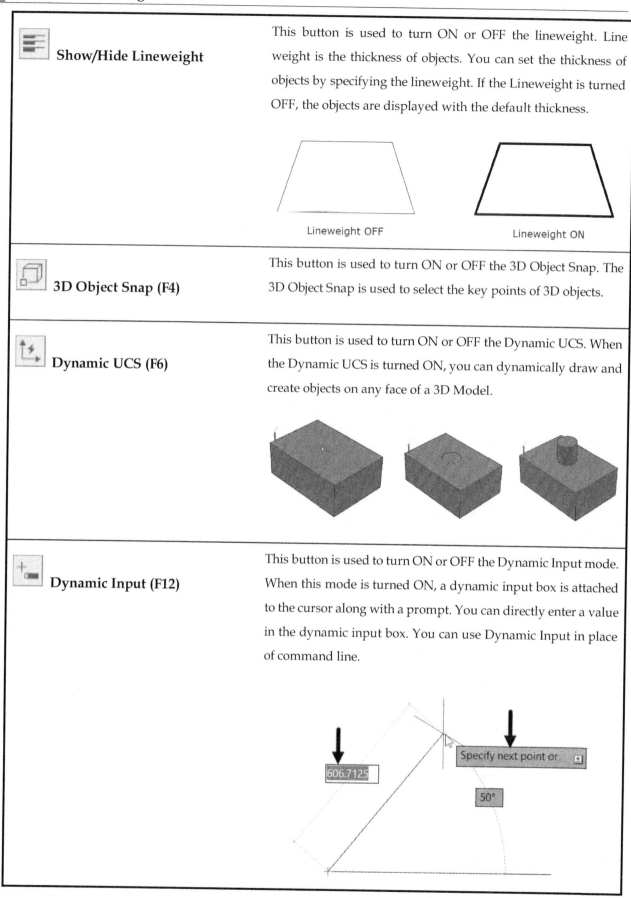 **Show/Hide Lineweight**	This button is used to turn ON or OFF the lineweight. Line weight is the thickness of objects. You can set the thickness of objects by specifying the lineweight. If the Lineweight is turned OFF, the objects are displayed with the default thickness.

Lineweight OFF   Lineweight ON

3D Object Snap (F4)	This button is used to turn ON or OFF the 3D Object Snap. The 3D Object Snap is used to select the key points of 3D objects.

Dynamic UCS (F6)	This button is used to turn ON or OFF the Dynamic UCS. When the Dynamic UCS is turned ON, you can dynamically draw and create objects on any face of a 3D Model.

Dynamic Input (F12)	This button is used to turn ON or OFF the Dynamic Input mode. When this mode is turned ON, a dynamic input box is attached to the cursor along with a prompt. You can directly enter a value in the dynamic input box. You can use Dynamic Input in place of command line.

Specify next point or

606.7125

50°

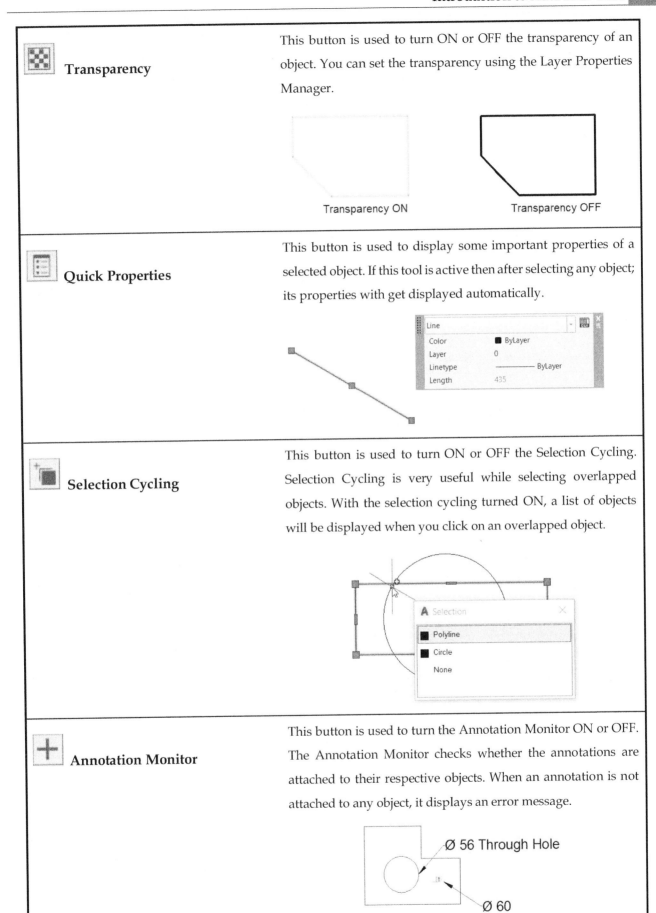 **Transparency**		This button is used to turn ON or OFF the transparency of an object. You can set the transparency using the Layer Properties Manager.

Transparency ON   Transparency OFF

Quick Properties

This button is used to display some important properties of a selected object. If this tool is active then after selecting any object; its properties with get displayed automatically.

Line	
Color	■ ByLayer
Layer	0
Linetype	—— ByLayer
Length	435

Selection Cycling

This button is used to turn ON or OFF the Selection Cycling. Selection Cycling is very useful while selecting overlapped objects. With the selection cycling turned ON, a list of objects will be displayed when you click on an overlapped object.

A Selection	✕
■ Polyline	
■ Circle	
None	

Annotation Monitor

This button is used to turn the Annotation Monitor ON or OFF. The Annotation Monitor checks whether the annotations are attached to their respective objects. When an annotation is not attached to any object, it displays an error message.

Ø 56 Through Hole

Ø 60

MODEL **Model or Paper Space**		This button is used switch between the Model space and Paper space. Model space is used to create drawings and Paper space is used to print drawings.
1:1 ▼ Annotation Scale		This button is used to control the size of annotative objects. Annotative objects are dimensions, texts, notes and other objects which can be sized as per the drawing scale.

Scale 1:1   Scale 2:1

Annotation Visibility	This button is used to display annotative objects that are not created in the current scale.
AutoScale	This button changes the annotation scale of objects.
Workspace Switching	This button is used to change the workspace.
Hardware Acceleration On/Off	This button is used to increase or decrease the graphics speed.
Isolate Objects	This button is used to Hide or Isolate objects in a drawing. If you hide an object, it will be hidden and all the other objects in the drawing will be visible. If you isolate an object, the other objects in the drawing will be hidden and the selected object will be visible.
Clean Screen	This button is used to hide the ribbon and toolbars from the window. This will increase the drawing area and provides more space to work on drawings.

Menu Bar

In AutoCAD, Menu Bar is not displayed by default. However, you can display the Menu Bar in other workspaces by clicking on the down-arrow located at the right side of the Quick Access Toolbar and selecting the **Show Menu Bar** option. The Menu Bar is located at the top of the window just below the title bar. It contains various menus such as File, Edit, View, Insert, Format, Tools, Draw, Dimensions, Modify, and so on. Clicking on any of the word on the Menu Bar displays a menu. The menu contains various tools and options. There are also sub-options available on the menu. These sub-options are displayed if you click on an option with an arrow. If you click on an option with (…), a dialog box will be displayed.

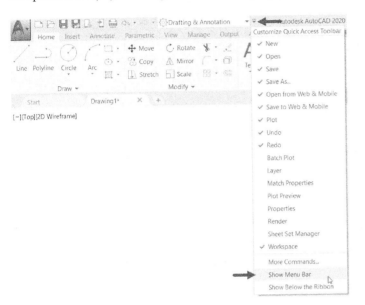

Changing the display of the Ribbon

You can change the display of the ribbon by clicking the arrow button located at the top of it. The ribbon can be displayed in three different modes as shown below.

Ribbon Minimized to Panel

Minimized to Panel Titles

Minimized to Tabs

Dialog Boxes and Palettes

Dialog boxes and Palettes are part of AutoCAD user interface. Using a dialog box or a palette, you can easily specify many settings and options. Examples of dialog boxes and palettes are a shown below.

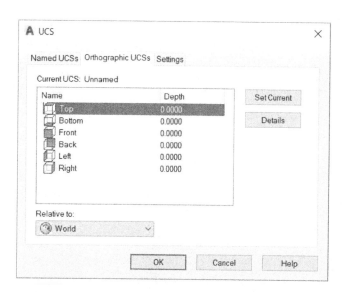

Dialog Box

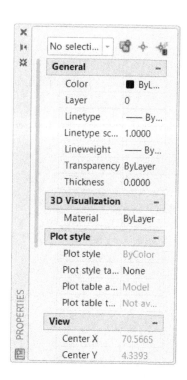

Palette

Tool Palettes

Tool Palettes provide you with another way of selecting tools and placing objects. You can display Tool Palettes by clicking **View > Palettes > Tool Palettes** on the ribbon. A Tool Palette is similar to a palette except that it has many palettes grouped in the form of tabs, as shown below. You can select tools from the Tool Palettes as well as drag and place objects (blocks) into the drawing. You can also create a new Tool Palette and add frequently used tools and objects to it.

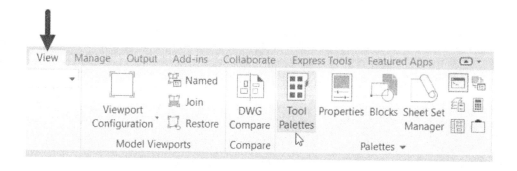

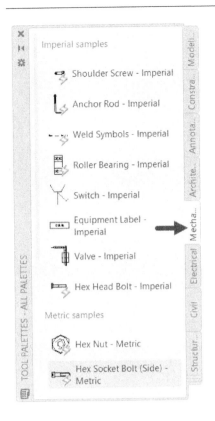

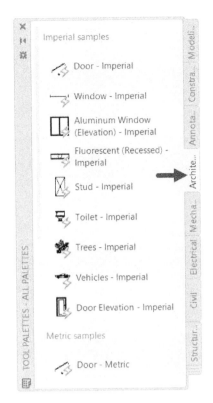

Shortcut Menus

Shortcut Menus are displayed when you right-click in the drawing window. AutoCAD provides various shortcut menus in order to help you access tools and options very easily and quickly. There are various types of shortcut menus available in AutoCAD. Some of them are discussed next.

Default menu

This shortcut menu is displayed whenever you right-click in the drawing window without invoking any command or selecting any object.

Edit Shortcut menu

This shortcut menu is displayed when you select an object from the drawing window and right-click. It consists of editing and selection options.

Command Mode shortcut menu

This shortcut menu is displayed when you select a command and right-click. It displays options depending upon the selected command. The shortcut menu below shows the options related to the **CIRCLE** command.

Grip shortcut menu

This shortcut menu is displayed when you select a grip of an object, move the cursor and right-click. It displays various operations that can be performed using grip.

Default Menu

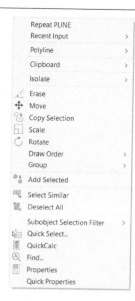

Edit Shortcut Menu

Command Mode Shortcut Menu

Grip Shorcut Menu

Selection Window

A selection window is used to select multiple elements of the drawing. In AutoCAD, you can select multiple elements by using two types of selection windows. The first type is a rectangular selection window. You can create this type of selection window by defining its two diagonal corners. When you define the first corner of the selection window on the left and second corner on the right side, the elements which completely fall under the selection window will be selected.

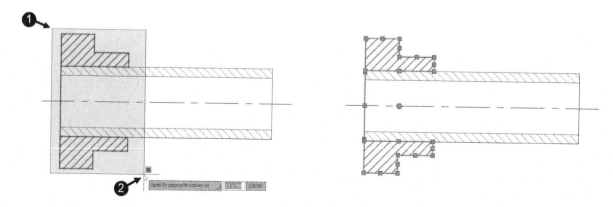

However, if you define the first corner on the right side and second corner of the left side, the elements, which fall completely or partially under the selection window, will be selected.

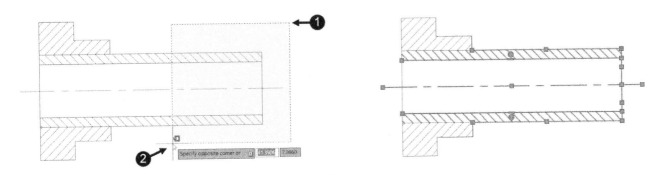

The second type of selection window is the Lasso. Lasso is an irregular shape created by clicking and dragging the pointer across the elements to select. If you drag the pointer from the left to right, the elements falling completely under the lasso will be selected.

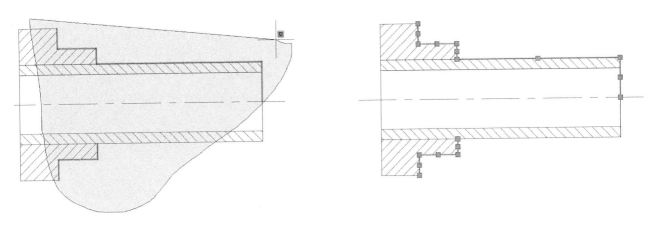

If you drag the pointer from right to left, the elements, which fall completely or partially under the lasso, will be selected.

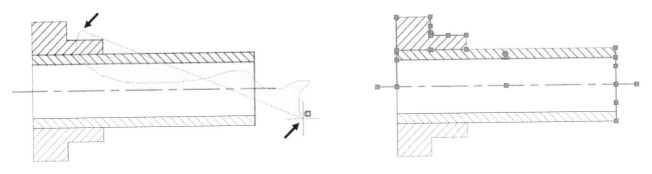

Starting a New Drawing

You can start an AutoCAD document by using the **Get Started** section or by using the **Select template** dialog box.

Get Section on the Initial Screen

To start a new drawing, click **CREATE** at the bottom of the initial screen, and then select a template from **Get Started > Templates** drop-down, as shown.

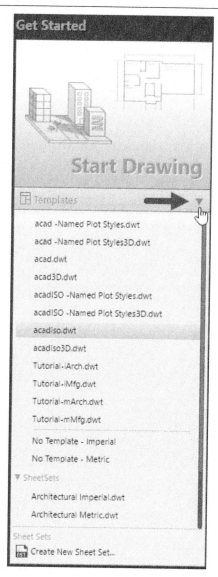

The Select Template dialog box

To start a new drawing, click the **New** button on anyone of the following:

- **Quick Access Toolbar**
- **Application Menu**

The **Select Template** dialog box appears when you click the **New** button. In this dialog box, select the **acad.dwt** (inch units) or **acadiso.dwt** (metric units) template for creating a 2D drawing. Select the **acad3D.dwt** or **acadiso3D.dwt** template for creating 3D models.

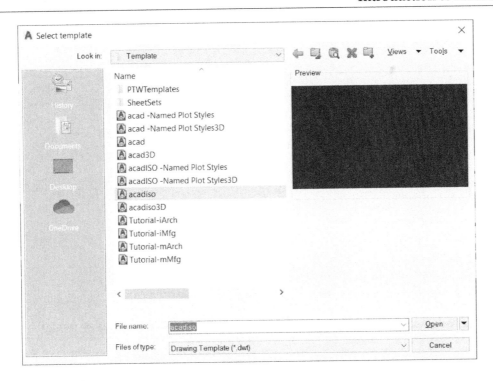

Command List

Various commands in AutoCAD are given in the table below:

Command	Alias	Description
APPLOAD		Invokes the **Load/Unload** Applications dialog box.
ADCENTER	DC	Opens the **DesignCenter** palette.
ALIGN	AL	Used to align objects with other objects.
ARC	A	Used to create an arc.
AREA		Displays the area of a selected closed object.
ARRAY	AR	Creates Rectangular, Path or Polar 2D arrays.
ASE		Displays the **dbConnect Manager** palette.

ATTDEF	ATT	Displays the **Attribute Definition** dialog box.
ATTEDIT	ATE	Used to edit Attributes.
AUDIT		Used to check and fix errors.
AUTOCONSTRAIN		Used to apply constraints automatically.
AUTOPUBLISH		Used to create a DWF file.
BACTION	AC	Used to add an action to a dynamic block.
BLOCK		Used to create a block.
BMAKE	B	Used to create a block.
BMPOUT		Used to create a Raster image out of the drawing.
BOUNDARY	BO	Used to create a hatch boundary.
BREAK	BR	Used to break an object.
CAL		Used to calculate mathematical expressions.
CHAMFER	CHA	Used to create chamfers.
CHPROP	CH	Displays the **Properties** palette.
CIRCLE	C	Used to create a circle.
COLOR	COL	Displays the **Select Color** dialog box.

COPYTOLAYER		Used to copy objects from one layer to another.
COPY	**CO**	Used to copy objects inside a drawing.
COPYCLIP	**CTRL+C**	Used to copy objects from one drawing to another.
CUSTOMIZE		Used to customize toolbars and palettes.
DASHBOARD		Displays the ribbon.
DASHBOARDCLOSE		Used to hide the ribbon.
DDEDIT	**ED**	Used to edit a note or annotation.
DIMSTYLE	**D**	Used to create or modify a dimension style.
DDMODIFY		Displays the Properties palette.
DELCONSTRAINT		Used to delete constraints.
OSNAP	**OS**	Used to set Object Snap settings.
DDPTYPE		Used to set the point style and size.
VIEW	**V**	Used to save views by names.
DGNEXPORT		Used to export the drawing to Microstation (DGN) format.
DGNIMPORT		Used to import a Microstation (DGN) format file.

DIMCONSTRAINT	DCON	Used to apply dimensional constraints to objects.
DIMLINEAR	DLI	Used to create a linear dimension.
DIMALIGNED	DAL	Used to create an aligned dimension.
DIMARC	DAR	Used to dimension the arc length.
DIMRADIUS	DIMRAD	Used to create at radial dimension.
DIMJOGGED	JOG	Used to create a jogged dimension.
DIMDIAMETER	DIMDIA	Used to create a diameter dimension.
DIMANGULAR	DAN	Used to create an angular dimension.
DIMORDINATE	DOR	Used to create ordinate dimension.
DIMCONTINUE	DIMCONT	Used to create continuous dimensions from an existing one.
DIMBASELINE	DIMBASE	Used to create baseline dimensions.
DIMINSPECT		Used to create an inspection dimension.
-DIMSTYLE		Update a dimension according the dimension style.
DIMSPACE		Used to adjust space between dimensions.
DIMBREAK		Used to break the extension line of a dimension when it intersects with another dimension.

DIMOVERRIDE		Used to override the system variables of a selected dimension.
DIMCENTER		Used to create a center mark of a circle.
DIMEDIT	DIMED	Used to edit a dimension.
DIMTEDIT	DIMTED	Used to edit the dimension text.
DIMDISASSOCIATE		Disassociates a dimension from the object.
DIST (DI)	DI	Used to measure the distance between two points.
DISTANTLIGHT		Used to create distant light.
DIVIDE	DIV	Places evenly spaced objects on a line segment
DONUT	DO	Used to create a donut.
DVIEW		Used to get the aerial view of a drawing.
DXBIN		Used to open a DXB file.
DXFIN		Used to open a DXF file.
DXFOUT		Used to save a file in DXF format.
ELLIPSE	EL	Used to create an ellipse.
ERASE	E	Used to erase objects.

EXIT		Used to close AutoCAD.
EXPLODE	X	Used to explode or ungroup objects.
EXPLORER		Displays Windows Explorer.
EXPORT	EXP	Used to export data.
EXTEND	EX	Used to extend an object upto another.
FILLET	F	Used to create a fillet at the corner.
FILTER		Used to set object selection filters.
GEOMCONSTRAINT	GCON	Used to apply geometric constraints.
GRADIENT		Used to apply gradient to a closed area.
GROUP	G	Used to group objects.
HATCH	H	Used to apply hatch to a closed area.
HATCHEDIT	HE	Used to edit hatch.
HELP		Display the Help window.
HIDE	HI	Changes the Visual Style to Hidden.
ID		Displays the coordinate values of a selected point.
IMAGEADJUST	IAD	Used to adjust images.

IMAGECLIP		Used to crop an image.
IMPORT		Used to import other forms of CAD data.
INSERT	I	Used to insert a block.
INSERTOBJ		Used to insert a object into the drawing.
ISOPLANE	CTRL+E	Used to set the current isometric plane.
JOIN	J	Used to joins end points of two linear or curved objects.
LAYCUR		The Layer of the selected objects will be made current.
LAYER	LA	Used to create a new layer and modify its properties.
LAYOUT		Used to modify layouts.
LENGTHEN	LEN	Used to increase the length of an object.
LIMITS		Used to set the drawing limits.
LIMMAX		Used to set the maximum limit of a drawing.
LINE	L	Used to create a line.
LINETYPE	LT	Used to set the linetype.
LIST	LI	Lists the properties of a selected object in the text window.

Command	Alias	Description
LOAD		Imports the shapes that can be used by the SHAPE command.
LTSCALE	LTS	Used to set the linetype scale.
MEASURE	ME	Used to place points or blocks at measured intervals on an object.
MENU		Used to load a customization file.
MENULOAD		Used to load or unload a customizable file.
MIRROR	MI	Used to create a mirror image of an object.
MLEDIT		Used to edit a multiline.
MLINE	ML	Used to create multiple parallel lines.
MLSTYLE		Used to create and modify a multiline style.
MOVE	M	Used to move selected objects.
MSLIDE		Used to create slide out of a drawing.
MSPACE	MS	Used to switch from paper space to model space.
MSTRETCH		Used to stretch multiple objects at a time.
MTEXT	MT or T	Used to write text in multiple lines.
MVIEW	MV	Used to create and modify layouts.

MVSETUP		Used to set drawing specifications for printing purpose.
NEW	**CTRL+N**	Used to open a new file.
NOTEPAD		Used to edit file in Notepad.
OFFSET	**O**	Creates a parallel copy of a selected object at a specified distance.
OOPS		Used to undo the ERASE command.
OPEN		Used to open an existing file.
OPTIONS	**OP**	Used to set various options related to the drawing.
ORTHO		Turns ON/OFF the Ortho Mode.
OSNAP	**OS**	Used to the **Object Snap** settings.
PAGESETUP		Used to specify the printing properties of a layout.
PAN	**P**	Used to drag a drawing to view its different portions.
PARAMETER	**PAR**	Used to assign expressions to a dimensional constraint.
PBRUSH		Opens the **Windows Paint** application.
PEDIT	**PE**	Used to edit polylines.
PLINE	**PL**	Used to create a polyline. A polyline is a single object which can have continuous lines and arcs.

PLOT	CTRL+P	Used to plot a drawing.
POINT	PO	Used to place a point in the drawing.
POLYGON	POL	Used to create a polygon.
PREVIEW	PRE	Used to preview the plotted drawing.
PROPERTIES	PR	Displays the **Properties** palette.
PSOUT		Used to create a postscript file.
PURGE	PU	Used to remove the unwanted data from the drawing.
QDIM		Used to create a quick dimension.
QSAVE		Used to save the current drawing.
QUICKCALC	QC	Displays the QuickCalc calculator.
QUIT		Used to close the current drawing session.
RAY		Used to create a line that starts from a selected point and extends upto infinity.
RECOVER		Used to repair and open the damaged files.
RECOVERALL		Used to repair a damaged file along with the attached external references.
RECTANG		Used to create a polyline rectangle.

REDEFI NE		Used to restore an AutoCAD command which has been overridden.
REDRAW	R	Refreshes the current viewport.
UNDEFI NE		Used to override an existing command with a new one.
REDO		Used to cancel the previous UNDO command.
REDRAWALL	RA	Refreshes all the viewports in a drawing.
REGEN	RE	Regenerates the current viewport of a drawing.
REGENALL	REA	Regenerates all the viewports of a drawing.
REGION	REG	Convert the area enclosed by objects into a region.
RENAME	REN	Used to rename blocks, viewports, dimension styles and so on.
REVCLOUD		Used to highlight a portion of drawing by creating a cloud around it.
RIBBON		Displays the ribbon.
RIBBONCLOSE		Hides the ribbon.
SAVE	CTRL+S	Saves the currently opened drawing.
SAVEAS		Saves the drawing with another name and location.

SAVEIMG		Used to save a rendered output file.
SCALE	SC	Used to increase or decrease the size of a drawing.
SCRIPT	SCR	Used to load a script file. A script is used to run various commands in a sequential manner.
SETVAR	SET	Used to list or change a system variable.
SHAPE		Used to insert a shape into a drawing.
SHELL		Used to enter MS-DOS commands.
SKETCH		Used to draw freehand sketches.
SOLID	SO	Used to create filled triangles or quadrilaterals.
SPELL	SP	Used to check the spelling of a text.
SPLINE	SPL	Used to create a spline (curved object).
SPLINEDIT	SPE	Used to edit a spline.
STATUS		Used to display the details of a drawing such as limits, model space usage, layers and so on.
STRETCH	S	Used to stretch objects.
STYLE	ST	Used to create or modify the text style.
TABLET	TA	Allows using a tablet for creating drawings.

TBCONFIG		Used to customize user interface.
TEXT		Used to enter text in the drawing.
THICKNESS	**TH**	Used to set a thickness value to 2D objects.
TOLERANCE –		Used to apply geometric tolerances to the drawing.
TOOLBAR	**TO**	Used to customize toolbars.
TRIM	**TR**	Used to trim unwanted portions of an object.
UCS –		Used to specify the location of the user coordinate system.
UNDO	**CTRL+Z (or) U**	Used to undo the last operation.
UNITS	**UN**	Set the units of the drawing
VIEW		Used to save and restore model space, layout, and preset views.
VPLAYER		Used to control the layer visibility in paper space.
VPORTS		Used to create multiple viewports in model space of paper space.
VSLIDE		Used to show an image slide file.
WBLOCK	**W**	Used to convert a block into a drawing.

WMFIN		Used to import a Windows Metafile. This file contains drawing data and image data. But only drawing data is imported.
WIPEOUT		Used to wipeout a portion of the drawing.
WMFOPTS		Used to specify options for importing a Windows Metafile.
WMFOUT		Used to save objects as Windows Metafile.
XATTACH	**XA**	Used to attach a drawing as an external reference.
XLINE – CREATES A CONSTRUCTION LINE	**XL**	Used to create construction lines. Construction lines extend to infinity and help in drawing objects.
XREF	**XR**	Used to attach a drawing as an external reference.
ZOOM	**Z**	Used to Zoom in or out of a drawing.

3D Commands

Command	Shortcut	Description
3DARRAY	**3A**	Used to create three dimensional arrays of a objects.
3DALIGN	**3AL**	Used align 3D objects.
3DFACE	**3F**	Used to create three sided or four 3D surface.
3DMESH		Used to create freeform 3D mesh.

3DCORBIT		Used to rotate a view in the 3D space with continuous motion.
3DDISTANCE		Used to control the distance.
3DEDITBAR		Used to add and edit control vertices on a NURBS surface or spline.
3DFLY		Used to view the 3D model as if you are flying through.
3DFORBIT		Used to freely rotate a view in 3D space.
3DMOVE	3M	Used to move the objects in 3D space.
3DORBIT	3DO	Used to rotate the view constrained along horizontal or vertical axis.
3DORBITCTR		Used to set the center for rotating view in 3D space.
3DPAN		Used to pan the 3D models horizontally or vertically. This is used when working in perspective view.
3DPOLY	3P	Used to create a 3D polyline.
3DPRINT	3DP	Used to print the model in 3D (plastic prototype).
3DROTATE		Used to rotate 3D objects in 3D space.
3DSCALE	3S	Used to increase or decrease the size of 3D object along the X, Y, Z directions.
3DSIN		Used to import a 3ds Max file.

3DDWF	Export the 3D model to a 3D DWF file.
3DWALK	Used to view the 3D model as if you are walking through it.
ANIPATH	Used to create an animation when you are navigating through the model.
BOX	Used to create a 3D box.
CONE	Used to create a 3D cone.
CONVERTOLDLIGHTS	Used to convert lights created in previous releases to the current format.
CONVERTOLDMATERIALS	Used to convert old materials to new format
CONVTONURBS	Used to convert a surface to NURBS. You can edit can easily edit a NURBS by using control vertices displayed on it.
CONVTOSOLID	Used to convert 3D meshes, polylines and circles to 3D solids.
CONVTOSURFACE	Used to convert objects to surfaces.
CVADD	Used to add control vertices to a NURBS surface or spline.
CVREMOVE	Used to remove control vertices from a NURBS surface or spline.

CVHIDE		Used to hide the control vertices of a NURBS surface or splines,
CVSHOW		Used to display the control vertices of a NURBS surface or splines.
CVREBUILD		Used to rebuild the control vertices of a NURBS surface.
CYLINDER		Used to create a 3D Cylinder.
EDGESURF		Used to create a mesh surface from four adjacent edges.
EXTRUDE	**EXT**	Used to extrude a closed region or polyline.
FLATSHOT		Used to create a 2D representation of a 3D model.
FREEPOINT		Used to create point light that emits light in all directions.
FREESPOT		Used to create a spot light without any target.
HELIX		Used to create a helical or spiral curve.
INTERFERE		Used to create a 3D solid at the interference point of the various solid objects.
INTERSECT	**IN**	Used to create a 3D solid at the intersection point of solid.
LIGHT		Used to create a light.

LIGHTLIST	Displays the lights available in the current 3D model.
LOFT	Used to create a 3D solid or surface between various cross sections.
MATERIALS	Displays the Material Browser.
MATERIALASSIGN	Used to assign a material to the model.
MATERIALMAP	Used to the control the texture.
MATERIALATTACH	Used to associate materials with layers.
MESH	Used to create 3D mesh objects.
MESHREFINE	Used to refine the mesh of 3D mesh objects.
MESHSMOOTH	Used to increase the smoothness of mesh objects.
MIRROR3D	Used to mirror 3D objects in 3D space.
OFFSETEDGE	Used to create a parallel copy of an edge at a specified distance.
PFACE	Used to create a 3D Polyface mesh by specifying vertices.
PLAN	Displays the top view of the 3D model.
PLANESURF	Used to create a planar surface.

POINTLIGHT		Used to create point light that emits light in all directions.
PRESSPULL		Used to extrude or subtract material.
PYRAMID		Used to create a pyramid.
-RENDER		Used to specify settings for rendering.
RENDERCROP		Used to render a rectangular portion of a 3D model.
RENDERENVIRONMENT		Used to control visual properties rendered image.
RENDEREXPOSURE		Used to control the lighting of a rendered image.
RENDERONLINE		Used to render an image in Autodesk 360 (cloud).
RENDERPRESETS		Used to specify preset values for rendering an image.
RENDERWIN		Displays the render window.
REVOLVE	**REV**	Used to create a revolved solid.
REVSURF		Used to create a revolved surface.
RMAT		Displays the Material Browser.
RPREF	**RPR**	Used to specify advanced render settings.
SECTION	**SEC**	Used to create section plane in a 3D model.

SLICE	**SL**	Used to slice a 3D model.
SOLPROF		Create a profile from a 3D model in a paperspace.
SOLIDEDIT		Used to edit faces and edges of a 3D solid.
SPACETRANS		Used to calculate equivalent model space and paper space distance.
SPHERE		Used to create a 3D sphere.
SPOTLIGHT		Used to create a spotlight that emits light like a torch.
STLOUT		Used to export a file to STL format.
SUNPROPERTIES		Displays the Sun properties palette.
SURFBLEND	**BLENDSRF**	Used to create a continuous blend surface between two surfaces.
SURFEXTEND		Used to lengthen a surface upto another surface.
SURFEXTRACTCURVE		Used to create Isoline curves on a surface, solid, or a face in U and V directions.
SURFFILLET		Used to create a surface fillet between two surface.
SURFOFFSET		Used to create parallel surface at a specified distance.
SURFNETWORK		Used to create a surface from various curves in U and V directions.

SURFPATCH		Used to create a surface using the edges forming a closed loop.
SURFSCULPT		Used to create a closed surface by trimming and combining the surfaces that form a region together.
SURFTRIM		Used to trim portions of a surface at intersections with other surfaces.
SURFUNTRIM		Used to untrim the trimmed surface.
SWEEP		Used to create 3D solid or surface by sweeping a profile along a path.
TABSURF		Used to create a mesh from a line or curve swept along a straight path
TORUS	**TOR**	Used to create a torus.
UNION	**UNI**	Used to combine various solids into one.
VISUALSTYLES		Used to create and modify visual styles.
VPOINT		Used to set the viewing direction of the 3D model.
WEDGE	**WE**	Used to create a wedge shape.
XEDGES		Used to create a 3D wireframe from a 3D solid.

Questions:

1. Where is **Application Menu** icon located in AutoCAD?
2. Where is **Status Bar** located in AutoCAD?
3. What are the two different color schemes in AutoCAD?
4. Where is **Navigation Bar** located?
5. Where is **ViewCube** located?
6. What are the three workspaces available in AutoCAD?

Chapter 2: Drawing Basics in AutoCAD

In this chapter, you will learn to do the following:

- ❖ **Draw lines, rectangles, circles, ellipses, arcs, polygons, and polylines**
- ❖ **Use the Erase, Undo and Redo tools**
- ❖ **Draw entities using the absolute coordinate points**
- ❖ **Draw entities using the relative coordinate points**
- ❖ **Draw entities using the tracking method**

Drawing Basics

This chapter teaches you to create simple drawings. You will create these drawings using the basic drawing tools. These tools include **Line**, **Circle**, **Polyline**, and **Rectangle** and so on and they are available in the **Draw** panel of the **Home** tab in the ribbon, as shown below. You can also invoke these tools by typing them in the command line, as shown.

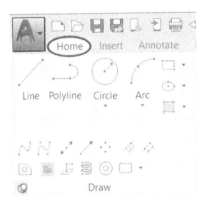

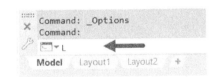

Drawing lines

You can draw a line by specifying its start point and end point using the **Line** tool. However, there are various methods to specify start and end points of a line. These methods are explained in the following examples.

Example (using the Absolute Coordinate System):

In this example, you will create lines by specifying points in the absolute coordinate system. In this system, you specify the points with respect to the origin (0,0). A point will be specified by entering its X and Y coordinates separated by a comma, as shown in figure below.

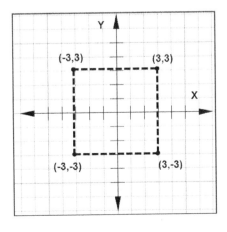

- Start AutoCAD 2020 by clicking the **AutoCAD 2020** icon on your desktop.
- On the Welcome screen, click **Start Drawing** > **Templates** > **acadISO-Named Plot Styles.dwt**, as shown. This starts a new drawing using the ISO template.

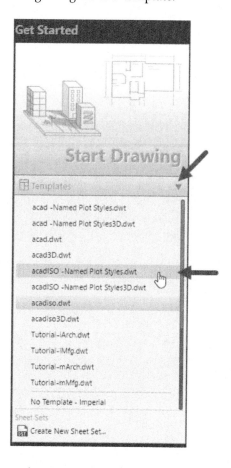

- Click **Zoom** > **Zoom All** on the **Navigation Bar**; the entire area in the drawing window will be displayed.

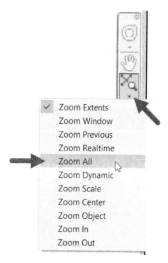

- Turn OFF the **Grid Display** by pressing the **F7** key.
- Click the **Customization** button on the status bar, and then select the **Dynamic Input** option from the flyout to display the **Dynamic Input** icon on the status bar.

- Turn OFF the **Dynamic Input** mode. You will learn about **Dynamic Input** later in this chapter.

- To draw a line, click **Home > Draw > Line** on the ribbon, or enter **LINE** or **L** in the command line.
- Follow the prompt sequence given next.

  Specify first point: Type **50,50** and press **ENTER**.
  Specify next point or [Undo]: Type **150,50** and press **ENTER**.
  Specify next point or [Undo]: Type **150,100** and press **ENTER**.
  Specify next point or [Close Undo]: Type **50,100** and press **ENTER**.
  Specify next point or [Close Undo]: Select the **Close** option; the drawing will be created as shown below.

(50,100)   (150,100)

(50,50)   (150,50)

- Click **Save** on the **Quick Access Toolbar** to display the **Save Drawing As** dialog box.

- Enter **Line-example1** in the dialog box and click on the **Save** button to save it, as shown.
- Click on ✕ icon to close the file, as shown.

Example (using Relative Coordinate system):

In this example, you will draw lines by specifying points in the relative coordinate system. In this method, you specify the location of a point with respect to the previous point. For this purpose, the symbol '@' is used before the point coordinates. This symbol means that the coordinate values are specified in relation with the previous point.

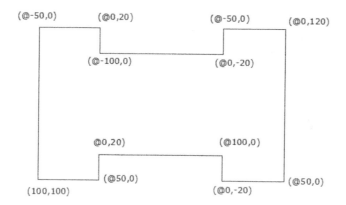

- Click on **New** button from **Quick Access Toolbar** to display the **Select template** dialog box, as shown.
- Select **acadISO –Named Plot Styles.dwt** template. Click **Open**.

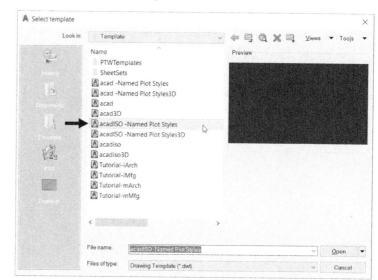

- Type **Z** in the command line to invoke the **ZOOM** command.
- Select the **All** option from the command line; the entire area in the drawing window will be displayed.
- Press the **F7** key to turn OFF the **Dynamic Input** mode, if active.

Alternatively, you can deactivate it from the status bar, as shown.

- Turn OFF the **Dynamic Input** mode, if active.
- Click **Home > Draw > Line** on the ribbon or enter **LINE** or **L** in the command line.
- Follow the prompt sequence given next.

Specify first point: Type **100,100** and press **ENTER**.
Specify next point or [Undo]: Type **@50,0** and press **ENTER**.
Specify next point or [Undo]: Type **@0,20** and press **ENTER**.
Specify next point or [Close Undo]: Type **@100,0** and press **ENTER**.
Specify next point or [Close Undo]: Type **@0, -20** and press **ENTER**.

Specify next point or [Close Undo]: Type **@50,0** and press **ENTER**.
Specify next point or [Close Undo]: Type **@0,120** and press **ENTER**.
Specify next point or [Close Undo]: Type **@-50,0** and press **ENTER**.
Specify next point or [Close Undo]: Type **@0,-20** and press **ENTER**.
Specify next point or [Close Undo]: Type **@-100,0** and press **ENTER**.
Specify next point or [Close Undo]: Type **@0,20** and press **ENTER**.
Specify next point or [Close Undo]: Type **@-50,0** and press **ENTER**.
Specify next point or [Close Undo]: Select the **Close** option.

- Save the file as **Line-example2.dwg**.
- Close the file.

Example (using Polar Coordinate system):

In the polar coordinate system, you specify the location of a point by entering two values: distance from the previous point and angle from the zero degrees. You enter the distance value along with the "@" symbol and angle value with the "<" symbol. Note that angles in AutoCAD are measured in anti-clockwise direction.

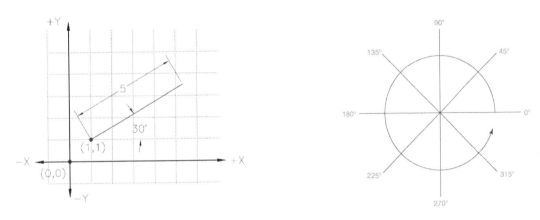

Drawing Task

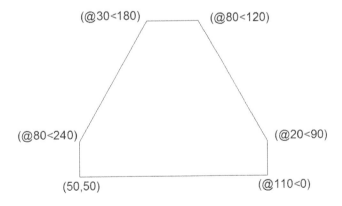

- Open a new file using the **acadISO -Named Plot Styles.dwt** template.
- Click **Zoom > Zoom All** on the **Navigation Bar**.
- Turn OFF the **Grid** icon on the status bar.
- Turn OFF the **Dynamic Input** mode, if active.
- Click **Home > Draw > Line** on the ribbon or enter **LINE** or **L** in the command line.
- Follow the prompt sequence given next.

Specify first point: Type **50,50** and press **Enter** key
Specify next point or [Undo]: Type **@110<0** and press **ENTER**.
Specify next point or [Undo]: Type **@20<90** and press **ENTER**.
Specify next point or [Close Undo]: Type **@80<120** and press **ENTER**.
Specify next point or [Close Undo]: Type **@30<180** and press **ENTER**.
Specify next point or [Close Undo]: Type **@80<240** and press **ENTER**.
Specify next point or [Close Undo]: Select the **Close** option

- Save the file as **Line-example3.dwg**.
- Close the file.

Example (using Direct Distance Entry):

In the direct distance entry method, you draw a line by entering its distance and angle values. Note that you need to turn ON the Dynamic Input.

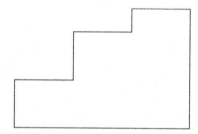

- Open a new file using the **acadISO -Named Plot Styles.dwt** template.
- Turn-off the **Grid** and **Snap Mode** at the Status Bar.
- Click **Zoom > Zoom All** on the **Navigation Bar**.
- Activate the **Dynamic Input** button on the Status Bar.

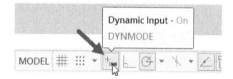

- Click **Home > Draw > Line** on the ribbon or enter **LINE** or **L** in the command line.
- Specify the first point of the line by typing **50,50** and pressing **ENTER**.
- Move the cursor horizontally toward right and type **150** as length.
- Press the **TAB** key and type **0** as angle, if required. Next, press **ENTER**.

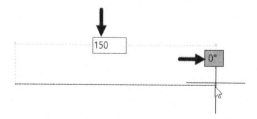

- Move the cursor vertically upwards and type **100** as length.
- Press the **TAB** key and type **90** as angle. Next, press **ENTER**.
- Move the cursor horizontally toward left and type **50**.
- Press the **TAB** key and type **180** as angle. Next, press **ENTER**.
- Move the cursor vertically downwards and type **20**.

- Press the **TAB** key and type **90** as angle. Next, press **ENTER**.
- Move the cursor horizontally toward left and type **50**.
- Press the **TAB** key and type **180** as angle. Next, press **ENTER**.
- Move the cursor vertically downwards and type **40**.
- Press the **TAB** key and type **90** as angle. Next, press **ENTER**.
- Move the cursor horizontally toward left and type **50**.
- Press the **TAB** key and type **180** as angle. Next, press **ENTER**.
- Select the **Close** option from the command line.
- Save and close the file.

Erasing, Undoing and Redoing

- Draw the sketch similar to the one shown below using the **Line** tool.

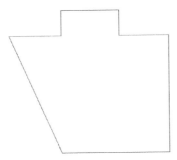

- Click **Home > Modify > Erase** on the ribbon or Enter **ERASE** or **E** in the command line.

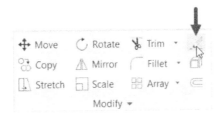

- Select the lines shown below and press **ENTER**; the lines will be erased.

- Click the **Undo** button on the **Quick Access Toolbar**; the lines will be restored.

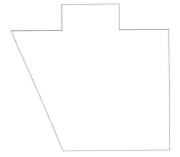

- Click the **Redo** button on the **Quick Access Toolbar**; the lines will be erased again.

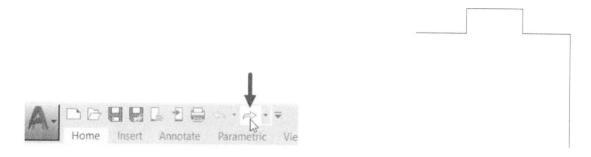

- Type **E** in the command line and press the **SPACEBAR**; the **ERASE** command will be invoked.
- Drag a selection window as shown below and press **ENTER**; the entities will be erased.

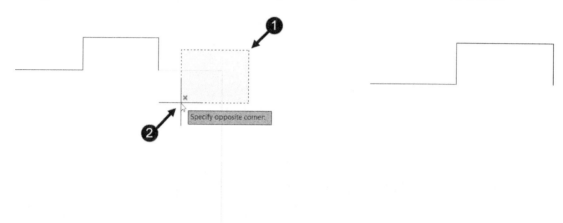

Drawing Circles

You can draw circles using the tools available in the **Circle** drop-down of the **Draw** panel. You can also type the **CIRCLE** command in the command line and create various types of circles. There are various methods to create circles. These methods are explained in the following examples.

Example (Center, Radius):

In this example, you will create a circle by specifying its center and radius value.

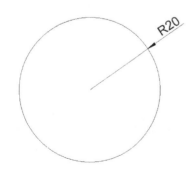

- Click **Home > Draw > Circle > Center, Radius** on the ribbon.
- Click at an arbitrary point in the drawing window to specify the center point.
- Type **20** as the radius and press **ENTER**.

Example (Center, Diameter):

In this example, you will create a circle by specifying its center and diameter value.

- Click **Home > Draw > Circle > Center, Diameter** 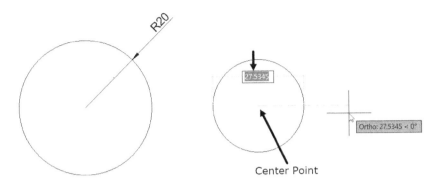 on the ribbon; the message, "Specify center point for circle or [3P 2P Ttr (tan tan radius)]:" appears in the command line.
- Pick a point in the drawing window which is approximately horizontal to previous circle.

Center Point

- Type **40** as the diameter and press **ENTER**; the circle will be created, as shown.

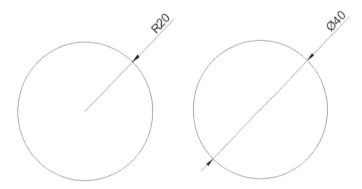

Example (2-Point):

In this example, you will create a circle by specifying two points. The first point is to specify the location of the circle and the second defines the diameter.

- Click **Home > Draw > Circle > 2-Point** on the ribbon; the message, "Specify first end point of circle's diameter:" appears in the command line.
  Now, you will create a circle by selecting the center points of the previous circles.
- Click on the down arrow next to the **Object Snap** button on the status bar to display the flyout. The options in this flyout are called Object Snaps. You will learn about these Object Snaps later in Chapter 3.
- Activate the **Center** option, if it is not already active.

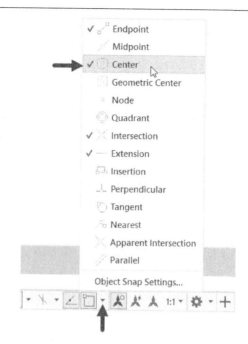

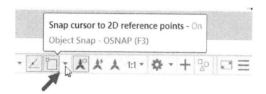

- Select the center point of the left side circle; the message, "Specify second end point of circle's diameter:" appears in the command line.
- Select the center point of the right-side circle; the circle will be created a shown below.

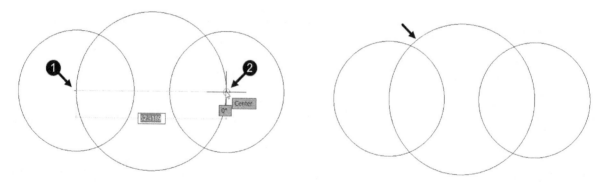

Example (3-Point):

In this example, you will create a circle by specifying three points. The circle will pass through these three points.

- Open a new file.
- Use the **Line** tool and create the drawing shown in figure below. The coordinate points are also given in the figure.

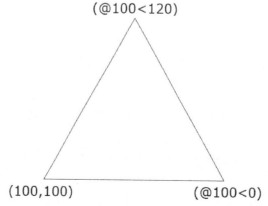

- Click **Home > Draw > Circle > 3-Point** 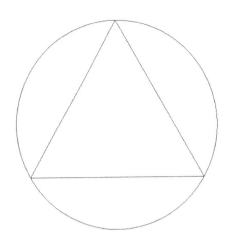 on the ribbon.
- Select the three vertices of the triangle; a circle will be created passing through the selected points.

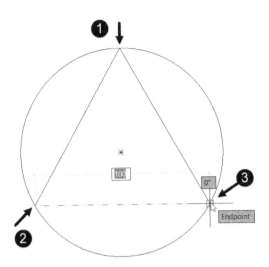

Example (Tan, Tan, Radius):

In this example, you will create a circle by selecting two objects to which it will be tangent, and then specifying the radius of the circle.

- Click **Home > Utilities > Measure > Radius** on the ribbon; the message, "**Select arc or circle:**" appears in the command line.
- Select the circle passing through the three vertices of the triangle; the radius and diameter values of the circle will be displayed above the command line.

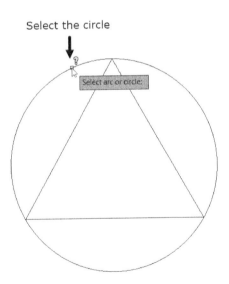

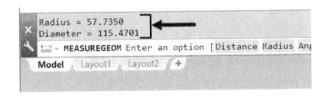

- Click **Home > Utilities > Quick Calculator** on the ribbon; the **Quick Calculator** appears.
- Type **57.7350** in the **Quick Calculator**, as shown.
- Click the "**/**" button and then the **2** button on the **Number Pad**, as shown.
- Click the "**=**" button; the value **28.8675** is displayed in the value box, as shown.

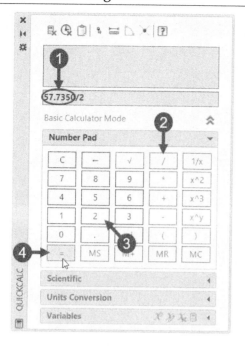
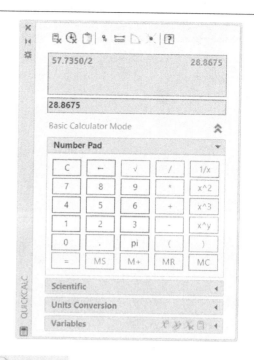

- Click **Home > Draw > Circle > Tan, Tan, Radius** 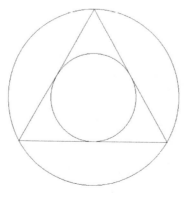 Tan, Tan, Radius on the ribbon; the message, "Specify point on object for first tangent of circle:" appears in the command line.
- Select the horizontal line of the triangle; the message, "Specify point on object for second tangent of circle:" appears in the command line.
- Select anyone of the inclined lines; the message, "Specify radius of circle" appears in the command line.
- Click the **Paste value to command line** button on the **Quick Calculator**; the value **28.8675** will be pasted in the command line.

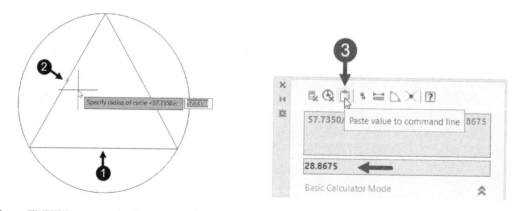

- Press **ENTER** to specify the radius; the circle will be created touching all three sides of the triangle.

- Save and close the file.

Example (Tan, Tan, Tan):

In this example, you will create a circle by selecting three objects to which it will be tangent.

- Click the **Open** button on the **Quick Access Toolbar**; the **Select File** dialog box appears.

- Browse to the location of **Line-example3.dwg** file and double-click on it; the file will be opened.
- Click **Home > Draw > Circle > Tan, Tan, Tan** on the ribbon.
- Select the bottom horizontal line of the drawing.
- Select the two inclined lines; a circle will be created tangent to the selected lines.

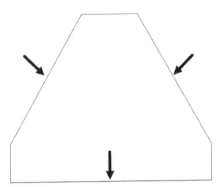 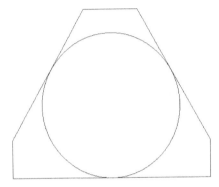

- Save and close the file.

Drawing Arcs

An arc is a portion of a circle. The total angle of an arc will always be less than 360 degrees, whereas the total angle of a circle is 360 degrees. AutoCAD provides you with eleven ways to draw an arc. You can draw arcs in different ways by using the tools available in the **Arcs** drop-down of the **Draw** panel. The usage of these tools will depend on your requirement. Some methods to create arcs are explained in the following examples.

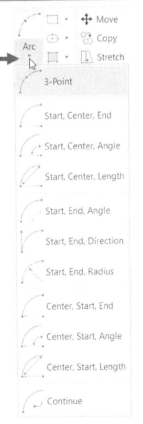

Example (3-Point):

In this example, you will create an arc by specifying three points. The arc will pass through these points.

- Open the **Line-example1.dwg** file.
- Expand the **Draw** panel in the **Home** tab and select the **Multiple Points** tool.

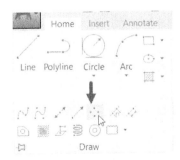

- Type **100,120** in the command line and press **ENTER**; the point will be placed above the rectangle.

(100,120)

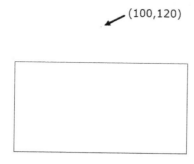

- Click on the drop-down next to the **Object Snap** button on the status bar, and then select the **Node** option from the flyout, as shown.

- Click **Home > Draw > Arc > 3-Point** on the ribbon; the message, "Specify start point of arc or [Center]:" appears in the command line.
- Select the top left corner of the rectangle.
- Select the point located above the rectangle.
- Select the top right corner of the rectangle; the three-point arc will be created.

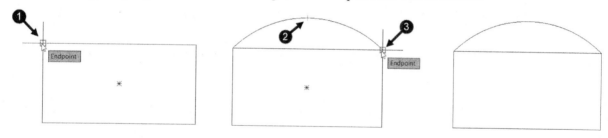

Example (Start, Center, End):

In this example, you will draw an arc by specifying its start, center and end points. The first two points define the radius of the arc and third point defines its included angle.

- Click **Home > Draw > Arc > Start, Center, End** on the ribbon; the message, "Specify start point of arc or [Center]:" appears in the command line.

  By default, the arc will be created in Counter-clockwise direction. Press and hold the **CTRL** key if you want to switch the direction.

- Pick an arbitrary point in the drawing window to specify the start point of an arc; the message, "Specify center point of arc:" appears.
- Pick a point to define the radius of the circle. You can also type the radius value and press **ENTER**; the message, "Specify end point of arc or [Angle chord Length]:" appears.
  You will notice that, as you move the cursor, the included angle of the arc changes.
- Pick a point to define the included angle of the arc. You can also type the angle value and press **ENTER**; the arc will be created.

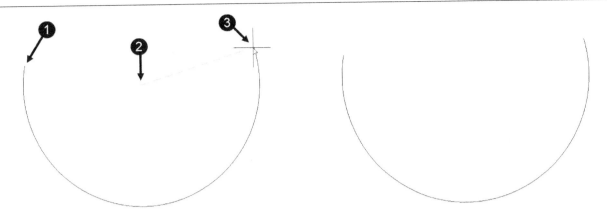

Example (Start, End, Direction):

- Use the **Line** tool and create the drawing shown in figure below. The dimensions are also given in the figure.

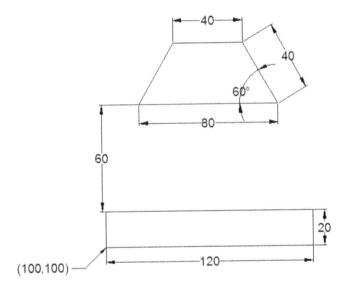

- Click **Home > Draw > Arc > Start, End, Direction** on the ribbon.
- Select the start and end points of the arc as shown in figure.
- Move the cursor vertically downward and click to specify the direction; the arc will be created.

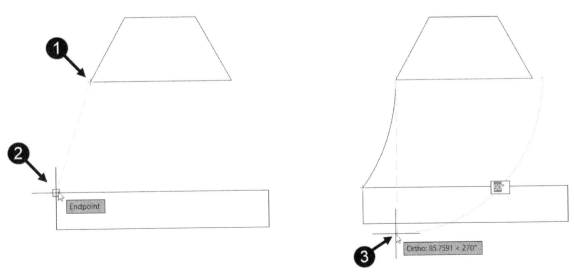

- Similarly, create another arc, as shown.

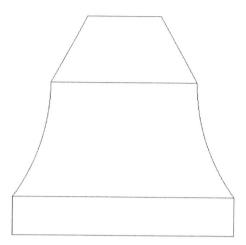

Drawing Splines

Splines are non-uniform curves which are used to create irregular shapes. In AutoCAD, you can create splines by using two methods: **Spline Fit** and **Spline CV**. These methods are explained in the following examples:

Example (Spline Fit):

In this example, you will create a spline using the **Spline Fit** method. In this method, you need to specify various points in the drawing window. The spline will be created passing through the specified points.

- Start a new drawing file.
- Use the **Line** tool and create a sketch similar to the one shown below.

- Expand the **Draw** panel in the **Home** tab and select the **Spline Fit** button; the message, "Specify first point or [Method Knots Object]:" appears in the command line.

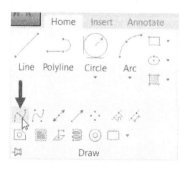
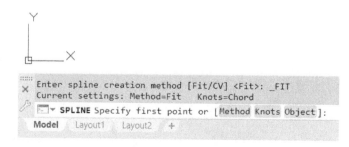

- Select the lower-left corner of the sketch; the message, "Enter next point or [start Tangency toLerance]:" appears in the command line.
- Select the top-left corner point of the sketch.

- Similarly, select the top-right and lower-right corners; a spline will be attached to the cursor.
- Press **ENTER** to create the spline.

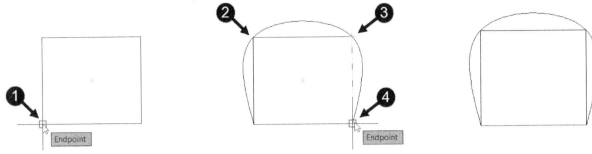

Example: (Spline CV):

In this example, you will create a spline by using the **Spline CV** method. In this method, you will specify various points called control vertices. As you specify the control vertices, imaginary lines are created connecting them. The spline will be drawn tangent to these lines.

- Expand the **Draw** panel in the **Home** tab and select the **Spline CV** button.

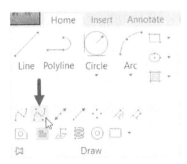

- Select the four corners of the sketch in the same sequence as in the earlier example.
- Press **ENTER**; a spline with control vertices will be created.

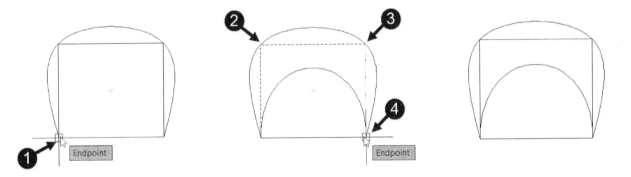

Drawing Ellipses

Ellipses are also non-uniform curves, but they have a regular shape. They are actually splines created in a regular closed shape. In AutoCAD, you can draw an ellipse in three different ways by using the tools available in the **Ellipse** drop-down of the **Draw** panel. The three different ways to draw ellipses are explained in following examples.

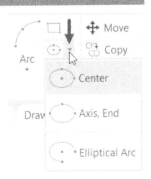

Example (Center)

In this example, you will draw an ellipse by specifying three points. The first point defines the center of the ellipse. Second and third points define the two axes of the ellipse.

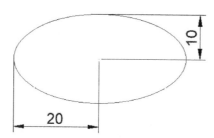

- Click **Home > Draw > Ellipse > Center** 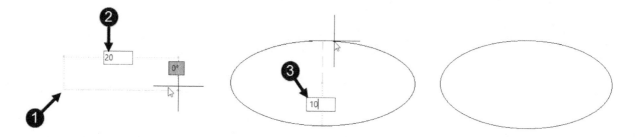 on the ribbon; the message, "Specify center of ellipse:" appears in the command line.
- Select an arbitrary point in the drawing window; the message, "Specify endpoint of axis:" appears command line.
- Move the cursor horizontally and type **20**. Next, press **ENTER**; the message, "Specify distance to other axis or [Rotation]:" appears in the command line.
- Type **10** and press **ENTER**; the ellipse will be created.

Example (Axis,End)

In this example, you will draw an ellipse by specifying three points. The first two points define the location and length of the first axis. The third point defines the second axis of the ellipse.

- Activate the **Dynamic Input** on the status, if it is not active.

- Click **Home > Draw > Ellipse > Axis, End** on the ribbon.
- Follow the prompt sequence given below:
  Specify axis endpoint of ellipse or [Arc Center]: Select an arbitrary point.
  Specify other endpoint of axis: Type **50** as length of the first axis and press **TAB**.
  Next, type **60** as angle and press **ENTER**.
  Specify distance to other axis or [Rotation]: Type **10** as radius of the second axis and press **ENTER**; the ellipse will be created inclined at **60**-degree angle.

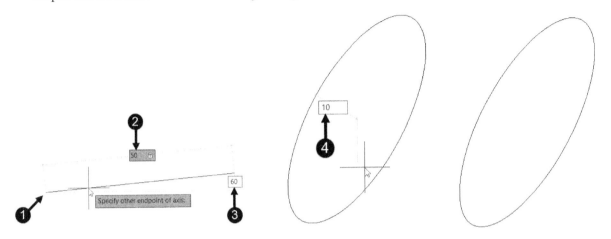

Example (Elliptical Arc)

In this example, you will draw an elliptical arc. To draw an elliptical arc, first you need to specify the location and length of the first axis. Next, specify the radius of the second axis; an ellipse will be displayed. Now, you need to specify the start angle of the elliptical arc. The start angle can be any angle between **0** and **360**. After specifying the start angle, you need to specify the end angle of the elliptical arc.

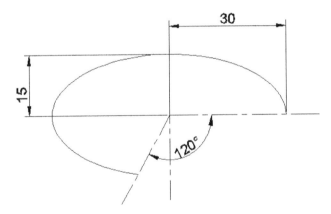

- Turn on the **Ortho Mode** on the Status bar.

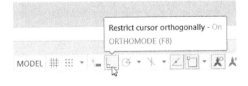

- Click **Home > Draw > Ellipse > Elliptical Arc** on the ribbon.
- Follow the prompt sequence given next:
  Specify axis endpoint of elliptical arc or [Center]: Select an arbitrary point.
  Specify other endpoint of axis: Move the cursor horizontally toward left and type **60**. Next, press **ENTER**.

Specify distance to other axis or [Rotation]: Move the cursor upward and type **15**. Next, press **ENTER**.

Specify start angle or [Parameter]: Type **0** and press **ENTER**.

Specify end angle or [Parameter Included angle]: Type **240** and press **ENTER**.

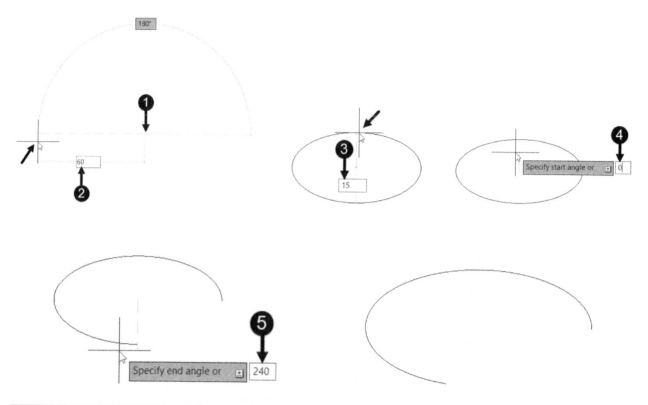

Drawing Polylines

A Polyline is a single object that consists of line segments and arcs. It is more versatile than a line as you can assign a width to it. In the following example, you will create a closed polyline.

Example:

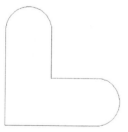

- Activate the **Ortho Mode** on the Status Bar.
- Click **Home > Draw > Polyline** on the ribbon or enter **PLINE** or **PL** in the command line; the message, "Specify start point:" appears in the command line.

- Select an arbitrary point in the drawing window.

- Follow the prompt sequence given next:

Specify next point or [Arc Halfwidth Length Undo Width]: Move the cursor horizontally toward right and type **100**. Next, press **ENTER**.

Specify next point or [Arc Close Halfwidth Length Undo Width]: Select the **Arc** option from the command line.

Specify endpoint of arc or [Angle CEnter Close Direction Halfwidth Line Radius Second pt Undo Width]: Move the cursor vertically upward and type **50**. Next, press **ENTER**.

Specify endpoint of arc or [Angle CEnter Close Direction Halfwidth Line Radius Second pt Undo Width]: Select the **Line** option from the command line.

Specify next point or [Arc Close Halfwidth Length Undo Width]: Move the cursor horizontally toward left and type **50**. Next, press **ENTER**.

Specify next point or [Arc Close Halfwidth Length Undo Width]: Move the cursor vertically upward and type **50**. Next, press **ENTER**.

Specify next point or [Arc Close Halfwidth Length Undo Width]: Select the **Arc** option from the command line

Specify endpoint of arc or [Angle CEnter Close Direction Halfwidth Line Radius Second pt Undo Width]: Move the cursor horizontally toward left and type **50**. Next, press **ENTER**.

Specify endpoint of arc or [Angle CEnter Close Direction Halfwidth Line Radius Second pt Undo Width]: Select the **CLose** option from the command line

Now, when you select a line segment from the sketch, the whole sketch will be selected. This is because the polyline created is a single object.

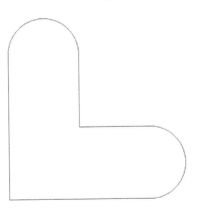
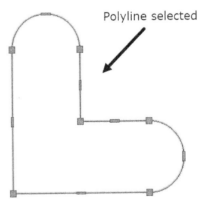

Polyline selected

Drawing Rectangles

A Rectangle is a four-sided single object. You can create a rectangle by just specifying its two diagonal corners. However, there are various methods to create a rectangle. These methods are explained in the following examples.

Example:

In this example, you will create a rectangle by specifying it corner points.

- Open a new file.
- Click **Home > Draw > Rectangle** on the ribbon or enter **RECTANG** or **REC** in the command line; the message, "Specify first corner point or [Chamfer Elevation Fillet Thickness Width]:" appears in the command line.

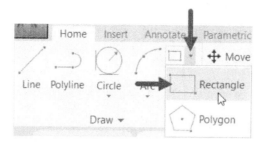

- Pick an arbitrary point in the drawing window; the message "Specify other corner point or [Area Dimensions Rotation]:" appears in the command line.
- Move the cursor diagonally toward right and click to create a rectangle.

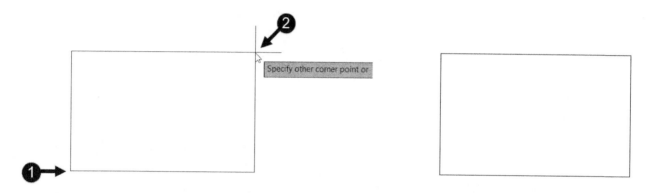

Example:

In this example, you will create a rectangle by specifying its length and width.

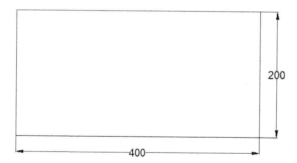

- Click **Home > Draw > Rectangle** on the ribbon, or enter **RECTANG** or **REC** in the command line.
- Specify the first corner of the rectangle by picking an arbitrary point in the drawing window.
- Follow the prompt sequence given next:

Specify other corner point or [Area Dimensions Rotation]: Select the **Dimensions** option from the command line
Specify length for rectangles: Type **400** and press **ENTER**.
Specify width for rectangles: Type **200** and press **ENTER**.
Specify other corner point or [Area Dimensions Rotation]: Move the cursor upwards and click to create the rectangle.

Example:

In this example, you will create a rectangle by specifying its area and width.

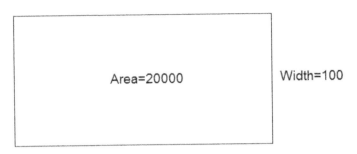

- Click **Home > Draw > Rectangle** on the ribbon, or enter **RECTANG** or **REC** in the command line.
- Specify the first corner of the rectangle by picking an arbitrary point.
- Follow the prompt sequence given next:

  Specify other corner point or [Area Dimensions Rotation]: Select the **Area** option from the command line

  Enter area of rectangle in current units: Type **20000** and press **ENTER**.

  Calculate rectangle dimensions based on [Length Width] <Length>: Select the **Width** option from the command line.

  Enter rectangle width: Type **100** and press **ENTER**; the length will be calculated automatically.

Example:

In this example, you will create a rectangle with chamfered corners.

- Click **Home > Draw > Rectangle** on the ribbon or enter **RECTANG** or **REC** in the command line.
- Follow the prompt sequence given next:

  Specify first corner point or [Chamfer Elevation Fillet Thickness Width]: Select the **Chamfer** option from the command line.

  Specify first chamfer distance for rectangles: Type **20** and press **ENTER**.

  Specify second chamfer distance for rectangles: Type **20** and press **ENTER**.

  Specify first corner point or [Chamfer Elevation Fillet Thickness Width]: Click at an arbitrary point in the drawing window to specify the first corner.

  Specify other corner point or [Area Dimensions Rotation]: Move the cursor diagonally toward right and click to specify the second corner.

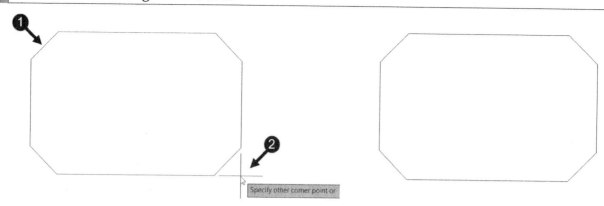

Example:

In this example, you will create a rectangle with rounded corners.

- Click **Home > Draw > Rectangle** on the ribbon or enter **RECTANG** or **REC** in the command line.
- Follow the prompt sequence given next:

  Specify first corner point or [Chamfer Elevation Fillet Thickness Width]: Select the **Fillet** option from the command line.
  Specify fillet radius for rectangles: Type **50** and press **ENTER**.
  Specify first corner point or [Chamfer Elevation Fillet Thickness Width]: Click at an arbitrary point in the drawing window to specify the first corner.
  Specify other corner point or [Area Dimensions Rotation]: Move the cursor diagonally toward right and click to specify the second corner.

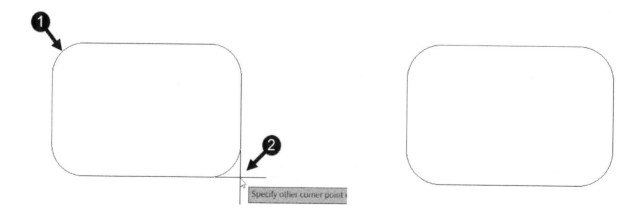

Example:

In this example, you will create an inclined rectangle.

- Click **Home > Draw > Rectangle** on the ribbon or enter **RECTANG** or **REC** in the command line.
- Specify the first corner of the rectangle by picking an arbitrary point.
- Follow the prompt sequence given next:

Specify other corner point or [Area Dimensions Rotation]: Select the **Rotation** option from the command line.
Specify rotation angle or [Pick points]: Type **60** and press **ENTER**.
Specify other corner point or [Area Dimensions Rotation]: Enter **400** and press **TAB** and then **300** in the Dynamic Input boxes.

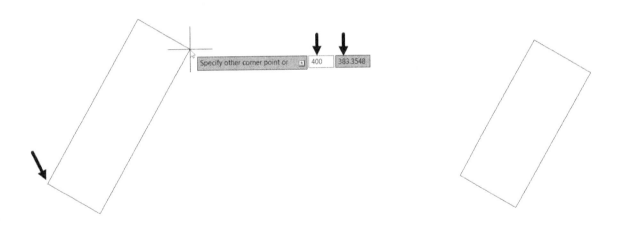

Drawing Polygons

A Polygon is a single object having many sides ranging from **3** to **1024**. In AutoCAD, you can create regular polygons having sides with equal length. There are two methods to create a polygon. These methods are explained in the following examples.

Example:

In this example, you will create a polygon by specifying the number of sides, and then specifying the length of one side.

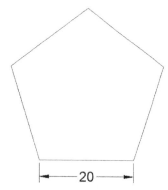

- Click **Home > Draw > Polygon** on the ribbon.

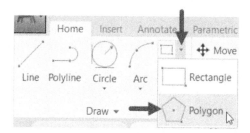

- Follow the prompt sequence given next.

  Enter number of sides <4>: Type **5** and press **ENTER**.
  Specify center of polygon or [Edge]: Select the **Edge** option from the command line.
  Specify first endpoint of edge: Select an arbitrary point.
  Specify second endpoint of edge: Type **20** and press **ENTER**.

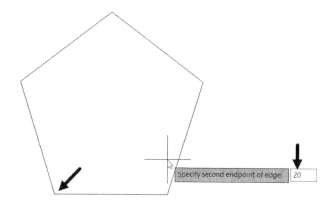
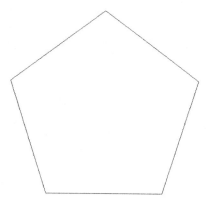

Example:

In this example, you will create a polygon by specifying the number of sides and drawing an imaginary circle (inscribed circle). The polygon will be created with its corners located on the imaginary circle. You can also create a polygon with the circumscribed circle. A circumscribed circle is an imaginary circle which is tangent to all the sides of a polygon.

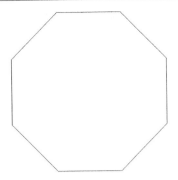

- Type **POL** in the command line and press **ENTER**; the **POLYGON** command will be invoked.
- Follow the prompt sequence given next:

   Enter number of sides <5>: Type **8** and press **ENTER**.
   Specify center of polygon or [Edge]: Select an arbitrary point
   Enter an option [Inscribed in circle Circumscribed about circle] <C>: Select the **Inscribed in circle** option from the command line.
   Specify radius of circle: Type **20** and press **ENTER**; a polygon will be created with its corners touching the imaginary circle.

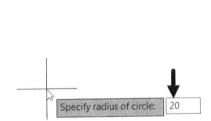

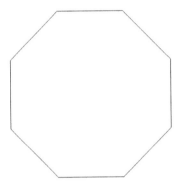

Questions:

1. Which key is pressed to turn off the Grid display?
2. Where is **Dynamic Input** button located?
3. What is the use of **Tan, Tan, Radius** tool?
4. Where is **Tan, Tan, Tan** tool available and for which this tool is used?
5. Which tool is used to create irregular shaped curves?
6. Which tool is used to create a hexagon?

Exercises

Exercise 1:

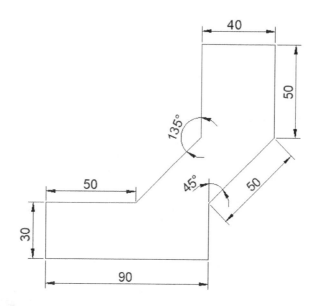

Exercise 2:

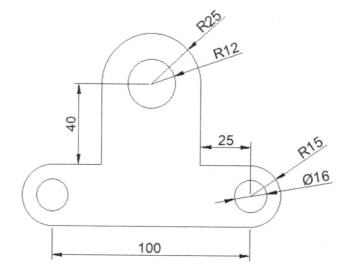

Exercise 3:

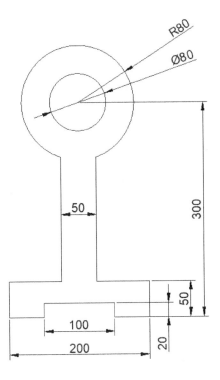

Chapter 3: Drawing Aids in AutoCAD

In this chapter, you will learn to do the following:

- **Use Grid and Snap**
- **Use Ortho Mode and Polar Tracking**
- **Use Object Snaps and Object Snap Tacking**
- **Create Layers and assign properties to it**
- **Zoom and Pan drawings**

Drawing Aids

This chapter teaches you to specify the drawing settings which will assist you to easily create a drawing in AutoCAD. Most drawing settings can be turned on or off from the status bar. You can also access additional drawing settings by right-clicking on the button located on the status bar.

Setting Grid and Snap

Grid is the basic drawing setting. It makes the drawing window appear like a graph paper. You can turn ON the grid display by clicking the **Grid Display** button on the status bar or just pressing **F7** on the keyboard. You can also adjust the grid size and the spacing between the grid lines by using the **Drafting Settings** dialog box.

Snap is used to drawing objects by using the intersection points of the grid lines. When you turn the Snap Mode ON, you will be able select only grid points. In the following example, you will learn to set the grid and snap settings.

Example:

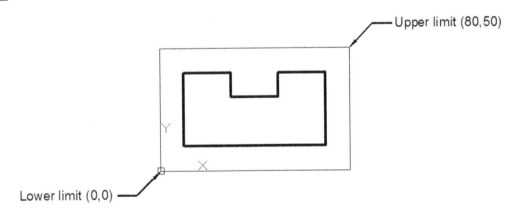

- Click **Application Menu > New**; the **Select template** dialog box appears.
- Select the **acadISO -Named Plot Styles.dwt** template if it is not selected by default.
- Click on the **Open** button, as shown.

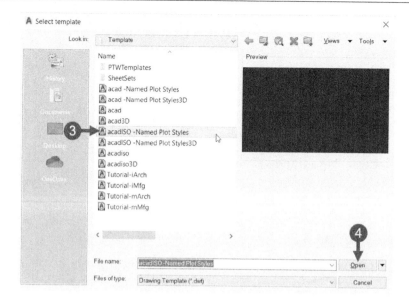

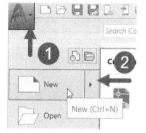

- Right-click on the **Grid Display** button located on the status bar.
- Click on the down arrow next to the **SNAPMODE** button and select the **Snap Settings** option. This **Drafting Settings** dialog box appears.

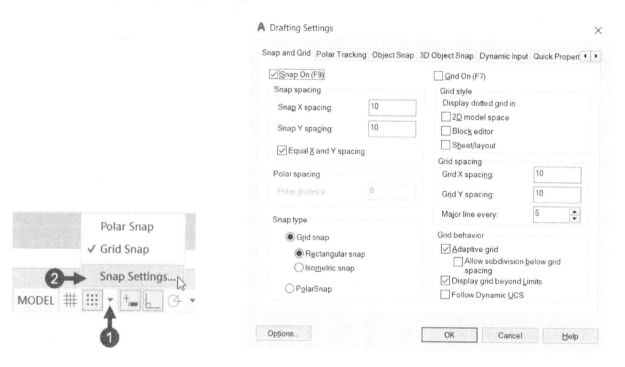

Alternatively, you can enter **DS** in the command line to display the **Drafting Settings** dialog box.

- Set **Grid X spacing** to **10** and press **TAB** key; the **Grid Y spacing** is updated with the same value.
- Set **Major line every** to **10**.

- Select the **Snap On** check box under **Snap and Grid** tab of dialog box, if it is not selected.
- Make sure that **Snap X spacing** and **Snap Y spacing** is set to **10**.

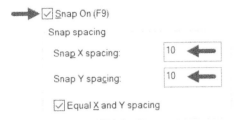

- Make sure that the **Grid snap** radio button is selected in the **Snap type** group.

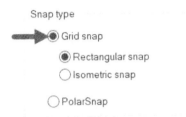

- Click **OK** on the dialog box.

Setting the Limits of a drawing

You can set the limits of a drawing by specifying its lower-left and top-right corners. By setting Limits of a drawing, you will define the size of the drawing area. In AutoCAD, limits are set to some default values. However, you can redefine the limits to change the drawing area as per your requirement.

- Type **Limits** at the command line and press **ENTER**.

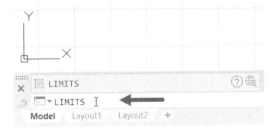

- Press **ENTER** to accept the lower limit as **0,0**.

  Now, you need to specify the upper limit.

- Type **80,50** and press **ENTER** key.
- Click **View > Navigate 2D > Zoom drop-down > All** on the ribbon; the drawing window will be zoomed to the limits.
- Click **Zoom > Zoom All** from the Navigation Bar; the drawing window will be zoomed to the limits.

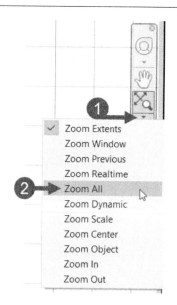

Tip : You can simply zoom the drawing area to the limit by followings the below given steps one-by-one:

Step 1: Press the **Z** key and then the **Enter** key.
Step 2: Now press the **A** key and then the **Enter** key.

Setting the Lineweight

Lineweight is the thickness of the objects that you draw. In AutoCAD, there is a default lineweight assigned to objects. However, you can set a new lineweight. The method to set the lineweight is explained below.

- Click on the **Customization** options on the Status bar and select the **LineWeight** option from the flyout displayed. This makes the **LineWeight** button visible on the status bar.

- Now, activate the **Show/Hide Lineweight** button located on the status bar.

- Right-click on the **Show/Hide Lineweight** button and select the **Lineweight Settings**; the **Lineweight Settings** dialog box appears.

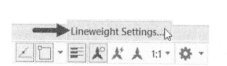

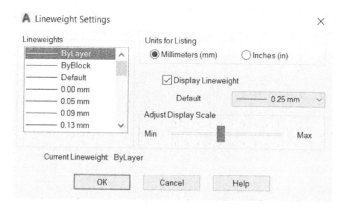

- Select **0.40** mm from the **Default** drop-down on the **Lineweight Settings** dialog box.
- Click **OK**.
- Type **L** at the command line and press **ENTER**.
- Type **10,10** and press **ENTER** to specify the first point.
- Make sure that the **Dynamic Input** ⊞ button in the status bar is active, as shown.
- Move the cursor horizontally toward right and click when the tooltip displays **60 < 0**, as shown.

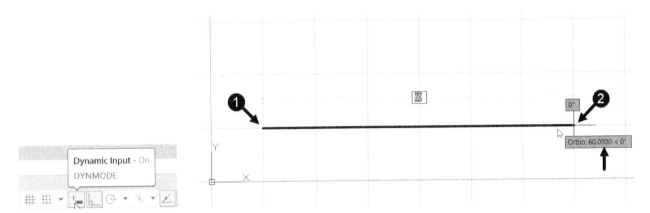

- Move the cursor vertically upwards and click when the tooltip displays **30<90**.
- Move the cursor horizontally toward left and click when the tooltip displays **20<180**.
- Move the cursor vertically downwards and click when the tooltip displays **10<270**.
- Move the cursor horizontally toward left and click when the tooltip displays **20<180**.
- Move the cursor vertically upwards and click when the tooltip displays **10<90**.
- Move the cursor horizontally toward left and click when the tooltip displays **20<180**.
- Right-click and select **Close**.

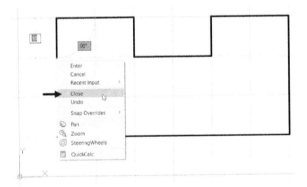

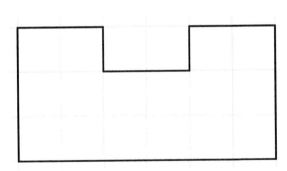

- Save and close the file.

Using the Ortho mode and Polar Tracking

Ortho mode is used to draw orthogonal (horizontal or vertical) lines. Polar Tracking is used to constrain the lines to angular increments. In the following example, you will create a drawing with the help of Ortho Mode and Polar Tracking.

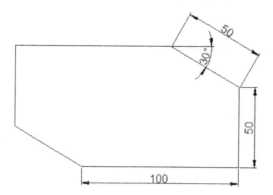

- Open a new AutoCAD file.
- Deactivate the **Grid Display** and **Snap Mode** buttons on the status bar.
- Click the **Ortho Mode** button on the status bar.
- Click **Zoom All** on the **Navigation Bar**.
- Click the **Line** button on the **Draw** panel.
- To specify the first point, type **50,50** and press **ENTER** key.
- Move the cursor toward right, type **100** and press **ENTER**; you will notice that a horizontal line is created.
- Move the cursor upwards, type **50** and press **ENTER**; you will notice that a vertical line is created.
- Click the **Polar Tracking** button on the status bar to activate it, as shown.
- Click on the drop down next to the **Polar Tracking** button and select **30** from the menu displayed, as shown.

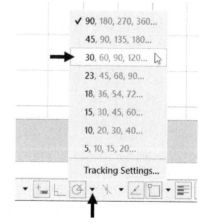

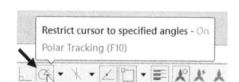

You will notice that a track line is displayed at 30-degree increments when you rotate the cursor.

- Move the cursor and stop when the tooltip displays <**150** angle value.

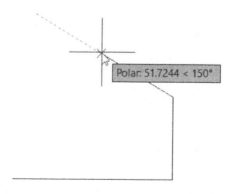

- Type **50** and press **ENTER** when the tooltip displays **<150°**.
- Move the cursor toward left.
- Type **100** and press **ENTER** when the tooltip displays **<180°**.
- Move the cursor downward.
- Type **50** and press **ENTER** when the tooltip displays **<270°**.
- Right-click and select **Close**.

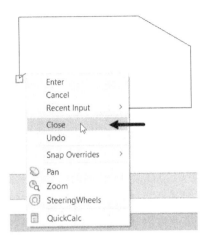
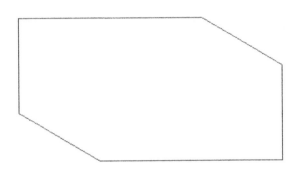

Using Layers

Layers are like a group of transparent sheets that are combined into a complete drawing. The figure below displays a drawing consisting of object lines and dimension lines. In this example, the object lines are created on the '**Object**' layer, and dimensions are created on the layer called '**Dimension**'. You can easily turn-off the '**Dimension**' layer for a clearer view of the object lines.

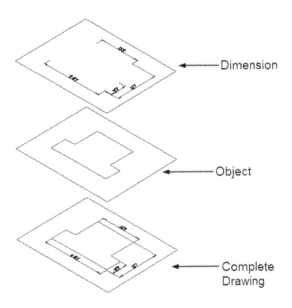

Layer Properties Manager

The **Layer Properties Manager** is used to create and manage layers. To open **Layer Properties Manager**, click **Home > Layers > Layer Properties** on the ribbon or enter **LA** in the command line.

The components of the **Layer Properties Manager** are shown below. The **Tree View** section is used for displaying layer filters, group, or state information. The **List View** section is the main body of the **Layer Properties Manager**. It lists the individual layers that currently exist in the drawing.

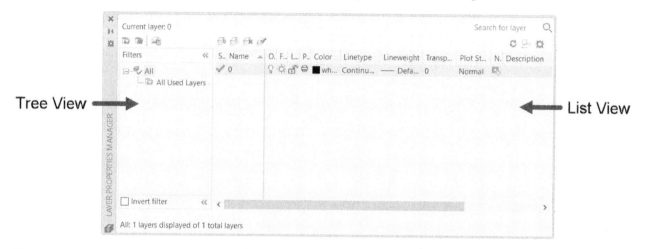

The **List View** section contains various properties. You can set layer properties and perform various operations in the **List View** section. A brief explanation of each layer property is given below.

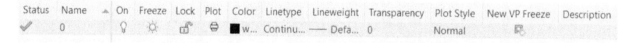

Status –Shows a green check when a layer is set to current.

Name - Shows the name of the layer.

On – Used to turn on/off the visibility of a layer. When a layer is turned on, it shows a yellow light-bulb. When you turn off a layer, it shows a grey light-bulb.

Freeze/Thaw – It is used to freeze the objects of a layer so that they cannot be modified. Also, the visibility of the object is turned off.

Lock/Unlock- It is used to lock the layer so that the objects on it cannot be modified.

Color – It is used to assign a color to the layer.

Linetype – It is used to assign a linetype to the layer.

Lineweight – It is used to set a lineweight(thickness) to the layer.

Transparency – It is used to set transparency to a layer. You set a transparency level from 0 to 90 for all objects on a layer.

Plot Style – It is used to override the settings such as color, linetype, and lineweight while plotting a drawing.

Plot – It is used to control which layer will be plotted.

New VP Freeze – It is used to create and freeze a layer in any new viewport.

Description – It is used to enter a detailed description about the layer.

Creating a New Layer

You can create a new layer by using anyone of the following methods:

1. Click the **New Layer** button on the **Layer Properties Manager**; a new layer with the name '**Layer1**' appears in **Name** field. Next, enter the name of the layer in the **Name** field.

2. Right-click in the **Name** field and select **New Layer** from the shortcut menu.
3. If you want to continue to create layers after creating one layer, then press **ENTER** or comma(,).

Making a layer current

If you want to draw objects on a particular layer, then you have to make it current. You can make a layer current using the methods listed below.

1. Select the layer from the List view and click the **Set Current** button on the **Layer Properties Manager**.

2. Double-click on the **Name** field of the layer.
3. Right-click on the layer and select **Set current**.
4. Select the layer from the **Layer** drop-down of the **Layer** panel, as shown.

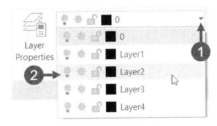

5. Click the **Make Current** button on the **Layers** panel, as shown. Next, select an object; the layer related to the selected object will become current.

Deleting a Layer

You can delete a layer by using anyone of the following methods:

1. Click the **Delete Layer** button or press **ALT+D**.

2. Right-click in the **Name** field and select **Delete Layer** from the shortcut menu.

You will learn more about layers in later chapters. You can find an example related to layers in the **Offset** tool section of chapter 4.

Using Object Snaps

Object Snaps are important settings that improve your performance and accuracy while creating a drawing. They allow you to select keypoints of objects while creating a drawing. You can activate the required Object Snap by using the **Object snap** shortcut menu. Press and hold the **SHIFT** key and right-click to display this shortcut menu.

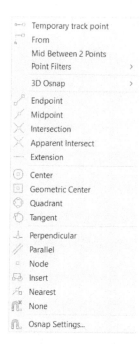

The following table gives you the functions of various Object Snaps.

Object Snap	Function
Endpoint	Snaps to the endpoints of lines and arcs. 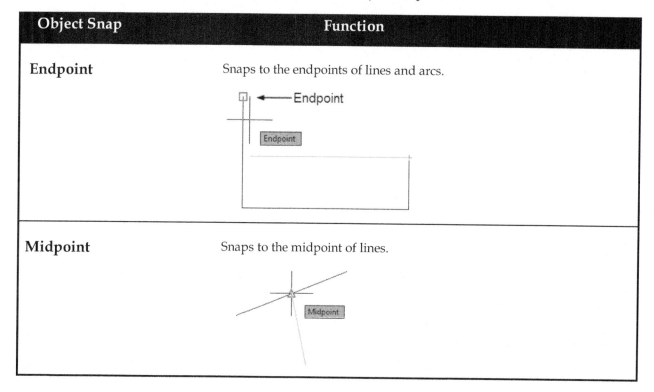
Midpoint	Snaps to the midpoint of lines.

Nearest	Snaps to the nearest point found along any object 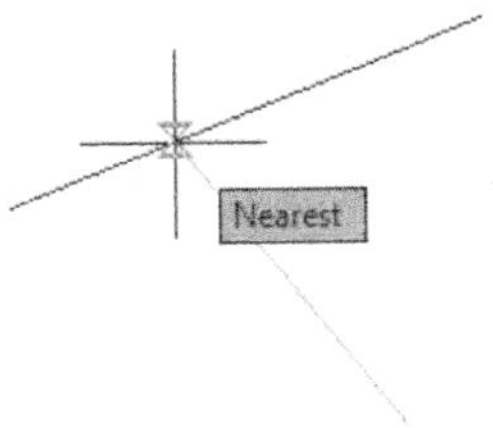
Center	Snaps to the centers of circles and arcs. 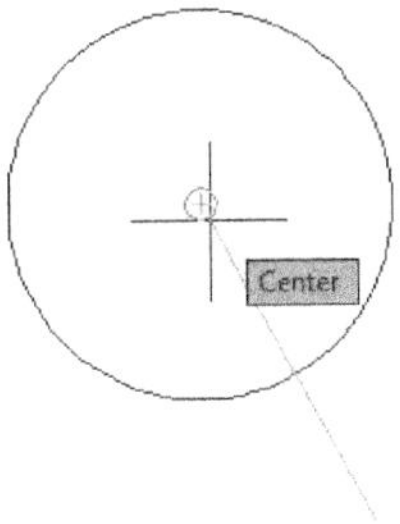
Tangent	Snaps to the tangent location of arcs and circles. 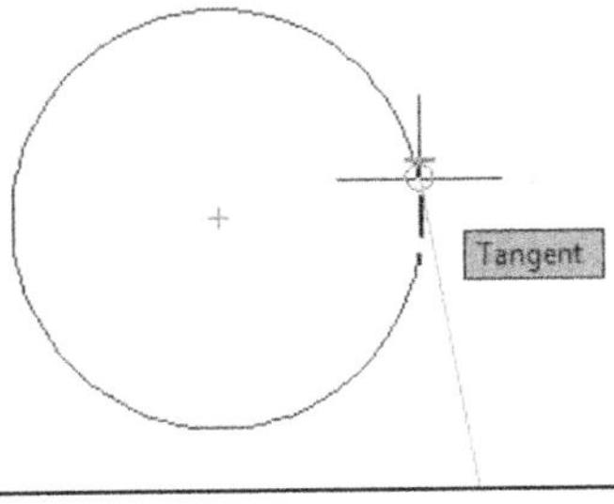
Quadrant	Snaps to four key points located on a circle. 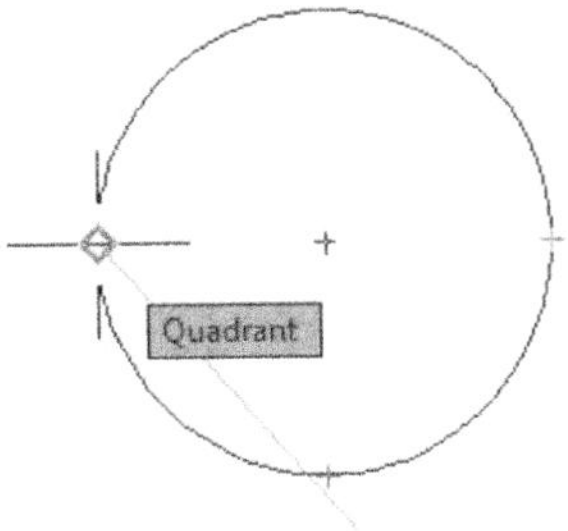
Intersection	Snaps to the intersections of objects. 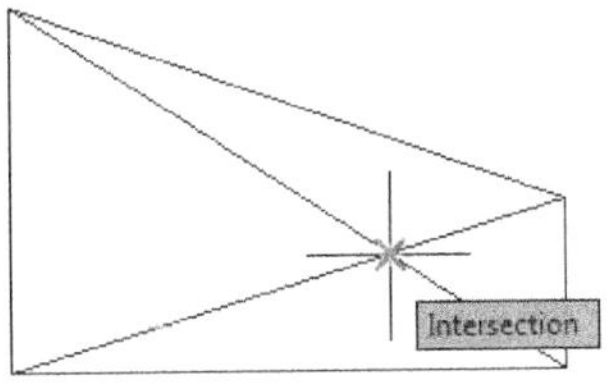

Apparent Intersection	Snaps to the projected intersection of two objects in 3D space.
Perpendicular	Snaps to a perpendicular location on an object.

Node	Snaps to points of dimensions lines, text objects, dimension text and so on.

Insert	Snaps to the insertion point of blocks, shapes and text.

None	Deactivates Object Snap.
Parallel	It is used to draw an object parallel to another object.

Extension	Creates a temporary extension line when the cursor passes through the endpoints of a line or an arc. You can pick points along the temporary extension lines.

From	Locates a point at a specified distance and direction from a selected reference point. 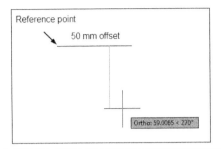
Midpoint Between 2 Points	Snaps to the middle point of two selected points. 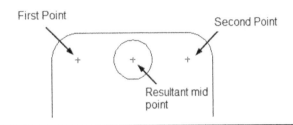
Temporary Track Point	It is used to locate a point by using trace lines from a reference point. 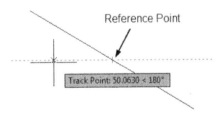

Running Object Snaps

Previously, you have learned to select Object Snaps from the shortcut menu. However, you can make Object Snap modes available continuously instead of selecting them every time. You can do this by using the **Running Object Snaps**. To use the Running Object Snaps, click on the down arrow next to the **Object Snap** button on the status bar and select the required object snap from the menu.

You can also select the **Object Snap Settings** option from the shortcut menu to open the **Drafting Settings** dialog box. In this dialog box, you can select the required Object Snaps by selecting check boxes.

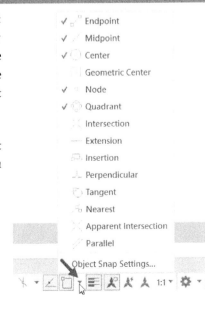

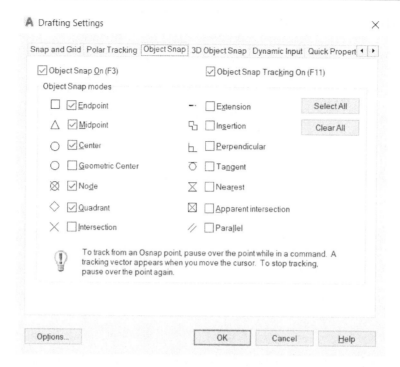

Cycling through Object Snaps

After setting the Running Object Snap settings, AutoCAD displays object snaps depending on the shape of the object. However, you can cycle through the object snaps by pressing the TAB. In the following example, you will learn to cycle through different object snaps.

Example:

- Click on the down arrow next to the **Object Snap** button and select the **Object Snap Settings** option; the **Drafting Settings** dialog box appears. Select the **Select All** check box and click the **OK** button.
- Draw the objects as shown below.

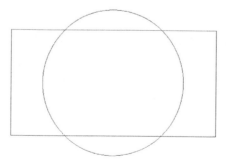

- Click the **Circle** button on the **Draw** panel.
- Place the cursor on the drawing. Press the **TAB** key; you will notice that the object snaps change.

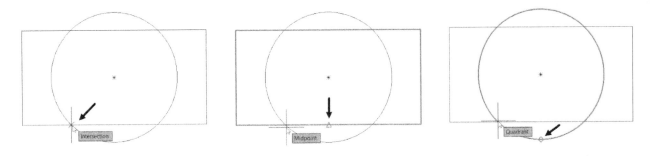

- Click when the **Center** snap is displayed and draw a circle.

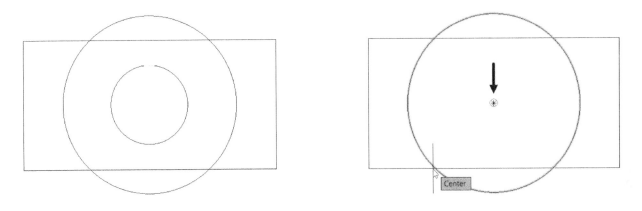

Using Object Snap Tracking

Object Snap tracking is the movement of cursor along the trace lines originating from the keypoints of objects. Object Snap Tracking works only when the **Object Snap** mode is turned on. In the following example, you will learn to use Object Snap Tracking for creating objects.

Example:

- Select the **Object Snap Tracking** button from the Status bar.

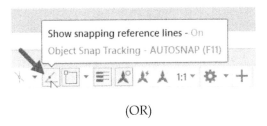

(OR)

- Open the **Drafting Settings** dialog box and click the **Object Snap** tab.
- Select the **Object Snap Tracking On** check box and click **OK** button.

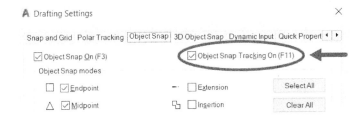

- Use the **Line** tool and draw the objects as shown below.

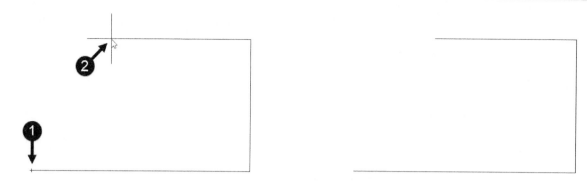

- Press the **ENTER** key twice to start drawing lines from the last point.
- Press the **F8** key to deactivate the **ORTHOMODE**, if it is active.
- Move the cursor and place it on the endpoint of the lower horizontal line.

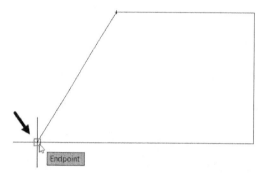

- Move the cursor vertically upwards; you will notice that a trace line is displayed as shown below.

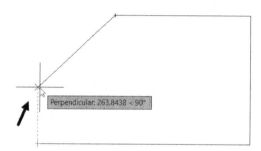

- Click on the trace line to create an inclined line.
- Snap the cursor to the endpoint of the lower horizontal line and click.

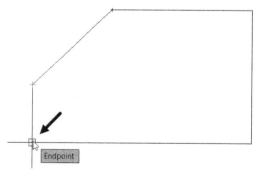

- Right-click and select **Enter**.
- Click the **Circle** button on the **Draw** panel of the ribbon.
- Place the cursor over the lower endpoint of the inclined line and move horizontally right; you will notice that a horizontal trace line is displayed.

- Move the cursor over bottom horizontal line to display a vertical trace line from its midpoint, as show below.

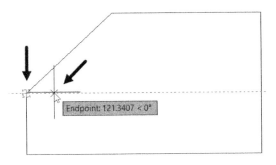
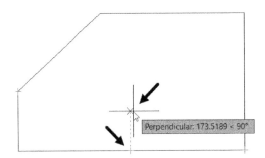

- Move the cursor vertically upwards where both trace lines intersect each other, as shown.
- Click at the intersecting point and create a circle, as shown below.

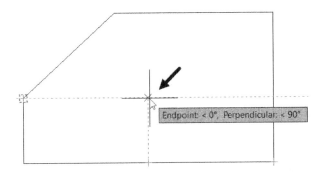
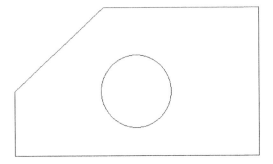

Using Zoom tools

Using the zoom tools, you can magnify or reduce a drawing. You can use these tools to view the minute details of a very complicated drawing. The Zoom tools can be accessed from the Menu Bar Navigation Bar, and Command line.

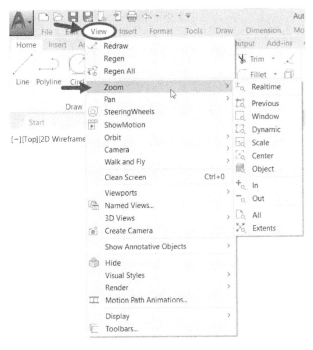

Menu Bar

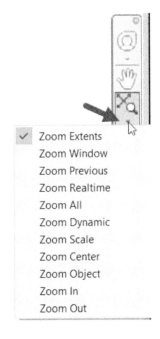

Navigation Bar

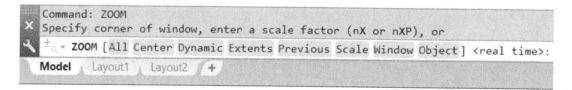

```
Command: ZOOM
Specify corner of window, enter a scale factor (nX or nXP), or
ZOOM [All Center Dynamic Extents Previous Scale Window Object] <real time>:
```

Model Layout1 Layout2 +

Command Line

Zooming with a Mouse Wheel

Zooming using the mouse wheel is one of the easiest methods.

- Roll the mouse wheel forward to zoom into a drawing.
- Roll the mouse wheel backwards to zoom out of the drawing.
- Press the mouse wheel and drag the mouse to pan the drawing.

Using Zoom Extents

Using the **Zoom Extents** tool, you can zoom to the extents of the largest object in a drawing.

- Click **Zoom > Zoom Extents** on the Navigation Bar.
- You can also double-click on the mouse wheel to zoom to extents.

Using Zoom-Window

Using the **Zoom-Window** tool, you can specify the area to be magnified by selecting two points representing a rectangle.

- Click **Zoom > Zoom Window** on the Navigation Bar.
- Create a window by selecting the first corner and the second corner; the area covered by the window will be magnified.

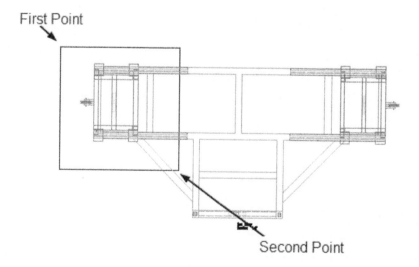

First Point

Second Point

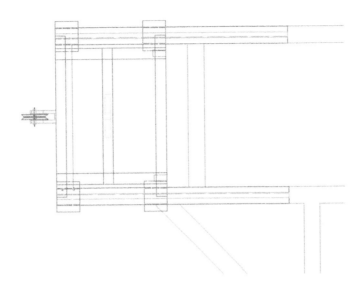

Using Zoom-Previous

After magnifying a small area of the drawing, you can use the **Zoom-Previous** tool to return to the previous display.

- Click **Zoom > Zoom Previous** on the Navigation Bar.

Using Zoom-Realtime

Using the **Zoom-Realtime** tool, you can zoom in or zoom out of a drawing in real time.

- Click **Zoom > Zoom Realtime** on the **Navigation Bar**; the cursor is changed to a magnifying glass with plus and minus symbols.
- Press and hold the left mouse button and drag the mouse forward to zoom into the drawing.
- Drag the mouse backward to zoom out of the drawing.

Using Zoom-All

The **Zoom All** tool is used to adjust the drawing space to the limits set by using the **LIMITS** command.

- Click **Zoom > Zoom All** on the **Navigation Bar**; the drawing will be zoomed to its limits.

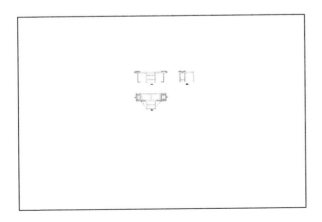

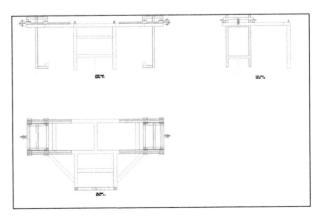

Using Zoom Dynamic

With the **Zoom Dynamic** tool, you can zoom to a particular portion of a drawing by using a viewing box.

- Click **Zoom > Zoom Dynamic** on the **Navigation Bar**; the drawing will be zoomed to its limits. Also, a viewing box is attached to the cursor.

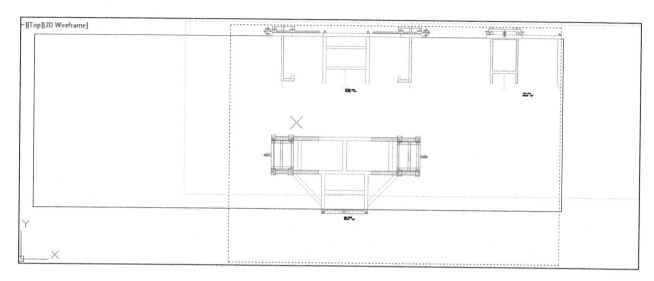

- Click and drag the cursor to define the shape of the viewing box.
- Left-click and move the cursor the area to be zoomed.

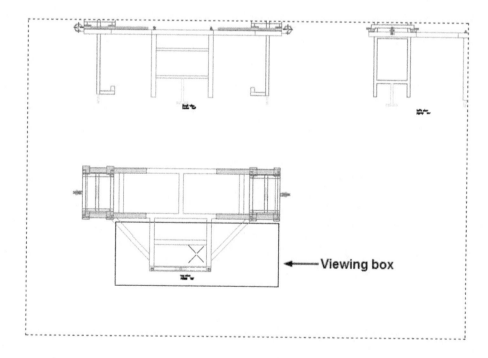

- Right-click and select **Enter**; the area covered by the viewing box is magnified.

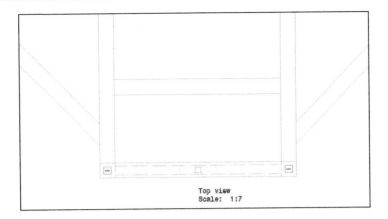

Top view
Scale: 1:7

Using Zoom-Scale

Using the **Zoom-Scale** tool, you can zoom in or zoom out of a drawing by entering zoom scale factors directly from your keyboard.

- Click **Zoom > Zoom Scale** on the Navigation Bar. The message, "**Enter a scale factor (nX or nXP)**" appears in the command line.
- Enter the scale factor **0.25** to scale the drawing to **25%** of the full view.
- Enter the scale factor **0.25X** to scale the drawing to **25%** of the current view.
- Enter the scale factor **0.25XP** to scale the drawing to **25%** of the paper space.

Using Zoom-Center

Using the **Zoom Center** tool, you can zoom to an area of the drawing based on a center point and magnification value.

- Click **Zoom > Zoom Center** on the Navigation Bar. The message, "**Specify Center point**" appears in the command line.
- Select a point in the drawing to which you want to zoom in; the message, "**Enter magnification or height**" appears in the command line.

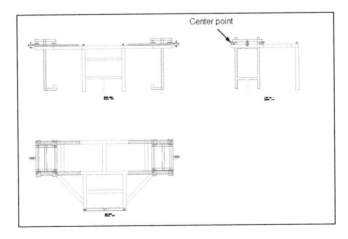

Center point

- Enter 10X in the command line to magnify the location of point the selected point by ten times.

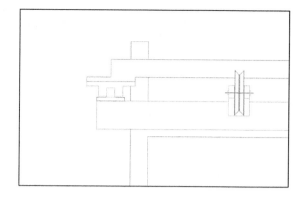

Using Zoom-Object

Using the **Zoom Object** tool, you can magnify a portion of the drawing by selecting one or more objects.

- Click **Zoom > Zoom Object** on the Navigation Bar.
- Select one or more objects from the drawing and press **ENTER**; the objects will be magnified.

Using Zoom-In

Using the **Zoom In** tool, you can magnify the drawing by a scale factor of 2.

- Click **Zoom > Zoom-In** on the Navigation Bar; the drawing is magnified to double.

Using Zoom-Out

The **Zoom-out** tool is used to de-magnify the display screen by a scale factor of 0.5.

Panning Drawings

After zooming into a drawing, you may want to view an area which is outside the current display. You can do this by using the **Pan** tool.

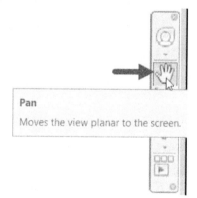

- Click **Pan** on the **Navigation Bar**, as shown.
- Press and hold the left mouse button and drag the mouse; a new area of the drawing which is outside the current view is displayed.

Questions:

1. Which tool is used to set the limits of the drawing area?
2. Which tool is used to make the line thickness visible?
3. Which key is pressed to activate/deactivate the Grid button/icon?
4. Which object snap is selected to snaps to the middle point of two selected points.
5. Which object snap is selected to snaps to four key points located on a circle.
6. Which button of **Line Property Manager** button is clicked to delete a layer?

Exercises

Exercise 1:

Exercise 2:

Chapter 4: Editing Tools in AutoCAD

In this chapter, you will learn the following tools:

- ❖ The **Move** tool
- ❖ The **Copy** tool
- ❖ The **Rotate** tool
- ❖ The **Scale** tool
- ❖ The **Trim** tool
- ❖ The **Extend** tool
- ❖ The **Fillet** tool
- ❖ The **Chamfer** tool
- ❖ The **Mirror** tool
- ❖ The **Explode** tool
- ❖ The **Stretch** tool
- ❖ The **Polar Array** tool
- ❖ The **Offset** tool
- ❖ The **Path Array** tool
- ❖ The **Rectangular Array** tool

Editing Tools

In previous chapters, you have learned to create some simple drawings using the basic drawing tools. However, to create complex drawings, you may need to perform various editing operations. The tools to perform the editing operations are available in the **Modify** panel of the **Home** ribbon. You can click the down arrow on this panel to find more editing tools. Using these editing tools, you can modify existing objects or use existing objects to create new or similar objects.

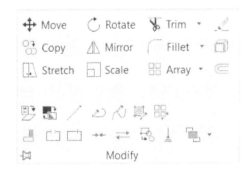

These editing tools are explained next, one-by-one.

The Move tool

The **Move**  tool is used to move a selected object(s) from one location to a new location without changing its orientation. To move objects, you need to select this tool and select the objects from the drawing area. After selecting objects, you need to specify the 'base point' and the 'destination point'.

Example:

Create the drawing as shown below.

- Click **Home > Modify > Move** on the ribbon or enter **M** in the command line.
- Select the circle located at the left-side, and then right-click to accept the selection.
- Select the center of the circle as the base point.
- Make sure that the **Ortho Mode** is activated.
- Move the cursor toward right and pick a point as shown below; the circle will be moved to the new location, as shown.

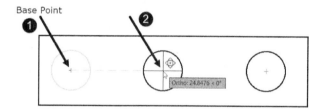

The Copy tool

The **Copy**  tool is used to copy objects and place them at a required location. This tool is similar to the **Move** tool, except that object will remain at its original position and a copy of it will be placed at the new location.

Example:

Draw a rectangle and two concentric circles of **100** mm and **150** mm diameter inside it, as shown.

- Click **Home > Modify > Copy** on the ribbon or enter **CO** in the command line.
- Select the two circles, and then right-click to accept the selection.
- Select the center of the circle as the base point.
- Make sure that the **Ortho Mode** is active.
- Move the cursor toward right.
- Type **300** and press **ENTER** the selected entities get copied and placed at the defined location, as shown.

The tool is still active and you can still place the copied entities at various locations, if required.

- Press the **Esc** key to deactivate the tool.

  Alternatively, you can select **Exit** from the command line to deactivate the **Copy** tool.

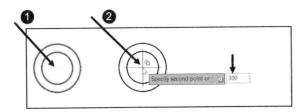
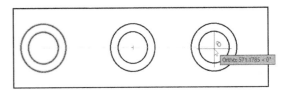

The Rotate tool

The **Rotate** ⟳ Rotate tool is used to rotate an object or a group of objects about a base point. To rotate objects, you need to invoke this tool and select the objects from the drawing window. After selecting objects, you need to specify the 'base point' and the angle of rotation. The object(s) will be rotated about the base point.

- Click **Home > Modify > Rotate** on the ribbon or enter **RO** in the command line.
- Select the circles/entities as shown below, and then right-click to accept the selection.

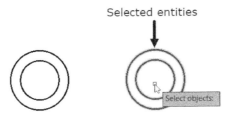

- Select the center of the other circle as the base point, as shown.

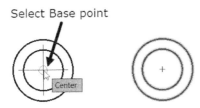

- Select the **Copy** option from the command line.
- Type **270** as the rotation angle and press **ENTER**, the selected circles will be rotated/copied at angle **270** angle.

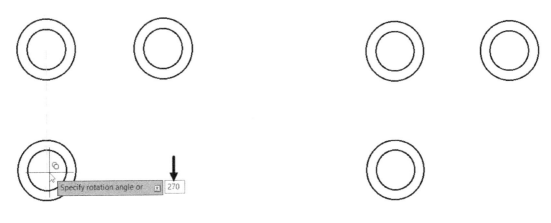

The Scale tool

The **Scale** ⬚ Scale tool is used to change the size of objects. You can reduce or enlarge the size without changing the shape of an object. To scale objects, you need to invoke this tool and select the objects from the drawing window. After selecting objects, you need to specify the 'base point' and the scale factor. The scale factor is the ratio between the original size of the object and the size to be achieved. For example, if you specify the scale factor as **2**, the size of the object will be doubled.

- Click **Home > Modify > Scale** on the ribbon or enter **SC** in the command line.
- Select the circles as shown below and right-click to accept the selection.
- Select the center point of the selected circles as the base point.

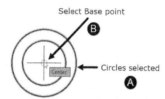

- Type **1.3** as the scale factor and press **ENTER**.

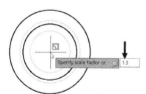
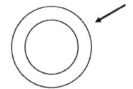

- Similarly scale the circles located at the top to **0.5**.

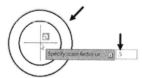

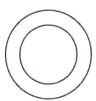

- Click **Home > Draw > Circle > Tan, Tan, Radius** on the ribbon.
- Click on two circles to define the tangent points, enter **200** as radius and press **ENTER**, as shown.

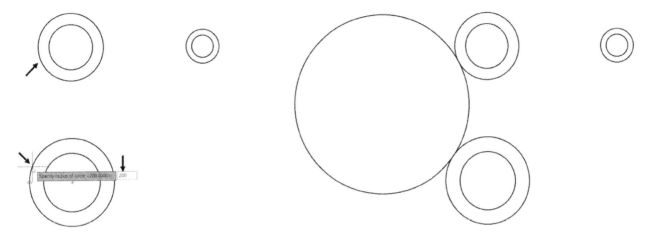

- Similarly, create other two circles of radius **200** and **300**, as shown.

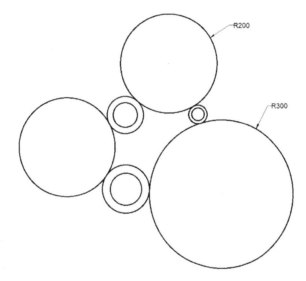

The Trim tool

When an object intersects with another object, you can remove its unwanted portion by using the **Trim** Trim tool. To trim an object, you need to first invoke the **Trim** tool, and then select the cutting edge (intersecting object) and the portion to be removed. If there are multiple intersection points in a drawing, you can simply select the **select all** option from the command line; all the objects in the drawing objects will act as 'cutting edges'.

- Click **Home > Modify > Trim** Trim on the ribbon or enter **TR** in the command line.

  Now, you need to select the cutting edges.

- Press **ENTER** to select all the objects as the cutting edges.

  Now, you need to select the objects to be trimmed.

- Click on the outer portion of the large circles one by one; the circles will be trimmed.

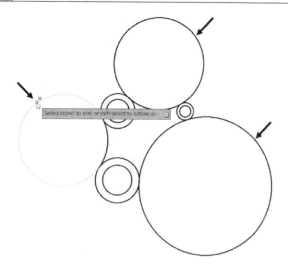
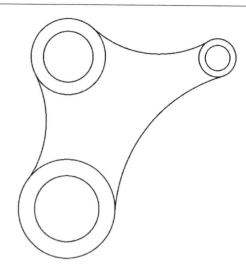

- Similarly, trim the other circles as shown below.

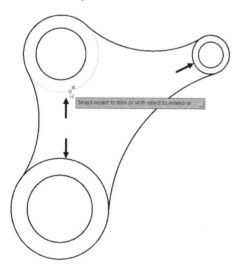
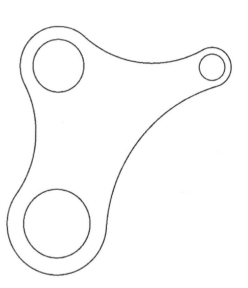

- Save and close the drawing.

The Extend tool

The **Extend** ⟶ Extend tool is similar to the **Trim** tool but its use is opposite of it. This tool is used to extend lines, arcs and other open entities to connect to other objects. To do so, you need to select the boundary up to which you want to extend the objects, and then select the objects to be extended.

- Start a new drawing.
- Create a sketch as shown below using the **Line** tool.
- Click **Home > Modify > Trim > Extend** on the ribbon or enter **EX** in the command line.

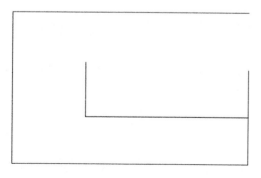
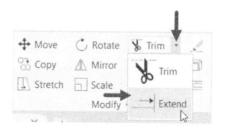

- Select the top horizontal line as the boundary edge and right-click.
- Now, select the open vertical lines one by one; the line will be extended up to the boundary edge.

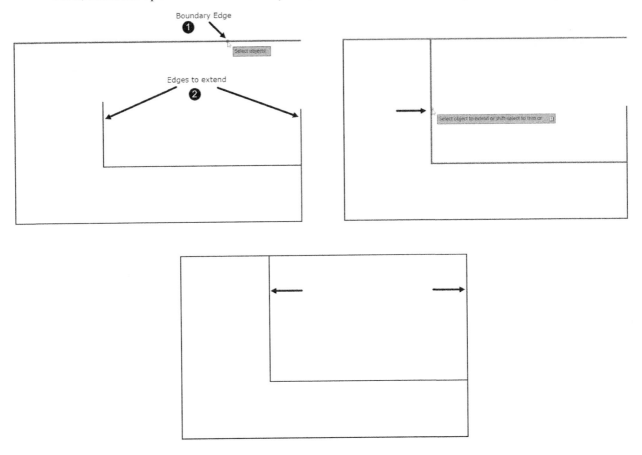

The Fillet tool

The **Fillet** Fillet tool is used to convert the sharp corners into round corners. To do so, you need to specify the radius and select the objects to be filleted. The following figure shows some examples of rounding the corners.

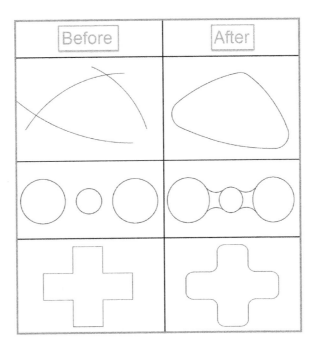

- Start a new drawing.
- Type **Limmax** in the command line and press **ENTER**.
- Set the maximum limit to **100,100** and press **ENTER**.
- Click **Zoom All** on the Navigation Bar.

  Alternatively, you can press **Z + ENTER** and then **A + ENTER**.

- Click **Home > Draw > Polyline** on the ribbon.
- Specify the start point as **50, 50**.
- Draw the lines as shown below.

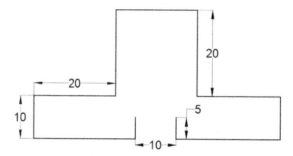

- Right-click and select **Enter**.
- Click **Home > Modify > Fillet** [Fillet] on the ribbon or enter **F** in the command line.
- Select the **Radius** option from the command line.
- Type **5** and press **ENTER**.
- Select all the close edges to create fillet, shown below.

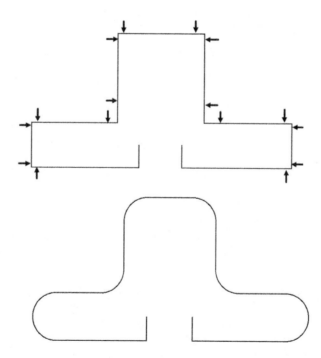

- Now, select the open vertical line to create fillet between them, as shown.

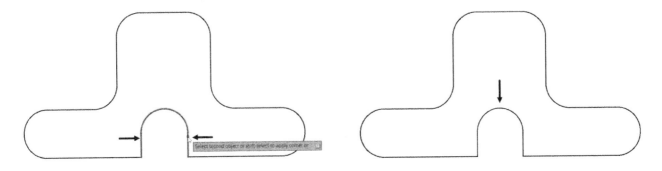

The Chamfer tool

The **Chamfer** `Chamfer` tool is used to replace the sharp corners with an angled line. This tool is similar to the **Fillet** tool, except that an angled line is placed at the corners instead of rounds.

- Click **Home > Modify > Fillet > Chamfer** `Chamfer` on the ribbon or enter **CHA** in the command line.
- Follow the prompt sequence given next:

  Select first line or [Undo Polyline Distance Angle Trim mEthod Multiple]: Select the **Distance** option from the command line.

  Specify first chamfer distance <0.0000>: Enter **3** as the first chamfer distance and press **ENTER**.

  Specify second chamfer distance <3.0000>: Press **ENTER** to accept **3** as the second chamfer distance

  Select first line or [Undo Polyline Distance Angle Trim mEthod Multiple]: Select the bottom left horizontal line, as shown.

  Select second line or shift-select to apply corner or [Distance Angle Method]: Select the vertical line connected to it.

Similarly, create chamfer to another corner on the right side, as shown.

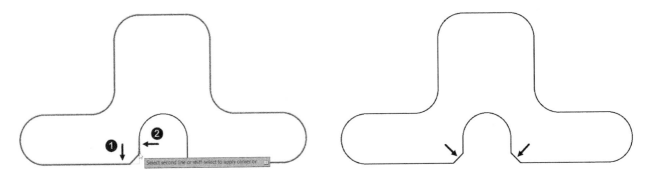

The Mirror tool

The **Mirror** `Mirror` tool is used to create a mirror image of objects. You can create symmetrical drawings using this tool. To mirror objects, you need to select the objects and specify the 'mirror line' about which the objects will be mirrored. You can specify the mirror line either by creating a line or selecting an existing line.

- Click **Home > Modify > Mirror** on the ribbon or enter **MI** in the command line.
- Select the drawing by clicking on it. Next, right-click.

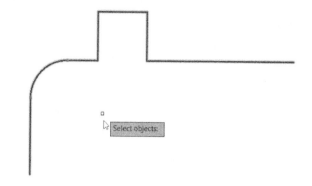

- Select the first point of the mirror line as shown below.

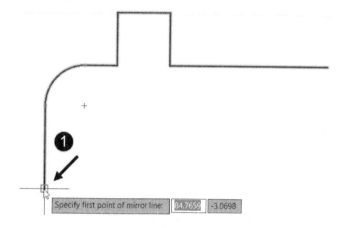

- Make sure that the **Ortho Mode is** active.
- Move the cursor toward right and click, as shown.
- Select the **No** option from the command line to retain the source objects.

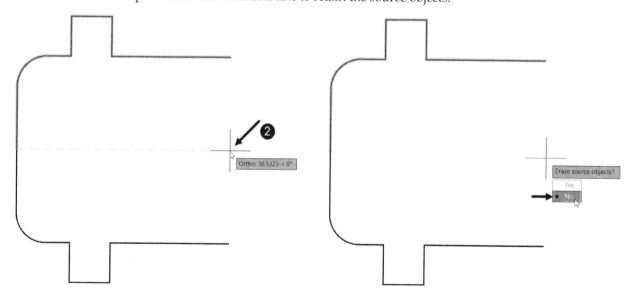

- Click **Home > Draw > Arc > Start, End, Direction** on the ribbon.
- Select the end point of top horizontal line and bottom horizontal line to create fillet both sides, as shown.
- Select the end point of the arc as shown below.

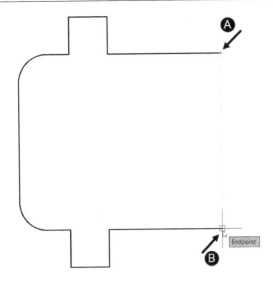

- Make sure that the **Ortho Mode** is active.
- Move the cursor toward right and click.

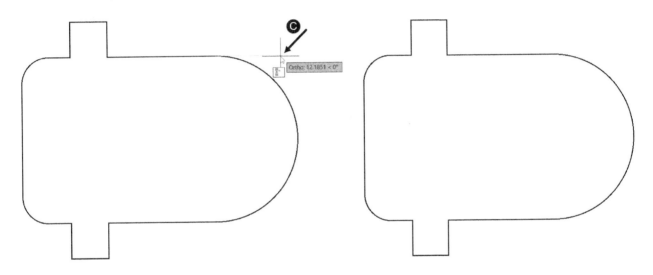

The Explode tool

The **Explode** tool is used to explode a group of objects into individual objects. For example, when you create a drawing using the **Polyline** tool, it acts as a single object. You can explode a polyline or rectangle or any group of objects using the **Explode** tool.

- Click on the portion of the drawing created using the **Polyline** tool; you will notice that it is selected as a single object.

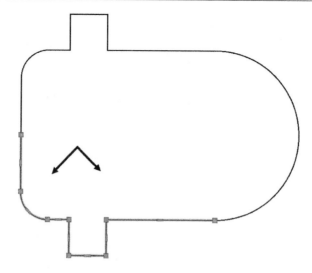

- Click **Home > Modify > Explode** on the ribbon or enter **X** in the command line.
- Select the polylines from the drawing.

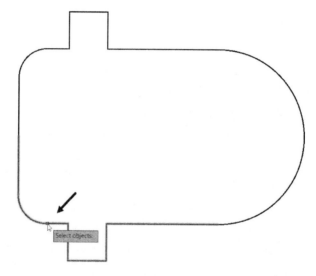

- Press **ENTER**; the polyline is exploded into individual objects.

  Now, you can select the individual objects of the polyline. You can also select the top polyline and few objects of bottom polyline to note the difference between top and bottom polyline (exploded), as shown.

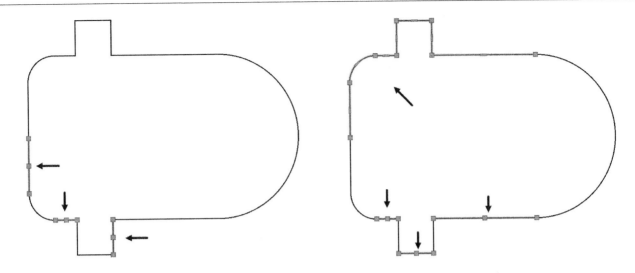

The Stretch tool

The **Stretch** ⬚ Stretch tool is used to lengthen or shorten drawings or parts of drawings. Note that you cannot stretch circles using this tool. Also, you need to select the portion of the drawing to be stretched by dragging a window.

- Click **Home > Modify > Stretch** on the ribbon or enter **STRETCH** in the command line.
- Drag a crossing window to select the objects of the drawing.

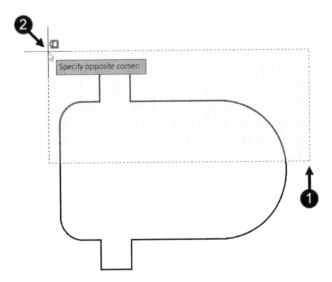

- Press **ENTER** or right-click to accept the selection.
- Select the base point as shown below.

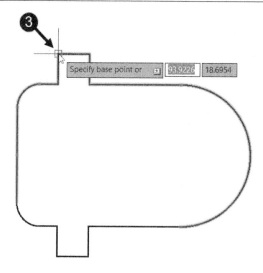

- Move the cursor upwards and click to stretch the drawing.

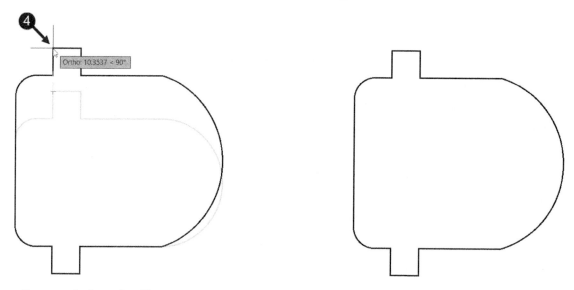

- Save and close the file.

The Offset tool

The **Offset** tool is used to create parallel copies of lines, polylines, circles, arcs and so on. To create parallel copy of an object, first you need to specify the offset distance, and then select the object. Next, you need to specify the side in which the parallel copy will be placed.

- Create the drawing shown below using the **Polyline** tool.

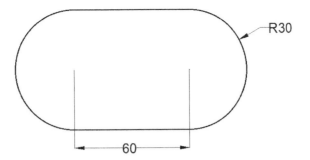

- Click **Home > Modify > Offset** 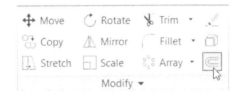 on the ribbon or enter **O** in the command line.

- Type **20** as the offset distance and press **ENTER**.
- Select the polyline loop.
- Click outside the loop to create the parallel copy.

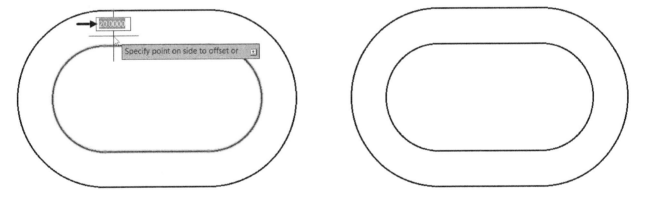

- Click **Home > Layer > Layer Properties** on the ribbon **LA** in the command line; the **Layer Properties Manager** appears.

- Click the **New layer**  button on the **Layer Properties Manager**. Enter **Centerline** in the **Name** field.

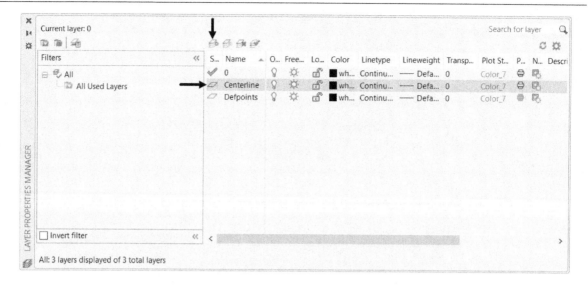

- Click the **Set Current** ![icon] button on the **Layer Properties Manager**; a new layer is created and is set as current.

- Click in the **Linetype** field of the current layer; the **Select Linetype** dialog box appears.

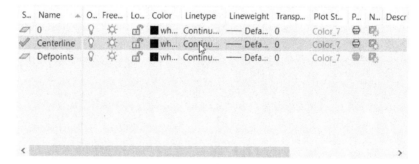

- On the **Select Linetype** dialog box, click the **Load** button; the **Load or Reload Linetypes** dialog box appears.

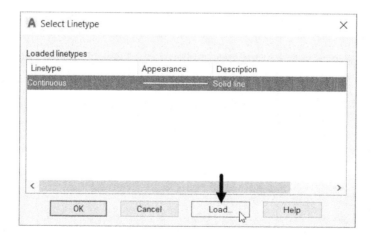

- Select the **CENTER2** linetype from this dialog box. Click **OK**; the linetype is added to the **Select Linetype** dialog box.

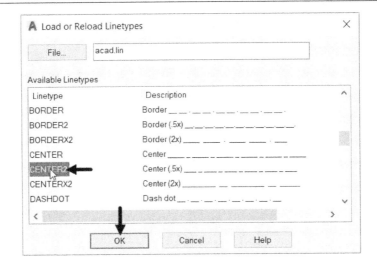

- Select the **CENTER2** linetype from the **Select Linetype** dialog box and click **OK**.
- Close the **Layer Properties Manager**.
- Click the **Offset** button on the **Modify** panel.
- Select the **Layer** option from the command line.
- Select the **Current** option from the command line; this ensures that the offset entity will be created with the currently set layer properties. If you select the **Source** option, the offset entity will be created with the properties of the source object.
- Type **10** as the offset distance and press **ENTER**.
- Select the outer loop of the drawing.
- Move the cursor inwards and click to create the offset entity.

Alternatively, you can select the inner loop and move the cursor outwards to create the offset entity.

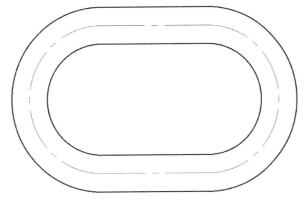

- Click on the **Layer** drop-down on the **Layer** panel of the ribbon.
- Select the **0** layer from the drop-down.

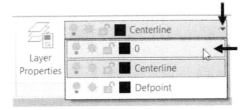

- Create a circle of **10** mm diameter, as shown.

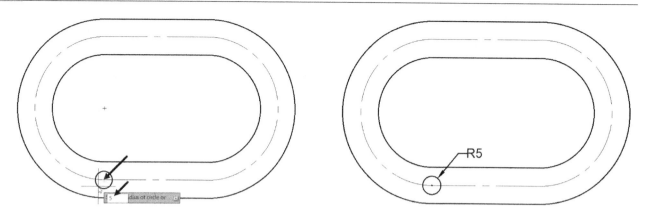

The Rectangular Array tool

The **Rectangular Array** Array tool is used to create an array of objects along the X and Y directions.

- Open a new AutoCAD file and draw the sketch shown below.

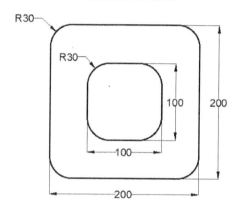

- Draw a circle of **30** mm diameter concentric to the fillet.

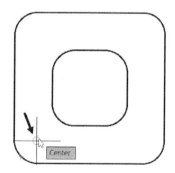 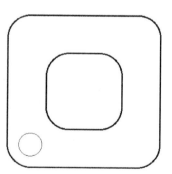

- Click **Home > Modify > Array > Rectangular Array** on the ribbon or enter **ARRAYRECT** in the command line.

- Select the small circle and right-click; a rectangular array with default values appears.

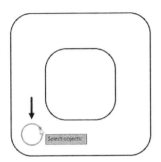

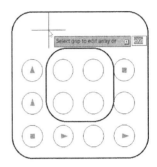

Also, the **Array Creation** tab appears, as shown.

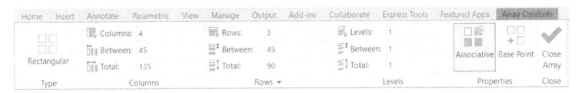

- Set the **Columns** count to **2**.
- Set the **Rows** count to **2**.
- Set the **Between** value in the **Columns** panel to **140**.
- Set the **Between** value in the **Rows** panel to **140**.

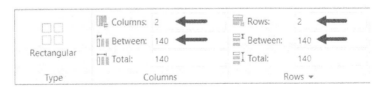

- Click **Close Array** Close Array on the ribbon.

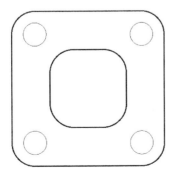

The Path Array tool

The **Path Array** 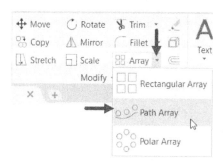 tool is used to create an array of objects along a path (line, polyline, circle, helix, spline etc.)

- Click **Home > Modify > Array > Path Array** on the ribbon or enter **ARRAYPATH** in the command line.

- Select the circle and right-click (in previously created while using the **Offset** tool).
- Select the centerline as the path; the preview of the path array appears in asymmetric order.
- Select the **Base Point** button from the **Properties** panel of the **Array Creation** tab.
- Next, select the center point of the circle with **5** mm radius; the path array will get arranged symmetrical, as shown.

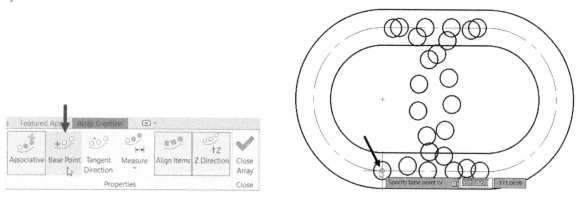

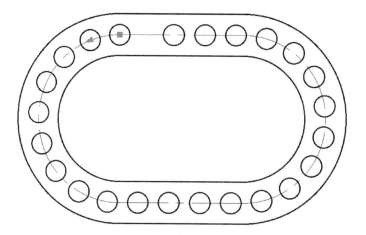

- Click the **Divide** method on the **Properties** panel; you need to enter the number of items in the path array.

If you select the **Measure** method, you need to enter the distance between the items in the path array.

- Set the Items count to **12**.

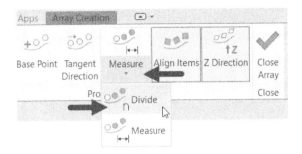

Notice that the **Align Items** button is active by default. As a result, the items are aligned with the path. If you deactivate this button, the items will not be aligned with the path.

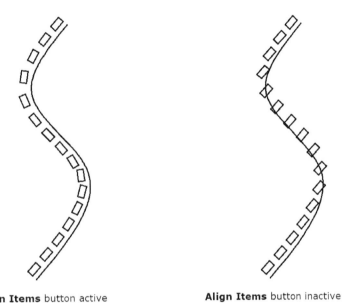

Align Items button active   **Align Items** button inactive

- Click the **Close Array** button.

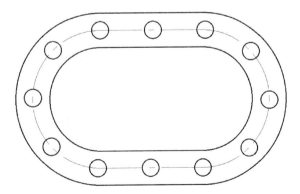

- Save and close the file.

The Polar Array tool

The **Polar Array** tool is used to create an arrangement of objects around a point in circular form. The following example shows you to create a polar array.

- Create two concentric circles of **180** and **70** diameters.

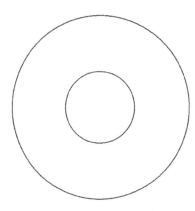

- Type **C** in the command line and press **ENTER**.
- Press and hold the **Ctrl** key, right-click and select **Quadrant** from the shortcut menu.

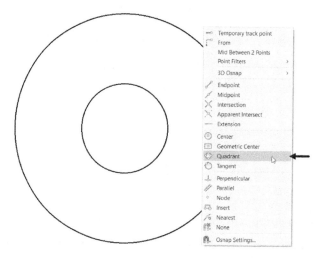

- Select the quadrant point of the circle as shown below.

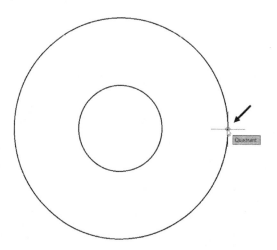

- Type **30** as radius and press **ENTER**.

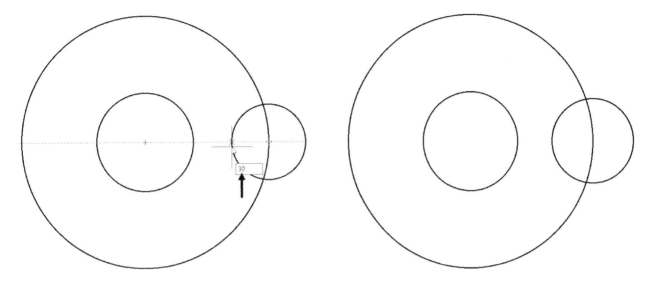

- Click **Home > Modify > Trim** on the ribbon.
- Select the large circle as the cutting edge and right-click.
- Select the circle on the quadrant as the object to be trimmed.

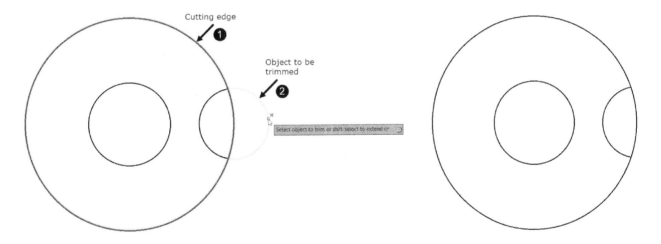

- Right-click and select **Enter**.
- Click **Home > Modify > Array > Polar Array** on the ribbon or **ARRAYPOLAR** in the command line.

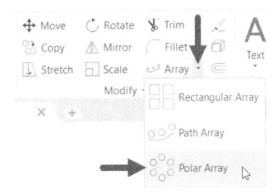

- Select the arc created after trimming the circle. Next, right-click to accept the selection.

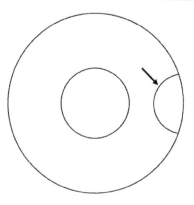

- Make sure that the **Object Snap** ![icon] is activated.
- Select the center of the large circle as the center of the array; the **Array Creation** tab appears in the ribbon.

- In the **Items** panel of the **Array Creation** tab, set the **Items** value to **4**.

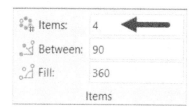

Note that the **Rotate Items** button is active in the **Properties** panel of the **Array Creation** tab. As a result, the array objects are rotated. If you deactivate this button, the polar array is created without rotating the objects as shown in figure.

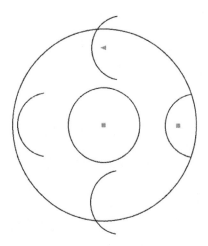

Also, the **Associative** button is active by default. This ensures that you can edit the array after creating it.

- Make sure that the **Associative** and the **Rotate Items** buttons are active. Next, click the **Close Array** button on the ribbon.

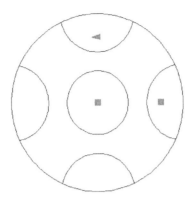

- Click the **Trim** button on the **Modify** panel.
- Press **ENTER** to select all objects as cutting edges.
- Trim the unwanted portions as shown below.

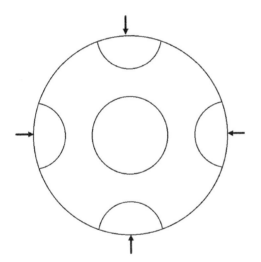
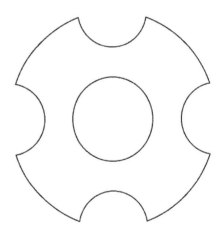

Editing Using Grips

When you select objects from the drawing window, small squares are displayed on them. These squares are called grips. You can use these grips to stretch, move, rotate, scale, and mirror objects, change properties, and perform other editing operations. Grips displayed on selecting different objects are shown below.

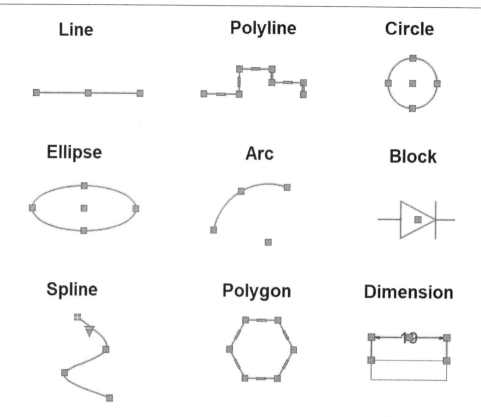

The following table gives you the details of the editing operations that can be performed when you select and drag grips.

Object	Grip	Editing Operation
Circle	Grip on circumference	<u>Scale</u>: Select anyone of the grips on the circumference and move the cursor to scale a circle.
	Center point grip	<u>Move</u>: Select the center grip of the circle and move the cursor.

Arc	**Grip on circumference**	**Stretch**: Select the grip on the circumference and move the cursor.
	Center point grip	**Move**: Select the center grip of the arc and move the cursor.
Line	**Midpoint Grip**	**Move**: Select the Midpoint grip and move the cursor
	Endpoint Grip	**Stretch/Lengthen**: Select an endpoint grip and move the cursor.

| Polylines, Rectangles , Polygons | Corner Grips | **Stretch**: Select the corner grips and move the cursor. 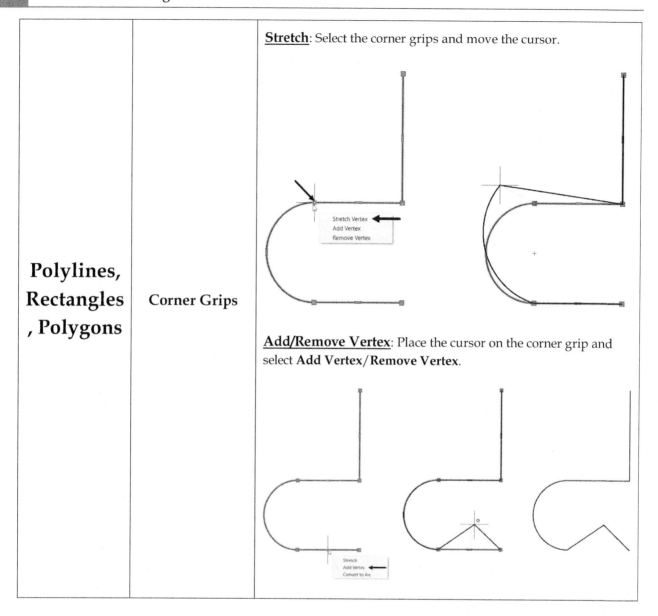

 Add/Remove Vertex: Place the cursor on the corner grip and select **Add Vertex/Remove Vertex**. |

	Midpoint Grips	**Convert to Arc**: Place the cursor on the midpoint grip and select **Convert to Arc**. 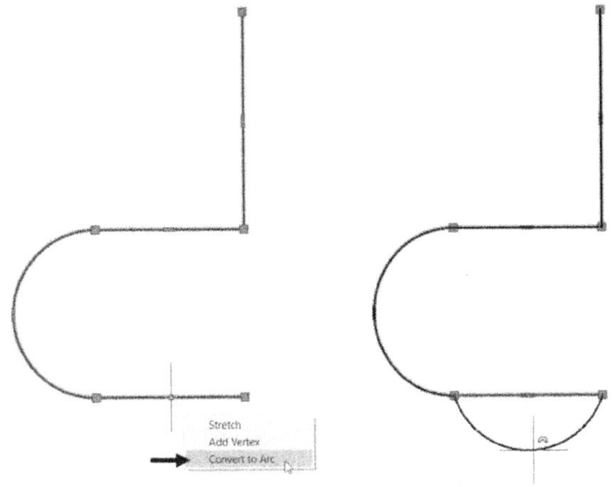 **Convert to Line**: Place the cursor on the midpoint grip of a polyline arc and select **Covert to Line**. 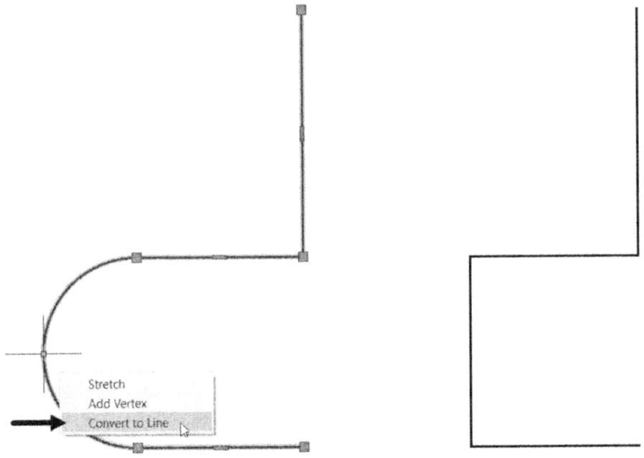
Ellipse	**Center Grip**	**Move**: Select the center grip and move the cursor. 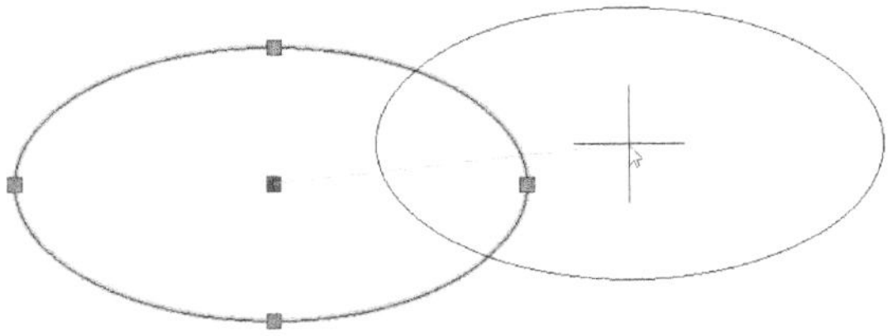
	Grips on circumference	**Stretch**: Select a grip on circumference and move the cursor. 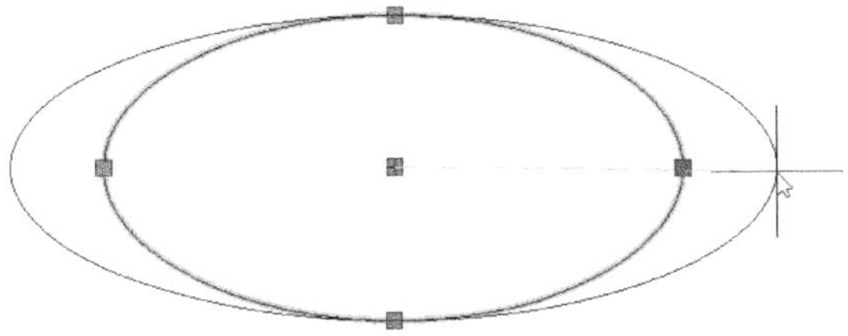

Spline	**Fit Points**	**Stretch**: Select a grip on the spline and move the cursor. 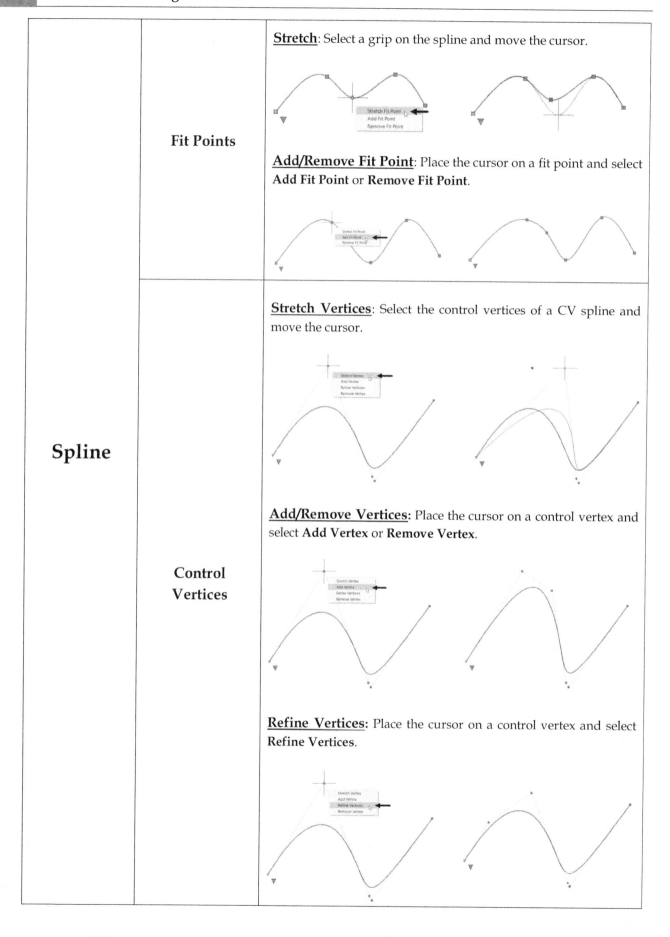 **Add/Remove Fit Point**: Place the cursor on a fit point and select **Add Fit Point** or **Remove Fit Point**.
	Control Vertices	**Stretch Vertices**: Select the control vertices of a CV spline and move the cursor. **Add/Remove Vertices**: Place the cursor on a control vertex and select **Add Vertex** or **Remove Vertex**. **Refine Vertices**: Place the cursor on a control vertex and select **Refine Vertices**.

Modifying Rectangular Arrays

You can use grips to edit rectangular arrays dynamically. Various array editing operations using grips are given next.

Moving a Rectangular array
- Create a rectangular array as shown below.

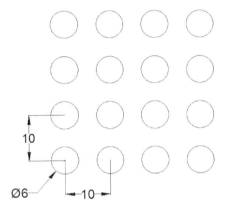

- Select the array; you will notice that grips are displayed on it.
- Select the grip located at the lower left corner and move the array as shown below.

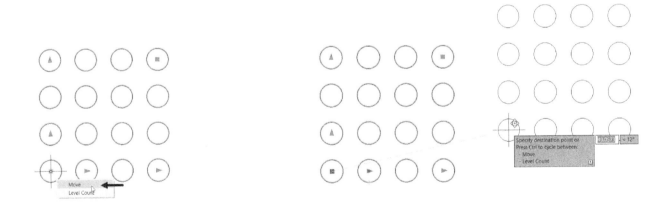

Adding/Removing Level to a Rectangular array
- Place the cursor on the lower left grip of the rectangular array; a shortcut menu appears.
- Select **Level Count** from the shortcut menu; the message, "**Specify number of levels**" appears in the command line.
- Type **4** and press **ENTER**.

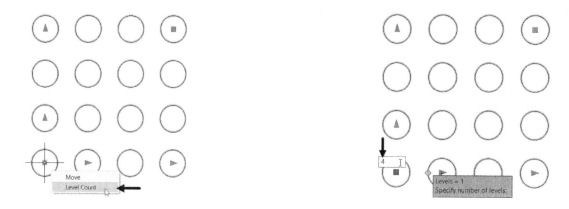

- Click the **Home** button near the **ViewCube** to view the levels.

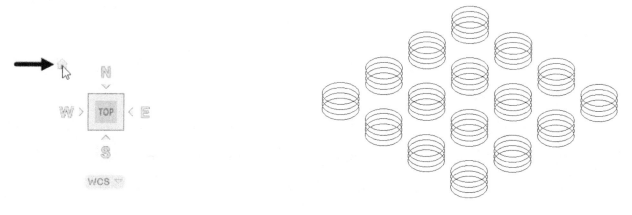

- Change the view to **Top** view by using the **In-Canvas** controls.

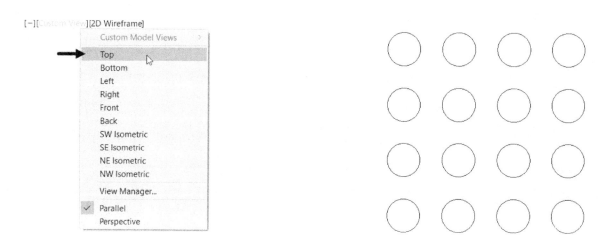

Changing the Column and Row Count

- To change the column and row count, place the cursor on the top right corner grip; a shortcut menu appears.
- Select **Row and Column Count** from the shortcut menu; the message, "**Specify number of rows and columns**" appears in the command line.
- Type **5** in the command line and press **ENTER**; the number of rows and columns are changed to **5**, as shown.

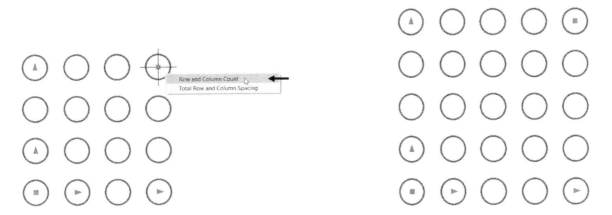

- If you only want to change the column count; place the cursor on the lower right corner grip of the array.
- Select **Colum Count** from the shortcut menu.
- Next, enter the number of columns or drag the cursor and click.

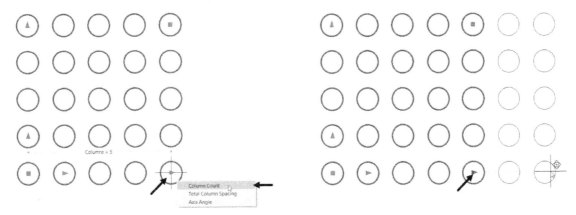

- To change the row count only, click the top left corner grip and drag the cursor. You can also enter the row count in the command line.

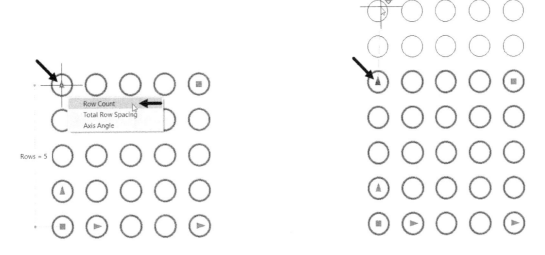

Changing the Column and Row Spacing

- To change the total column and row spacing, place the cursor on the top right corner grip and select **Total Row and Column Spacing** from the shortcut menu.

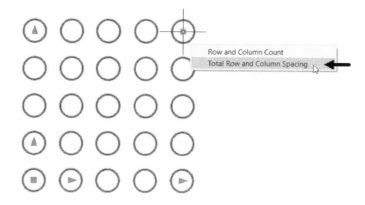

- Type the **60** in the command line; the spacing between the columns and rows is adjusted to fit the total length.

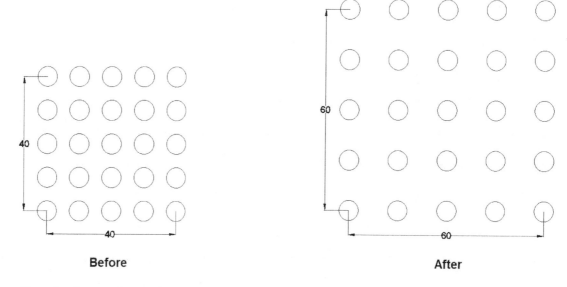

Before   **After**

- To only change the total column spacing, place the cursor on the lower right corner grip and select **Total Column Spacing** from the shortcut menu.

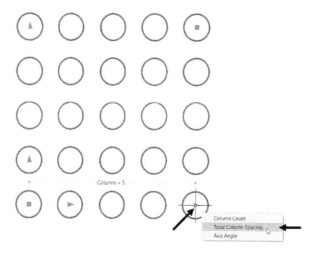

- Next, enter the total column distance or drag the cursor and click.

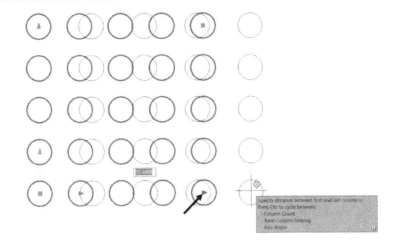

- If you want to change the distance between the individual columns, click the second column grip and drag the cursor, as shown.

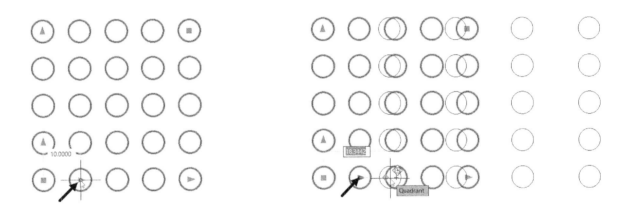

- You can also enter the distance in the command line.
- Similarly, you can change the total row spacing and distance between the individual rows by using the grips shown below.

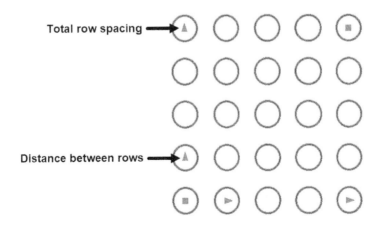

Changing the Axis Angle of the Rectangular Array

- To change the Axis angle of the rows, place the cursor on the lower right corner grip and select **Axis angle** from the shortcut menu.
- Type the angle and press **ENTER**. Note that the angle is calculated from the first column of the array. For example, if you enter **65** as the axis angle, the rows will be inclined 65 degrees from the first column, as shown.

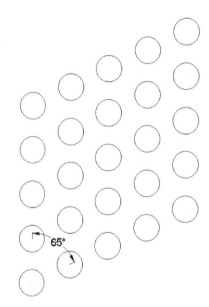

- Similarly, you can the axis angle of the columns by using the top left corner grip.

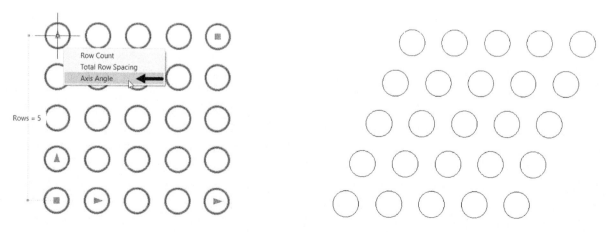

Editing the Source Item of the Rectangular Array

Create a rectangular array as shown below.

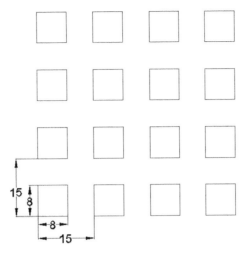

- Select the rectangular array; the **Array** tab appears in the ribbon.
- Click the **Edit Source** button on the **Option** panel; the message, "**Select item in array**" message appears in the command line.
- Select the lower left triangle of the rectangular array; the **Array Editing State** message box appears.

- Click **OK**; the array editing state is activated.
- Draw a circle and trim the unwanted portion as shown below.

- Click on the **Save Changes** button on the **Edit Array** panel of the ribbon, as shown.

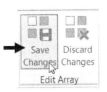

Modifying Polar Arrays

Similar to editing rectangular arrays, you can also edit a polar array by using grips. Various array editing operations using grips are given next.

Changing the Radius of a Polar array

- Create the polar array as shown below.
- Select the polar array; grips will be displayed on it.
- Place the cursor on the base grip, as shown in figure.
- Select **Stretch Radius** from the shortcut menu.

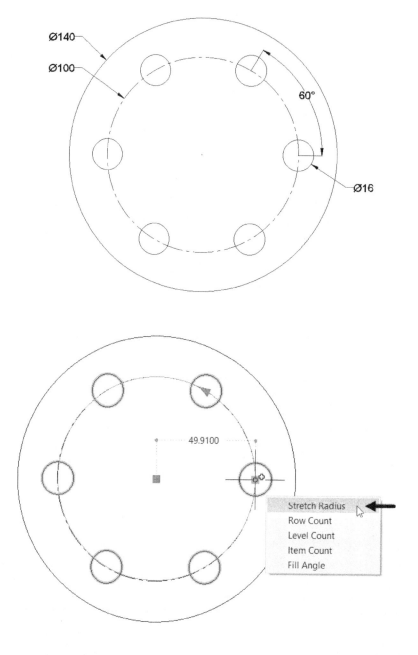

- Move the cursor outward or inward and click. You can also enter a new radius value of the polar array.

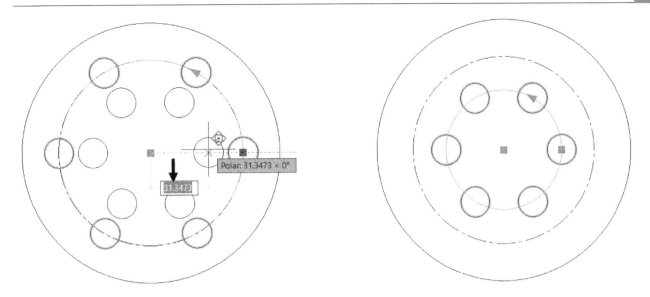

Changing the Row Count of a Polar array

- Place the cursor on the base grip of the array and select **Row Count** from the shortcut menu.
- Move the cursor outward and click. You can also enter the number of the rows in the command line.

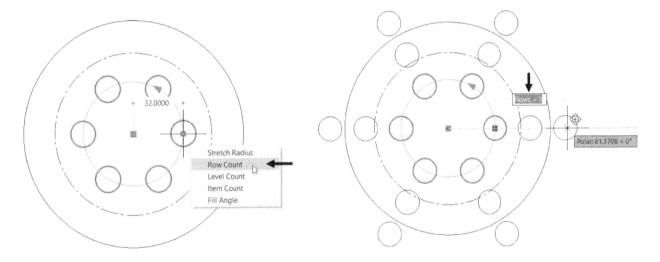

- You can again change the **Row Count** by using the last row grip.

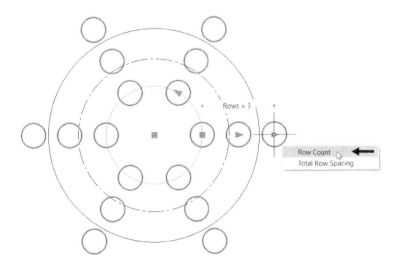

Changing the Row Spacing

- To change the total row spacing, place the cursor on the last row grip and select **Total Row Spacing**.

- Next, move the cursor and click. You can also enter the total row spacing value in the command line.

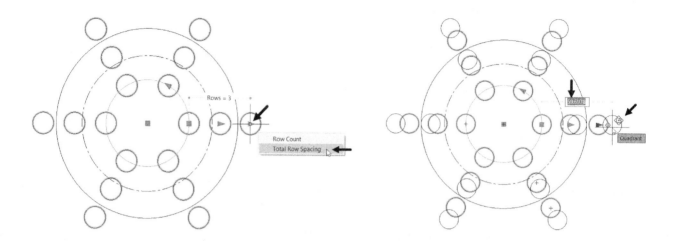

- To change the distance between the individual rows, click the second-row grip and move the cursor outward. You can also enter the distance in the command line.

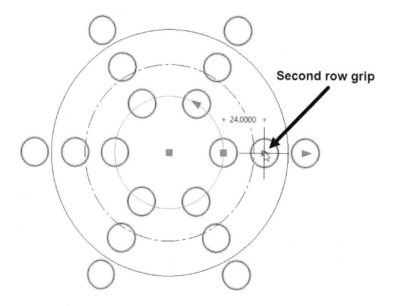

Changing the Angle between the Items

- To change the angle between the items, click the second radial grip.
- Next, move the cursor or enter the new angle value, as shown.

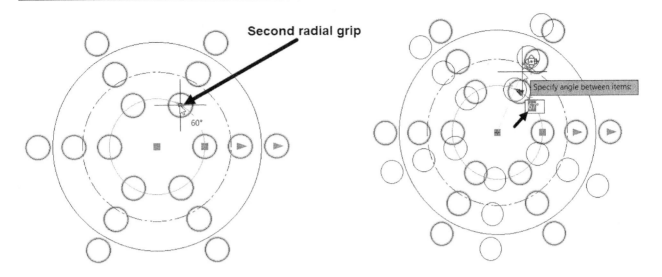

Changing the Fill angle of the array

- The default fill angle of a polar array is **360** degrees. To change the fill angle, place the cursor on the base grip and select **Fill Angle** from the shortcut menu.

- Enter a new value for the fill angle or drag the cursor and click.

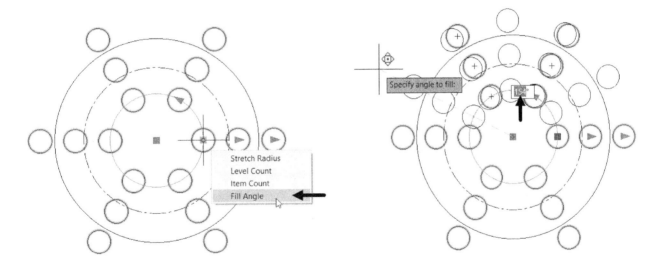

Changing the Item count of a Polar array

- Select the polar array and enter a new item count in the **Items** box of the **Array** ribbon.

Questions:

1. Which tools is to enlarge or reduce size of object?
2. Which tool is used to remove unwanted portion of object?
3. Which tool is used to extend an object to connect with another object?
4. Which tool is use to convert sharp corner into round corner?
5. Which tool is used to create an array of objects along a path?
6. Which tool is used to create an array of objects along the X and Y directions?

Exercises

Exercise 1:

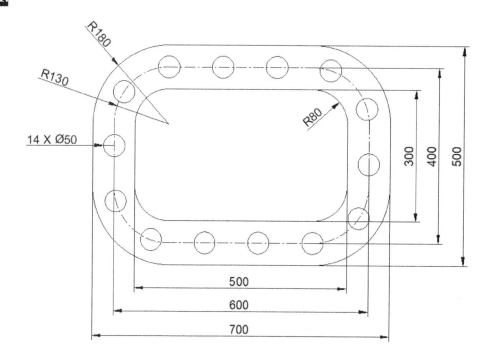

Exercise 2:

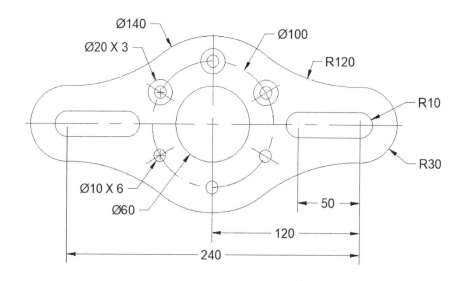

Exercise 3:

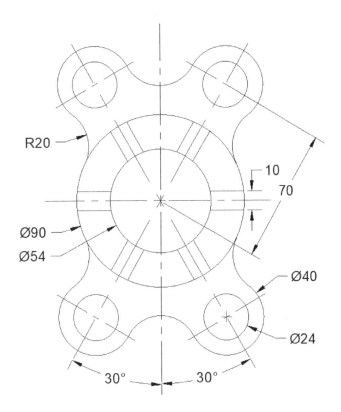

Exercise 4:

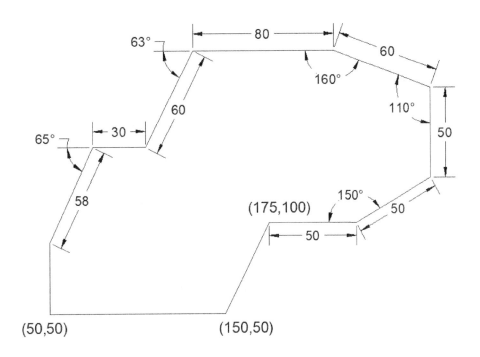

Exercise 5:

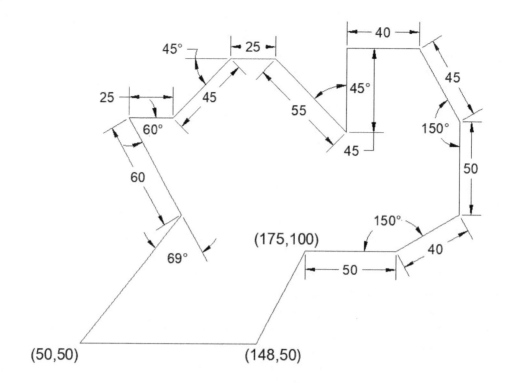

Chapter 5: Multi View Drawings in AutoCAD

In this chapter, you will learn concept of drawing views. The drawing views are generated to show accurate shape and size of the object that can be dimensioning properly.

In this chapter, you will learn about:

❖ **Orthographic Views**

❖ **Auxiliary Views**

❖ **Named Views**

Multi View Drawings

To manufacture a component, you must create its engineering drawing. The engineering drawing includes various views of the object, showing its accurate shape and size that can be clearly dimensioned. This can be done by creating the orthographic views of the object.

In the first section of this chapter, you will learn how to create orthographic views of an object. The second section introduces you to auxiliary views. The auxiliary views describe the features of a component, which are located on an inclined plane or surface.

Creating Orthographic Views

Orthographic Views are standard representations of an object on a drawing sheet. It is the method to generate information related all the hidden and visible features of an object. These views are generated by projecting an object onto three different planes (top plane, front plane, and side plane). These three views are projected and aligned with each other. You can project an object by using two different methods:

- **First Angle Projection**

- **Third Angle Projection**.

Projection	Symbol
First Angle	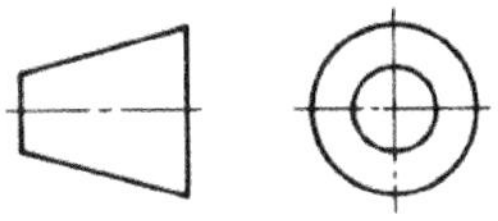
Third Angle	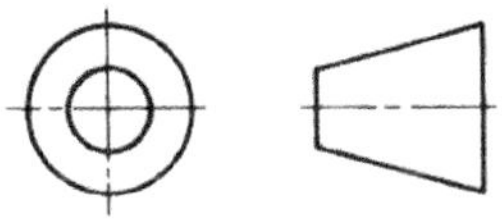

First Angle Projection
➤ Orthographic views created while projecting an object using the **First Angle Projection** method.
➤ The object is kept in the first quadrant.
➤ The object lies between the observer and plane of projection
➤ The plane of projection is assumed to be non-transparent
➤ When views are drawn in their relative position; **Top view** comes below **Front View** and **Right View** drawn to the left side of the elevation

Below is the figure in which orthographic views are created while projecting an object using the **First Angle Projection** method.

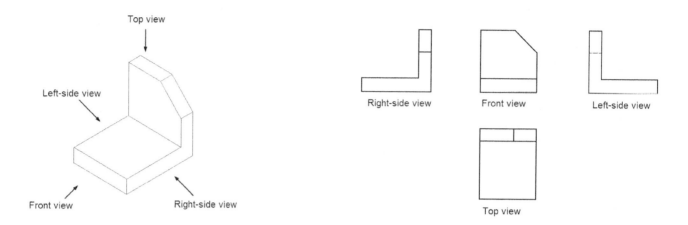

Third Angle Projection

Orthographic views created while projecting an object using the **Third Angle Projection** method.

➢ The object is kept in the third quadrant.

➢ The plane of projection lies between the observer and object

➢ The plane of projection is assumed to be transparent

➢ When views are drawn in their relative position, **Top view** comes above **Front View** and **Right View** drawn to the right side of the elevation.

Below is the figure in which orthographic views are created while projecting an object using the **Third Angle Projection** method.

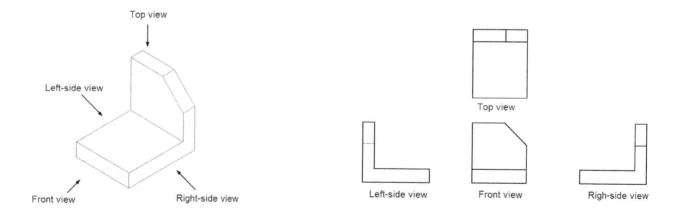

Example:

In this example, you will create the orthographic views of the part shown below. The views will be created by using the **Third Angle Projection** method.

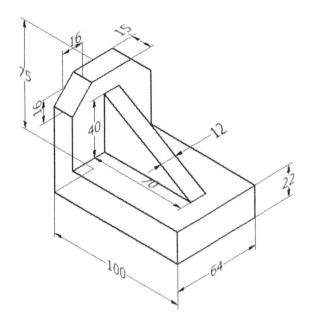

> ➤ Open a new drawing.
> ➤ Click the **Layer Properties** button on the **Layer** panel; the **Layer Properties Manager** appears.
> ➤ Click the **New Layer** button on the **Layer Properties Manager** to create new layers.
> ➤ Create two new layers with the following properties.

Layer Name	Linetype	Lineweight
Construction	Continuous	0.00 mm
Object	Continuous	0.30 mm

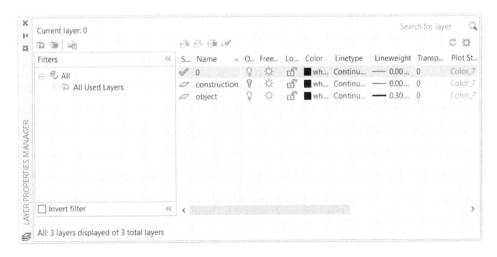

> ➤ Right-click on the **Construction** layer and select **Set current**, as shown.

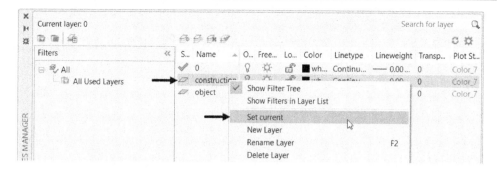

> ➢ Close the **Layer Properties Manager**.
> ➢ Activate the **Ortho Mode** on the status bar.
> ➢ Click **Zoom > Zoom All** on the Navigation Bar.
>
> Next, you need to draw construction lines. They are used as references to create actual drawings. You will create these construction lines on the **Construction** layer so that you can hide them when required.
>
> ➢ Click **Home > Draw > Construction Line** on the ribbon or enter **XLINE** in the command line.

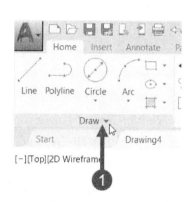

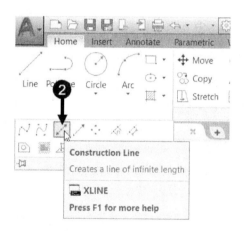

> ➢ Click anywhere in the lower left corner of the drawing window.
> ➢ Move the cursor upward and click to create a vertical construction line.
> ➢ Move the cursor toward right and click to create a horizontal construction line.
> ➢ Press **ENTER** to exit the tool.
> ➢ Click the **Offset** button on the **Modify** panel.
> ➢ Type **100** as the offset distance and press **ENTER**.
> ➢ Select the vertical construction line.
> ➢ Move the cursor toward and click to create an offset line.
> ➢ Right-click and select **Enter** to exit the **Offset** tool.
> ➢ Press the **SPACEBAR** on the keyboard to start the **Offset** tool again.
> ➢ Type **75** as the offset distance and press **ENTER**.
> ➢ Select the horizontal construction line.
> ➢ Move the cursor above and click to create the offset line.
> ➢ Press **ENTER** to exit the **Offset** tool.
> ➢ Similarly, create other offset lines as shown below.

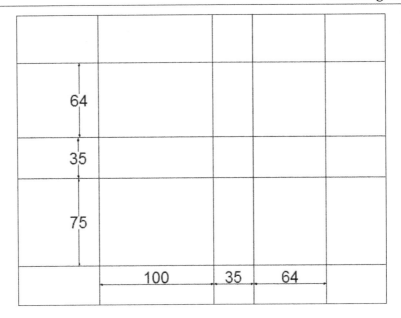

➤ Set the current layer to **Object**.

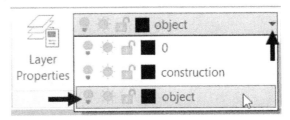

Now, you need to create object lines.

➤ Click the **Line** button on the **Draw** panel.
➤ Create an outline of the front view by selecting the intersection points between the construction lines.

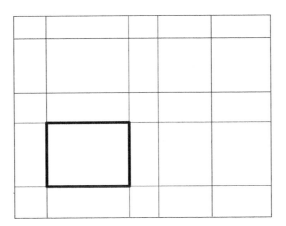

➤ Right-click and select **Enter** to exit the **Line** tool.

➤ Activate the **Show/Hide Lineweight** button on the status bar.

➤ Similarly, create the outlines of the top and side views.

Next, you need to turn off the **Construction** layer.

➢ Click on the **Layer** drop-down in the **Layer** panel.
➢ Click the light-bulb of the **Construction** layer; the layer will be turned off.

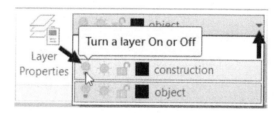

➢ Use the **Offset** tool and create two parallel lines on the front view, as shown below.

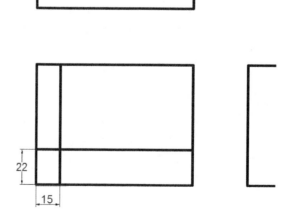

➢ Use the **Trim** tool and trim the unwanted lines of the front view as shown below.

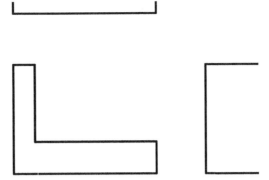

> ➤ Use the **Offset** tool to create the parallel line as shown below.

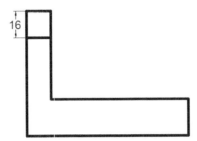

- Use the **Offset** tool and create offset lines in the Top view as shown below.

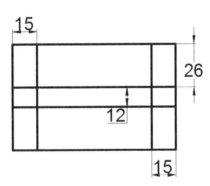

- Use the **Trim** tool and trim the unwanted objects.

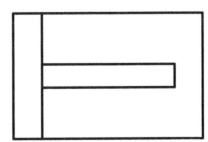

- Create other offset lines and trim the unwanted portions as shown below.

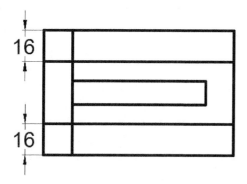
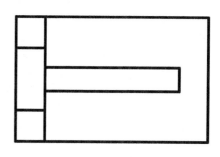

- Click the **Line** button on the **Draw** panel.
- Press and hold the **SHIFT** key and right-click. Select the **From** option.

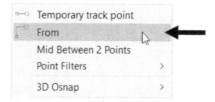

- Select the endpoint of the line in the front view as shown below.

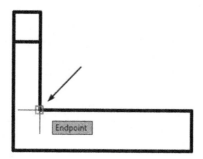

- Move the cursor on the vertical line and enter **40** in the command line; the first point of the line is specified at a point **40** mm away from the endpoint. Also, a rubber band line will be attached to the cursor.
- Move the cursor onto the endpoint on the top view as shown below.

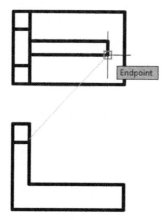

- Move the cursor vertically downward; you will notice that track lines are displayed.
- Move the cursor near the horizontal line of the front view and click at the intersection point as shown below. Press **ENTER** to exit the tool.

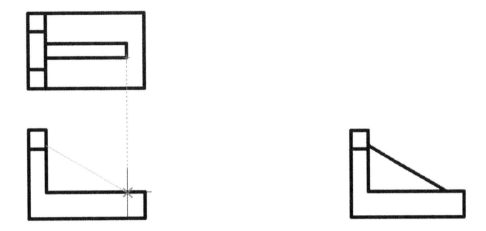

Next, you need to create the right-side view. To do so, you need to draw a **45-** degree miter line and project the measurements of the top view onto the side view.

> ➤ Click on the **Layer** drop-down in the **Layer** panel.
> ➤ Click the light-bulb icon of the **Construction** layer; the **Construction** layer is turned on.
> ➤ Select the **Construction** layer from the **Layer** drop-down to set it as the current layer.
> ➤ Draw an inclined line by connecting the intersection points of the construction lines as shown below.

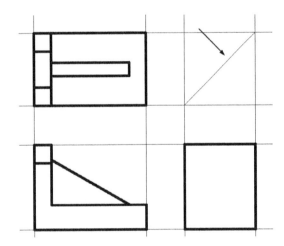

> ➤ Click the **Construction Line** button on the **Draw** panel.
> ➤ Select the **Hor** option from the command line and create the projection lines as shown below.

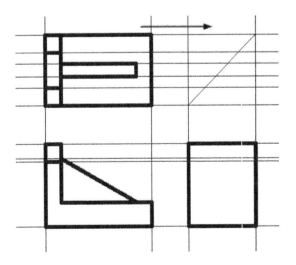

- ➤ Right-click to exit the **Construction Line** tool.
- ➤ Press **ENTER** and select the **Ver** option from the command line.
- ➤ Create the vertical projection lines as shown below.
- ➤ Use the **Trim** tool trim the extend portions of the construction lines.

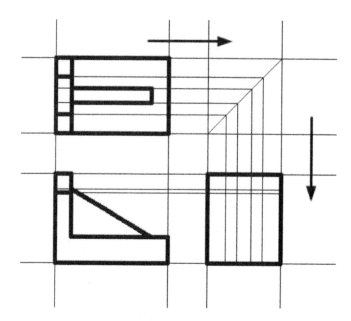

- ➤ Set the **Object** layer as current.
- ➤ Click the **Offset** button on the **Modify** panel.
- ➤ Select the **Through** option from the command line.
- ➤ Select the lower horizontal line of the side view.

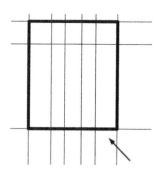

- ➤ Select the end point on the front view as shown below.

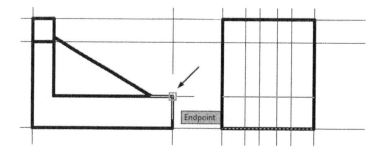

- ➤ Right-click and select **Enter**.
- ➤ Use the **Line** tool bend create the objects in the side view as shown below.

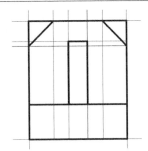

> ➤ Turn off the **Construction** layer by clicking on the light-bulb of the **Construction** layer.
> ➤ Trim the unwanted portions on the right-side view.

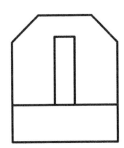

The drawing after creating all the views is shown below.

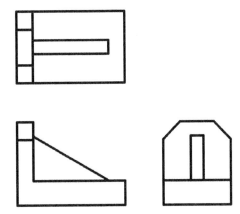

> ➤ Save the file as **ortho_views.dwg**. Close the file.

Creating Auxiliary Views

Most of the objects are represented by using orthographic views (front, top and/or side views). But many objects have features located on inclined faces. You cannot get the true shape and size for these features by using the orthographic views. To see an accurate size and shape of the inclined features, you need to create an auxiliary view. An auxiliary view is created by projecting the object onto a plane other than horizontal, front or side planes. The following figure shows an object with an inclines face. When you create orthographic views of the object, you will not be able to get the true shape of the hole on the inclined face.

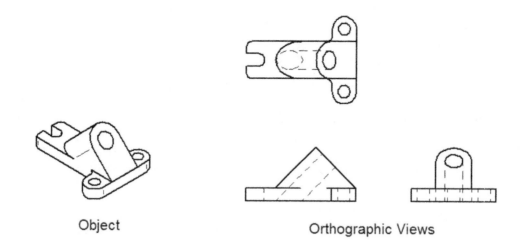

Object   Orthographic Views

To get the actual shape of the hole, you need to create an auxiliary view of the object as shown below.

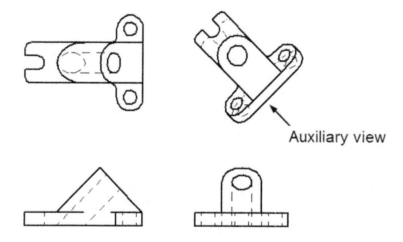

Auxiliary view

Example:

In this example, you will create an auxiliary view of the object shown below.

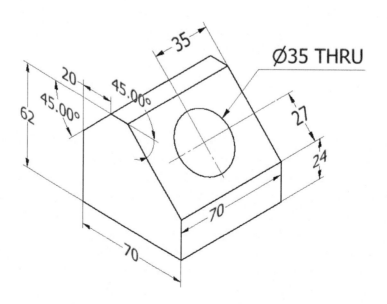

➤ Open a new AutoCAD file.
➤ Create four new layers with the following properties.

Layer Name	Linetype	Lineweight
Construction	Continuous	0.00 mm
Object	Continuous	0.50 mm
Hidden	HIDDEN	0.30 mm
Centerline	CENTER	0.30 mm

➤ Select the **Construction** layer from the **Layer** drop-down in the **Layer** panel.
➤ Create a rectangle at the lower left corner of the drawing window, as shown in figure.

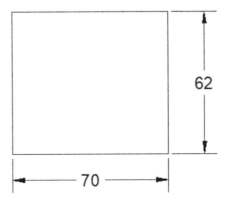

➤ Select the rectangle and click the **Copy** button from the **Modify** panel.
➤ Select the lower left corner of the rectangle as the base point.
➤ Make sure that the **Ortho mode** is activated.
➤ Move the cursor upward and type **25** in the command line. Next, press **ENTER**.
➤ Press **ESC** to exit the **Copy** tool.

➤ Click the **Rotate** button on the **Modify** panel and select the copied rectangle. Press **ENTER** to accept.
➤ Select the lower right corner of the rectangle as the base point.
➤ Type **45** as the angle and press **ENTER**.

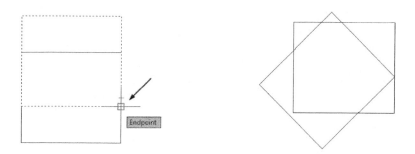

➤ Create another rectangle approximately **60** mm above the previous one, as shown.

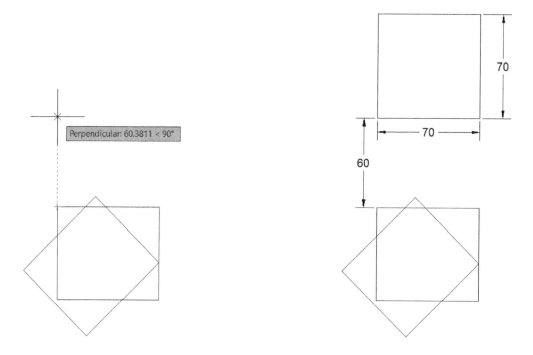

The rectangle located at the top is considered as top view and the below it is the front view.

➤ Click the **Explode** button on the **Modify** panel and select the newly created rectangle. Next, right-click to explode the rectangle.

➤ Use the **Offset** tool and offset the vertical lines of the rectangle.

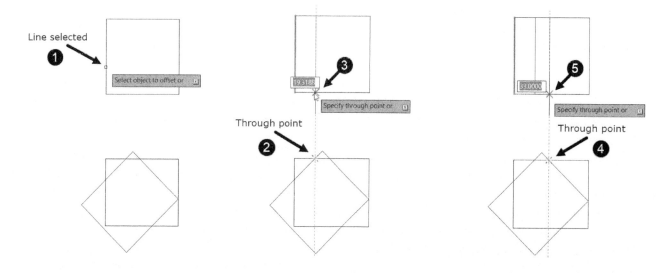

➢ Select the **Object** layer from the **Layer** drop-down in the **Layer** panel.
➢ Create the object lines in the front and top views as shown below.

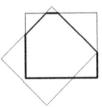

➢ Select the **Construction** layer from the **Layer** panel.
➢ Click the **Construction Line** button on the **Draw** panel.
➢ Select the **Offset** option from the command line. Next, select the **Through** option.
➢ Select the inclined line on the front view. Next, select the intersection point as shown below.

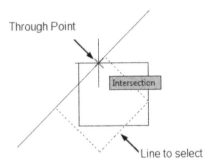

➢ Similarly, create other construction lines as shown below.

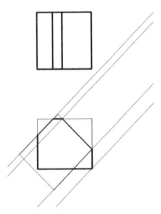

➢ Create other construction lines as shown below.

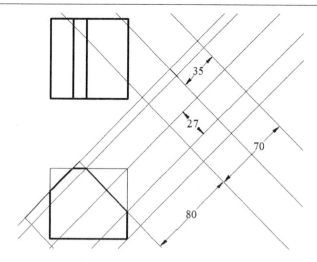

> ➤ Set the **Object** layer as current layer. Next, create the object lines using the intersection points between the construction lines.
> ➤ Use the **Circle** tool and create a circle of the **35** mm.

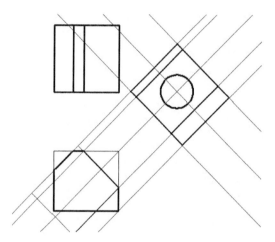

> ➤ Set the **Construction** layer as current layer. Create projection lines from the circle.
> ➤ On your own, create the other object lines, hidden lines, and center lines, as shown below.

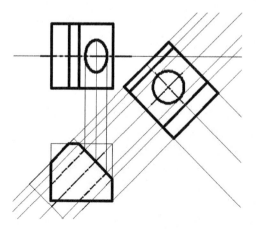

> ➤ Drawing after hiding the **Construction** layer is shown below.

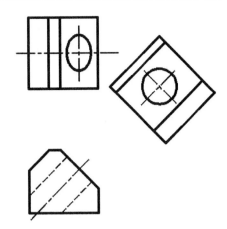

Creating Named views

While working with a drawing, you may need to perform numerous zoom and pan operations to view key portions of a drawing. Instead of doing this, you can save these portions with a name. Then, restore the named view and start working on them.

- Open the **ortho_views.dwg** file.
- Click on the **View** tab from the Ribbon.
- Right click on the Ribbon and click **Show Panels > Named Views,** to display **Named Views** panel on the Ribbon, if not displayed by default.
- To create a named view, click **View > Named Views > View Manager** on the ribbon; the **View Manager** dialog box appears, as shown.

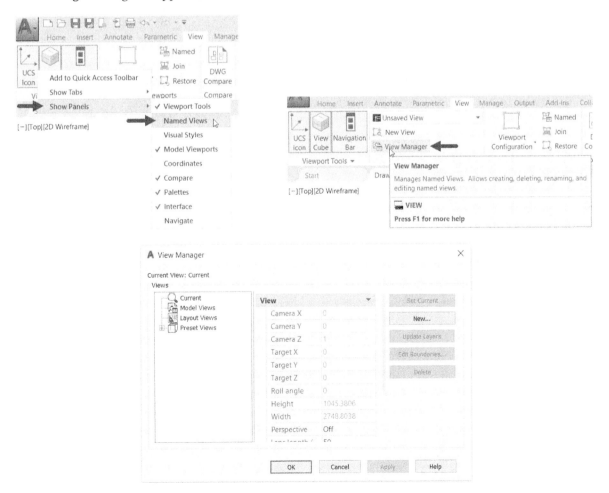

> Click the **New** button on the **View Manager** dialog box; the **New View/Shot Properties** dialog box appears.
> Select the **Define Window** radio button from the **Boundary** section of the **New View/Shot Properties** dialog box.
> Create a window on the front view, as shown below.

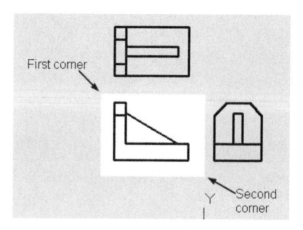

> Press **ENTER** to accept.
> Enter **Front** in the **View name** box.

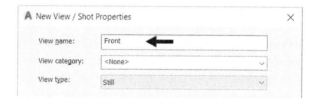

> Click **OK** on the **New View/Shot Properties** dialog box.
> Similarly, create the named views for the top and right views of the drawing.

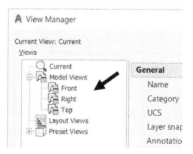

> To set the **Top** view to current, select it from the **Views** tree and click the **Set Current** button on the dialog box. Next, click **OK** on the **View Manager** dialog box; the **Top** view will be zoomed and fitted to the screen.

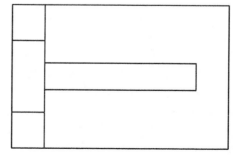

Questions:

1. In which projection method, the plane of projection lies between the observer and object?
2. In which projection method, the plane of projection is assumed to be non-transparent?
3. Where is **Right View** drawn in **Third View** projection method?
4. In which projection method, the object lies between the observer and plane of projection?
5. In which projection method, **Top View** comes below **Front View** and **Right View** drawn to the left side of the elevation?
6. In which quadrant the object is kept in the **Third View** projection method?

Exercises

Exercise 1:

Create the orthographic views of the object shown below.

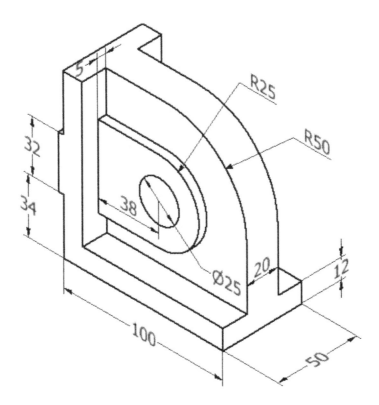

Exercise 2:

Create the orthographic views of the object shown below.

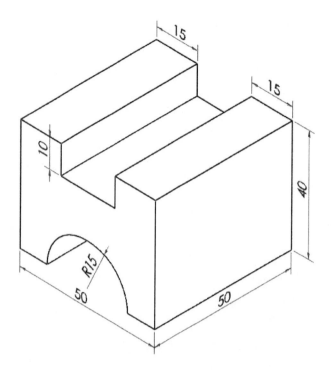

Exercise 3:

Create the orthographic and auxiliary views of the object shown below.

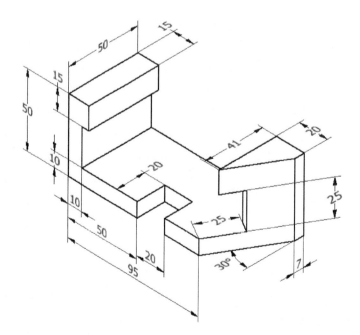

Chapter 6: Dimensions & Annotations in AutoCAD

This chapter covers the various options used for creating dimensions and annotations to the sketch quickly and easily.

The topics covered in this chapter are:

- ❖ **Creating Dimensions**
- ❖ **Creating Dimension Style**
- ❖ **Adding Leaders**
- ❖ **Adding Dimensional Tolerances**
- ❖ **Adding Geometric Tolerances**
- ❖ **Editing Dimensions**

Dimensioning

In previous chapters, you learned how to draw create drawings. However, while creating a drawing, you also need to apply the size information. You can provide the size information by applying dimensions to the drawings. In this chapter, you will learn how to create various types of dimensions. You will also learn about some standard ways and best practices of dimensioning.

Creating Dimension

In AutoCAD, there are many tools available for creating dimensions. You can access these tools from the Ribbon, Command line, and Menu Bar.

The functions of various dimensioning tools are discussed below, one-by-one:

Dimension   [DIM]

This tool is used to create the dimensions according to the entity selected.

- Click **Annotate > Dimensions > Dimension** on the ribbon.
- Select a line entity, move the cursor and click to place the linear dimension, as shown.

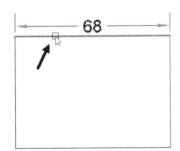
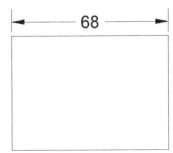

- Select a circle, move the cursor and click to place the diameter dimension, as shown.
- Select an arc, move the cursor and click to place the radial dimension, as shown.
- Similarly, select two lines and place the angular dimension, as shown.

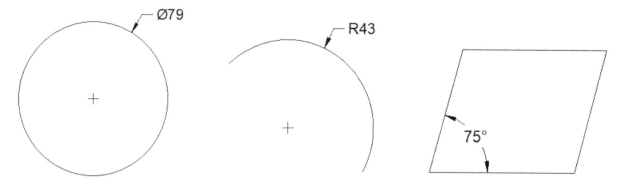

Linear   [DLI]

Linear   This tool is used to create horizontal and vertical dimensions.

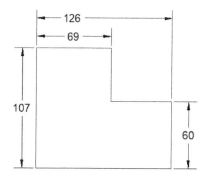

- Click **Annotate > Dimensions > Dimension > Linear** Linear on the ribbon.
- Select the first and second points of the dimension.
- Move the cursor in horizontal direction to create a vertical dimension (or) move in the vertical direction to create a horizontal dimension.
- Click to place the dimension.

Aligned   [DAL]

Aligned   This tool is used to create a linear dimension parallel to the object.

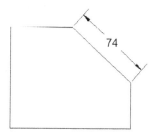

- Click **Annotate > Dimensions > Dimension > Aligned** Aligned on the ribbon.
- Select the first and second points of the dimension line.
- Move the cursor and click to place the dimension.

Angular [DAN]

 Angular   This tool is used to create an angular dimension.

- Click **Annotate > Dimensions > Dimension > Angular**  Angular on the ribbon.
- Select the first line and second line, as shown.
- Move the cursor and place angle dimension, as shown.

- To create an angle dimension on an arc, select the arc and place the dimension.

- To create an angle dimension on a circle, select two points on the circle and place the angle dimension, as shown.

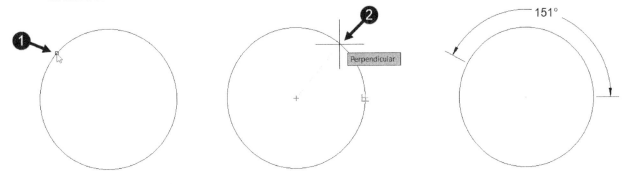

Arc Length [DAR]

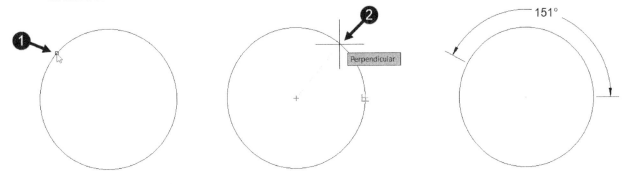 Arc Length   This tool is used to dimension the total or partial length of an arc.

- Click **Annotate > Dimensions > Dimension > Arc Length** Arc Length on the ribbon.

- Select an arc from the drawing.
- If you want to dimension only a partial length of an arc, select **Partial** option from the command line.
- Next, select the two points on the arc, as shown.
- Move cursor and click to place the dimension.

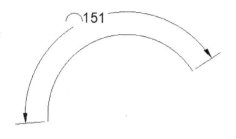

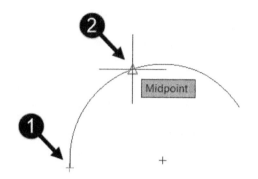

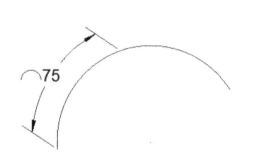

Radius　　　　　　　　　[DRA]

This tool is used to create a radial dimension of a circle or an arc.

- Click **Annotate > Dimensions > Dimension > Radius** on the ribbon.
- Select a circle or an arc and place the dimension, as shown.

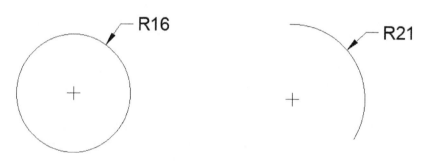

Diameter　　　　　　　　[DIA]

This tool is used to dimension a circle or an arc, as shown.

- Click **Annotate > Dimensions > Dimension > Diameter** on the ribbon.
- Select a circle or an arc and place the dimension.

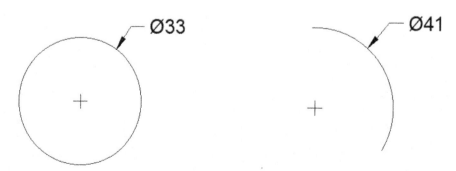

Jogged [DJO]

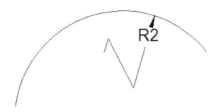 It is used to create jogged dimensions. A jogged dimension is created when it is not possible to show the center of an arc or circle.

- Click **Annotate > Dimensions > Dimension > Jogged** on the ribbon.
- Select an arc or circle.
- Select a new center point of the circle or arc.
- Locate the dimension and the jog location.

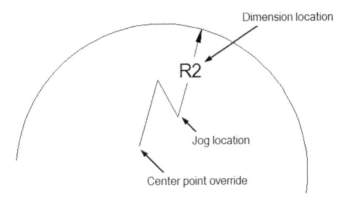

Ordinate [DOR]

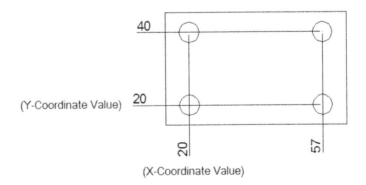 It is used to create ordinate dimensions based on the current position of the User Coordinate System (UCS).

- Click **Annotate > Dimensions > Dimension > Ordinate** on the ribbon.
- Select the point of the object.
- Move the cursor in the vertical direction and click to place the X-Coordinate value.
- Move the cursor in the horizontal direction and click to place the Y-Coordinate value.

⊢⊣ Continue   It is used to create a linear dimension from the second extension line of the previous dimension.

- Create a linear dimension by selecting the first and second points.

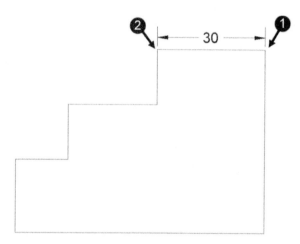

- Click **Annotate > Dimensions > Continue** ⊢⊣ Continue on the ribbon; a chain dimension is attached to the cursor.

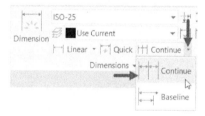

- Select the third and fourth point of the chain dimension.
- Place the chain dimension. Next, right-click and select **Enter**.

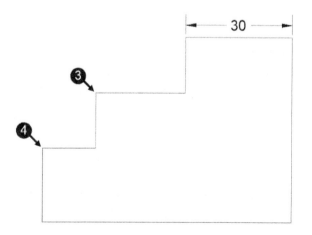
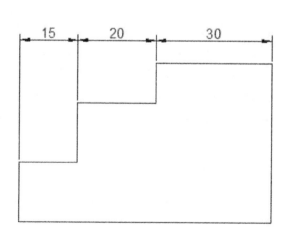

⊢⊣ Baseline   It is used to create dimensions by using the previously created dimension.

- Create a linear dimension, as shown.

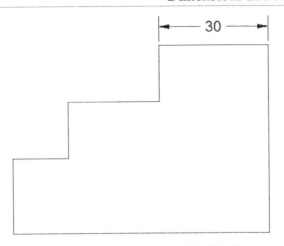

- Click **Annotate > Dimensions > Continue > Baseline** Baseline on the ribbon.
- Select the base dimension, if it is not already selected.
- Select the other two points for the baseline dimension.
- Next, right-click and select **Enter**.

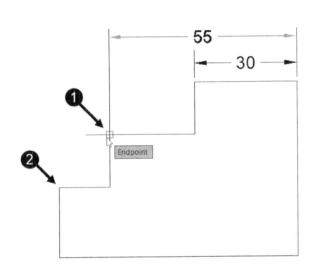

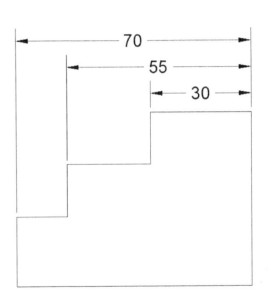

Dimension, Dimjogline [DJL]

It is used to create a jogged linear dimension.

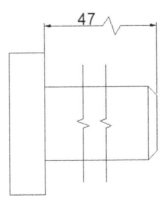

- Click **Annotate > Dimensions > Dimension, Dimjogline** on the ribbon.

- Select the linear dimension to add jog.
- Specify the location of the jog on the dimension.

Center Mark   [DCE]

It is used to place a center mark inside a circle or an arc. The type of center mark will depend on the value of the **DIMCEN** variable. For a positive value, center marks are created and for a negative value, centrelines are created.

- Click **Annotate > Centerlines > Center Mark** on the ribbon.
- Select an arc or a circle; the center mark will be placed at its center, as shown.

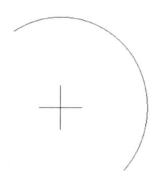
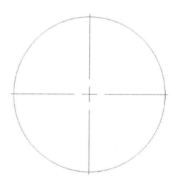

Quick Dimension   [QDIM]

Quick   It is used to dimension one or more objects at the same time.

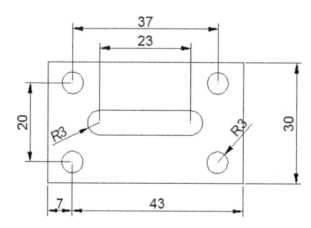

- Click **Annotate > Dimensions > Quick Dimension** Quick on the ribbon.
- Select one or more objects from a drawing.
- Right-click and place the dimensions.

Adjust Space [DIMSPACE]

 It is used to adjust the space between linear and angular dimensions.

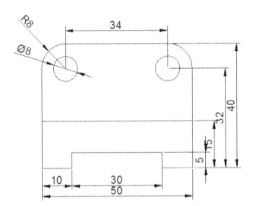 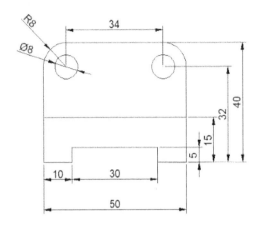

- Click **Annotate > Dimensions > Adjust Space** on the ribbon.
- Select the base dimension from which the other dimensions are to be adjusted.
- Select the dimensions to be adjusted.
- Right-click to accept.
- Enter the space value or select the Auto option; the dimensions will be adjusted with respect to the base dimension.

Break [DIMBREAK]

It is used to create breaks in dimension, extension, and leader lines.

- Click **Annotate > Dimensions > Break** on the ribbon.
- Select the dimension to add a break.
- Select the cutting object; the dimension will be broken by the cutting object.
- Right-click to exit the tool.

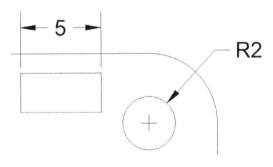 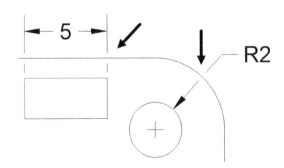

Inspect **[DIMINSPECT]**

It is used to create an inspection dimension. The inspection dimension describes how frequently the dimension should be checked to ensure the quality of the product.

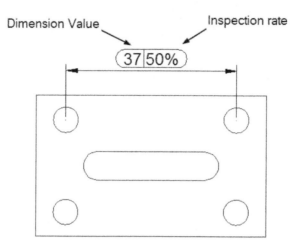

- Click **Annotate > Dimensions > Inspect** on the ribbon; the **Inspection Dimension** dialog box appears.

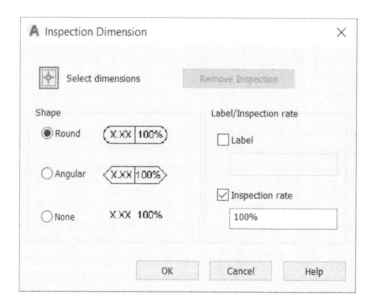

- Click the Select dimensions button on the dialog box and select the dimension to apply the inspection rate.
- Right-click to accept.
- Select the shape of the inspection from the Shape section.
- Enter the Inspection rate. 100% means that the value will be checked every time during the inspection process. 50% means half the times.
- If required, select the Label check box and enter the inspection label.
- Click OK.

Example:

In this example, you will create the drawing as shown below and add dimensions to it.

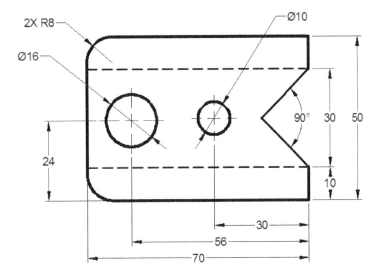

- Create four new layers with the following settings.

Layer	Linetype	Lineweight
Construction	Continuous	0.00 mm
Object	Continuous	0.50 mm
Hidden	HIDDEN2	0.30 mm
Dimensions	Continuous	Default

- Set the maximum limit of the drawing to **100,100**.
- Click **Zoom All** on the **Navigation Bar**.
- Create the drawing on the **Object** and **Hidden** layers.

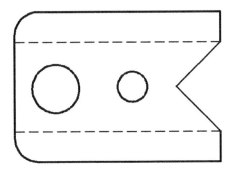

- Select the **Dimensions** layer from the **Layer** drop-down in the **Layer** panel of the **Home** tab, as shown.

Alternatively, you can select it from the **Layer** drop down available in the **Dimensions** panel of the **Annotate** tab, as shown.

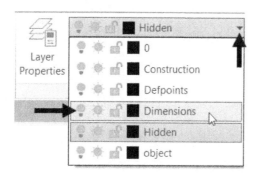
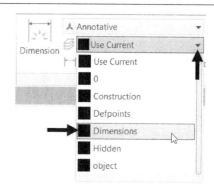

Creating a Dimension Style

The appearance of the dimensions depends on the dimension style used. You can create a new dimension style using the **Dimension Style Manager** dialog box. In this dialog box, you can specify various settings related to appearance and behaviour of dimensions. The following example demonstrates you to create a dimension style.

➤ Click the inclined arrow on the **Dimensions** panel of the **Annotate** tab of ribbon or enter **D** in the command line; the **Dimension Style Manager** dialog box appears.

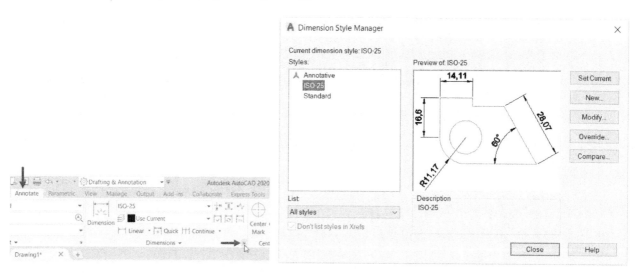

The basic nomenclature of dimensions is given below.

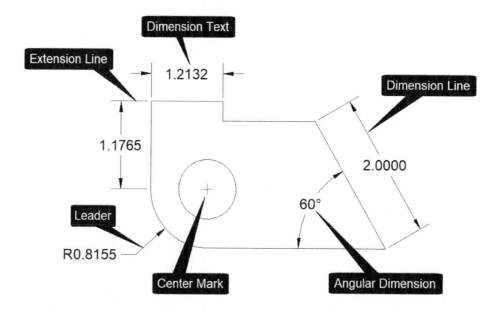

By default, the **ISO-25** or the **Standard** dimension style is active. If the default dimension style does not suit the dimensioning requirement, you can create a new dimension style and modify the nomenclature of the dimensions.

- To create a new dimension style, click the **New** button on the **Dimension Style Manager** dialog box; the **Create New Dimension Style** dialog box get visible.

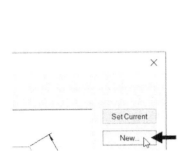
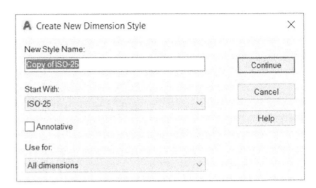

- Enter **Mechanical** in the **New Style Name** edit box of the **Create New Dimension Style** dialog box.
- Select **ISO-25** from the **Start With** drop-down, if it is not selected.
- Click on the **Continue** button to display the **New Dimension Style: Mechanical** dialog box.

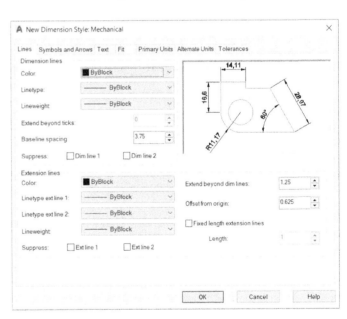

- In the **New Dimension Style: Mechanical** dialog box, click the **Primary Units** tab.
- Ensure that the **Unit Format** is set to **Decimal**.
- Select **0** from the **Precision** drop-down, as shown.
- Select **'.'(Period)** from the **Decimal separator** drop-down, as shown.

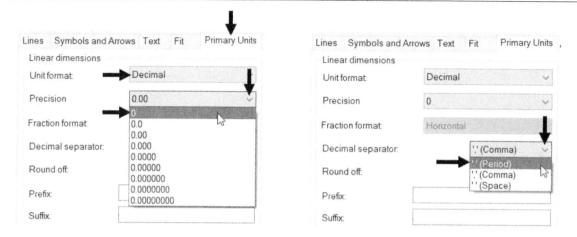

Study the other options in the **Primary Units** tab. Most of them are self-explanatory.

- Click the **Text** tab.
- Ensure that the **Text height** value is set to **2.5**.
- In the **Text placement** section, set the **Vertical** and **Horizontal** values to **Centered**.
- Set the **Text alignment** to **Horizontal**.

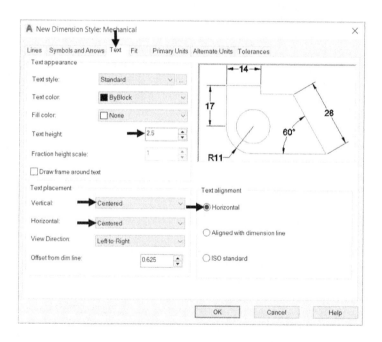

Study the other options in the **Text** tab. These options let you to change the appearance of the dimension text.

- Click the **Lines** tab from the dialog box.
- In this tab, notice the two options in the **Extension lines** section: **Extend beyond dim lines** and **Offset from origin.**

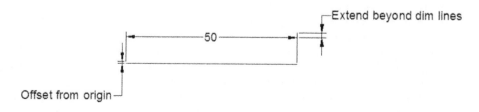

- Set **Extend beyond dim lines** and **Offset from origin** to **1.25**.
- Set the **Baseline spacing** in the **Dimension lines** section to **5**.

On your own, examine the different options in this tab. The options in this tab are used to change the appearance and behaviour of the dimension lines and extension lines.

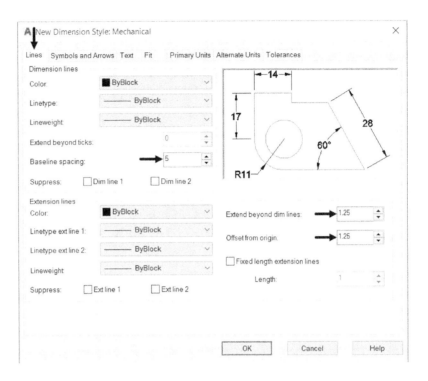

- Click on the **Symbols and Arrows** tab and set **Arrow size** to **3** and **Center Marks** to **3**.
- Select the **Line** option in the **Center marks** section.

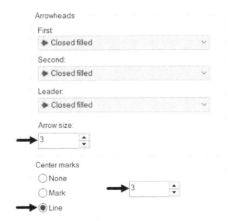

Notice the different options in this tab. The options in this tab are used to change the appearance of the arrows and symbols. Also, you can set the appearance of the center marks and centrelines of circles and arcs.

- Click **OK** from the **New Dimension Style: Mechanical** dialog box to accept the settings.
- Next, click on the **Set Current** from the **Dimension Style Manager** dialog box to set the **Mechanical** dimension style as current.
- Click **Close** to close the dialog box.

- Now click on the **Center Mark** button (**Annotate > Centerlines > Center Mark**).

- Select a circle from the drawing to apply the center mark.
- Press the SPACEBAR to invoke the **Center Mark** tool again and select the other circle.

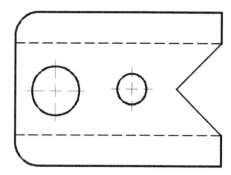

- Type **DLI** in the command line and press **ENTER** to activate the **DIMLINEAR** tool.

  Alternatively, you can select **Annotate > Dimensions > Linear** from the Ribbon.

- Select the lower right corner of the drawing.
- Select the end point of the center mark of the small circle; the dimension is attached to the cursor.
- Place the dimension as shown below.

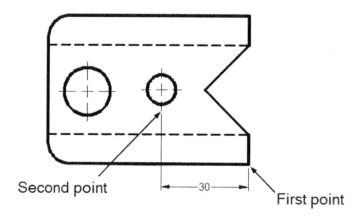

- Click **Annotate > Dimension > Continue > Baseline** on the ribbon; a dimension is attached to the cursor.
- Select the end point of the center mark of the large circle; another dimension is attached to the cursor.
- Select the lower left corner of the drawing.
- Press **ENTER** twice.

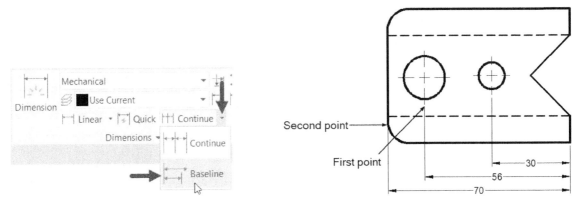

- Click **Annotate > Dimensions > Linear > Angular** from the ribbon.
- Select the two angled lines and place the angular dimension.

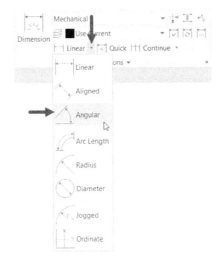

- Click **Annotate > Dimensions > Linear > Diameter** on the ribbon and apply diameter dimensions to the circles.
- Type **DRA** in the command line and press **ENTER** to activate the **DIMRADIUS** tool.
- Select the fillet located at the top left corner; the radial dimension is attached to the cursor.
- Select **Mtext** from the command line and type **2X** and press **SPACEBAR**.
- Click in the drawing window to update and place the dimension text.
- Next, place the radial dimension at **45** degrees.
- Similarly, apply the other dimensions, as shown below.

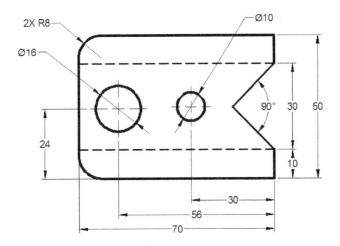

Note: By selecting the **Dimension** tool from **Dimensions** panel of the **Annotate** tab, you can create the dimensions as per the entity selected.

Adding Leaders

A Leader is a thin, dark, solid line terminating with an arrowhead at one end and a dimension, note, or symbol at the other end. In the following example, you will learn to create a leader style, and then create a leader.

Example:

- Draw a square of **24** mm length.
- Create a circle of **10.11** mm diameter at center of the square.

- Click **Home > Draw > Arc > Center, Start, Angle** on the ribbon.
- Select the center point of the circle.
- Move the cursor horizontally toward right.
- Type **6** as the radius and press **ENTER**.
- Type **270** as the included angle and press **ENTER**.

- Click on the down arrow of the **Annotation** panel in **Home** tab to expand it, as shown.
- Click on the **Multileader Style** icon to display the **Multileader Style Manager** dialog box.

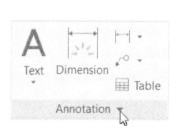
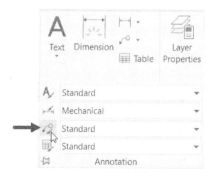

- Click on the **New** button of the **Multileader Style Manager** dialog box; the **Create New Multileader Style** dialog box get visible.

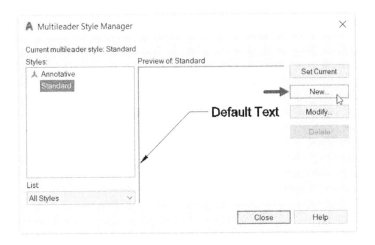

- In the **Create New Multileader Style** dialog box, enter **Hole callout** in the **New style name** edit box and select **Standard** from the **Start with** drop-down.

- Click on the **Continue** button; the **Modify Multileader Style** dialog box get visible.
- Under the **Leader Format** tab, set the **Arrowhead Size** to **2.5**.

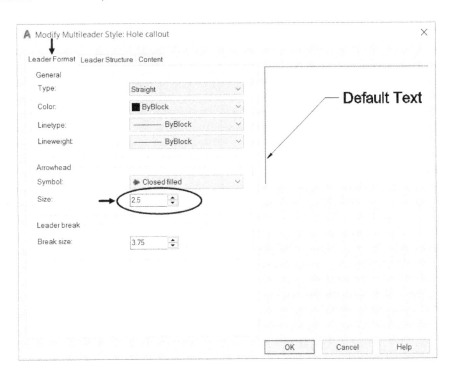

The other options in this tab are used to set the appearance of the multileader lines and the arrow head.

- Click on the **Leader Structure** tab and set the **Landing distance** to **5**.

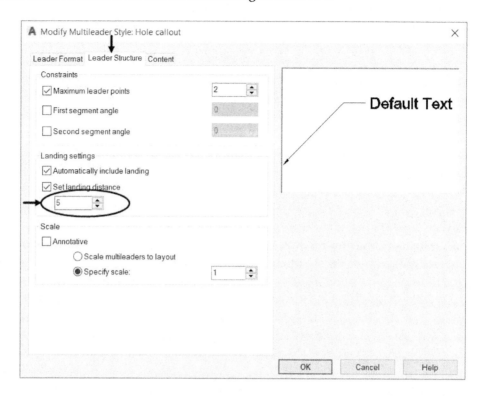

- Click on the **Content** tab and set the **Text height** to **2.5**.

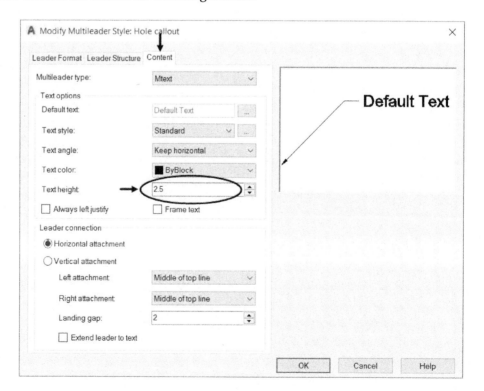

The other options in this tab are used to define the appearance of the text or block that will be attached at the end of the leader line.

- Click **OK** from the **Modify Multileader Style** dialog box.
- Click **Set Current** from the **Multileader Style Manager** dialog box.

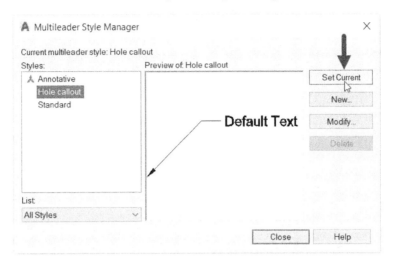

- Click **Close** to close the dialog box.
- Click **Annotate > Leaders > Multileader** on the ribbon.

- Click on the down-arrow with the **Polar tracking** button at the status bar and select **45** from the menu.
- Select a point in the first quadrant of the arc.
- Move the cursor in the top right direction and click to create the leader.

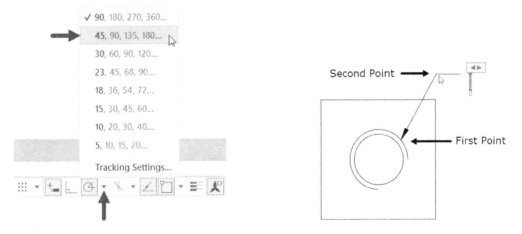

- Type **M12X1.75 - 6H 16** in the text editor.
  Next, you need to insert the depth symbol before **16**.
- Place the cursor before **16** and click the **Symbol** button on the **Insert** panel of the **Text Editor** ribbon; a menu appears.

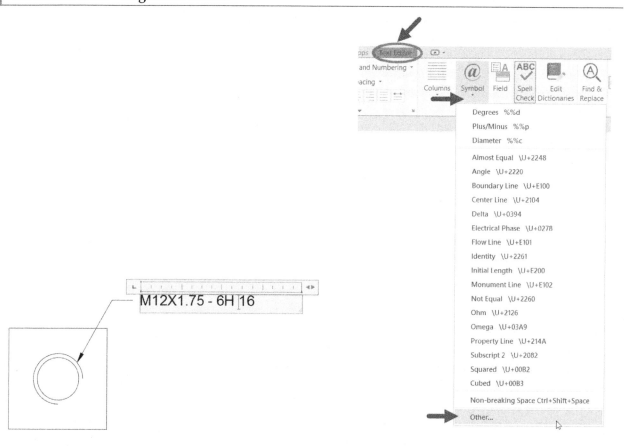

- Click **Other** on the menu; the **Character Map** dialog box appears.
- In the **Character Map** dialog box, select **GDT** from the **Font** drop-down.
- Select the **Depth** symbol from the fonts table.

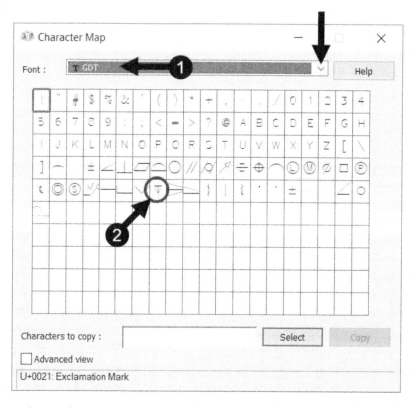

- Click **Select** and **Copy** buttons.

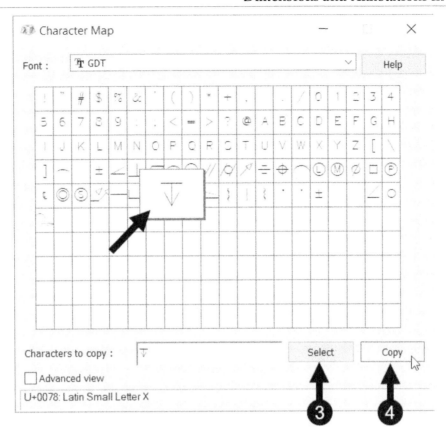

- Close the **Character Map** dialog box.
- Right-click and select **Paste**; the depth symbol is pasted in the text editor.
- Adjust the spacing so that the complete text is in one line.

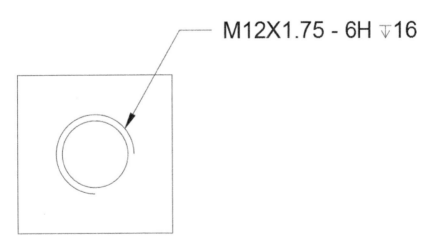

Adding Dimensional Tolerances

During the manufacturing process, the accuracy of a part is an important factor. However, it is impossible to manufacture a part with the exact dimensions. Therefore, while applying dimensions to a drawing we provide some dimensional tolerances which lie within acceptable limits. The following example shows you how to add dimension tolerances in AutoCAD.

Example:

Create the drawing as shown below. Do not add dimensions to it.

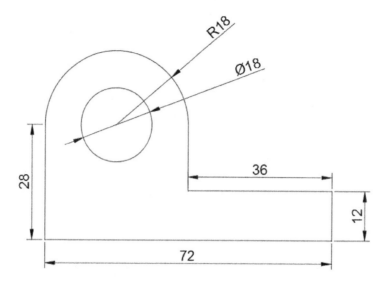

- Create a new dimension style with the name **Tolerances**.
- In the **New Dimension Styles** dialog box, click the **Tolerances** tab.
- In the **Tolerances** tab, set the **Method** as **Deviation**.
- Set **Precision** as **0.00**.
- Set the **Upper Value** and **Lower Value** to **0.05**.
- Set the **Vertical Position** as **Middle**.

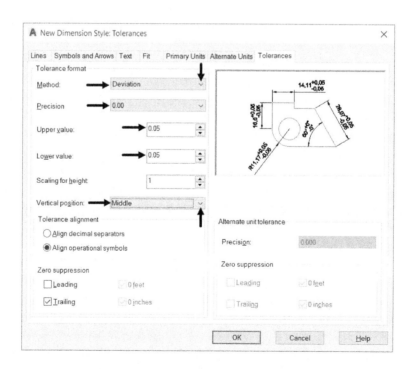

- Specify the following settings in the **Primary Units**, **Text**, and **Symbols and Arrows** tab, as shown:

Primary Units tab:

Unit format: Decimal

Precision: 0.00

Decimal Separator: '.'Period

Text tab:

Text height: 2.5

Text placement: Centered (in Vertical & Horizontal)

Text alignment: Horizontal

Symbols and Arrows tab:

Arrow Size: 2.5

Center marks: Line

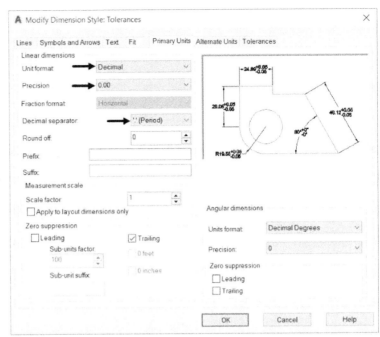

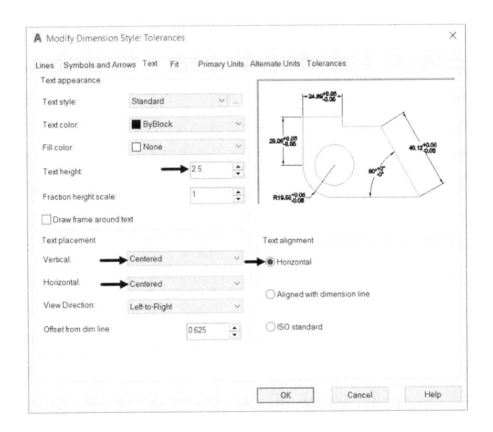

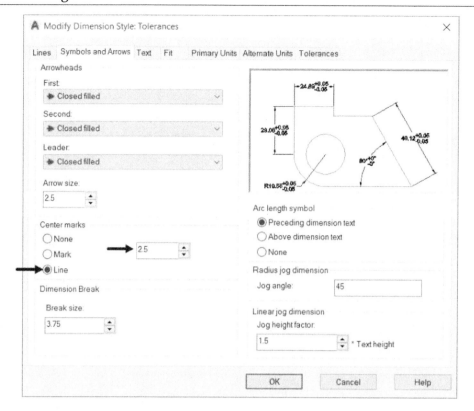

- Click **OK** from **New Dimension Styles** dialog box.
- Click **Set Current** and **Close** on the **Dimension Style Manager** dialog box.
- Apply dimensions to the drawing.

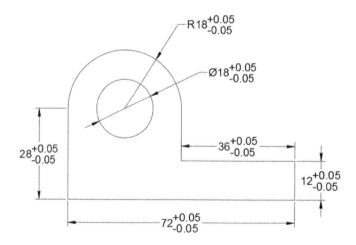

Geometric Dimensioning and Tolerancing

Earlier you have learned how to apply tolerances to the size (dimensions) of a component. However, the dimensional tolerances are not sufficient for manufacturing a component. You need to give tolerance values to its shape, orientation and position as well. The following figure shows a note which is used to explain the tolerance value given to the shape of the object.

Note: The vertical face should not taper
over 0.08 from the horizontal face

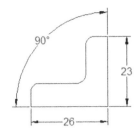

Providing a note in a drawing may be confusing. To avoid this, we use Geometric Dimensioning and Tolerancing (GD&T) symbols to specify the tolerance values to shape, orientation and position of an object. The following figure shows the same example represented by using the GD&T symbols. In this figure, the vertical face to which the tolerance frame is connected, must be within two parallel planes 0.08 apart, perpendicular to the datum reference (horizontal plane).

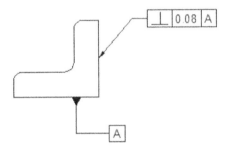

The Geometric Tolerancing symbols that can be used to interpret the geometric conditions are given in the table below.

Purpose		Symbol
To represent the shape of a single feature.	Straightness	——
	Flatness	▱
	Cylindricity	⌭
	Circularity	○
	Profile of a surface	⌓
	Profile of a line	⌒

To represent the orientation of a feature with respect to another feature.	Parallelism	//
	Perpendicularity	⊥
	Angularity	∠
To represent the position of a feature with respect to another feature.	Position	⊕
	Cocentricity and coaxiality	◎
	Run-out	↗
	Total Run-out	↗↗
	Symmetry	=

Example:

In this example, you will apply geometric tolerances to the drawing shown below.

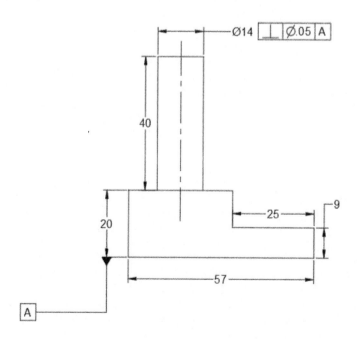

- Create the drawing as shown below.

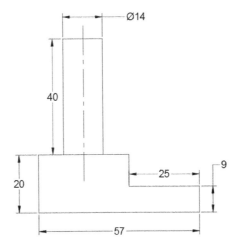

- Click on the **Dimensions** down-arrow from the **Annotate** tab to expand it, as shown.
- Next click on the **Tolerance** button, as shown; the **Geometric Tolerance** dialog box get displayed.

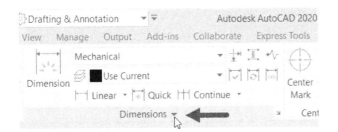
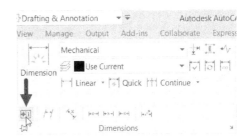

- In the **Geometric Tolerance** dialog box, click on the upper box of the **Sym** group; the **Symbol** dialog box appears.

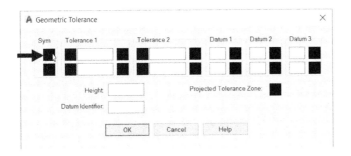
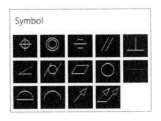

- In the **Symbol** dialog box, click the **Perpendicularity** symbol; the symbol appears in the **Sym** group.

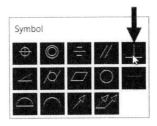

- Click in the top left box of the **Tolerance 1** group; the diameter symbol appears in the box.
- Enter **.05** in the box next to the diameter symbol.

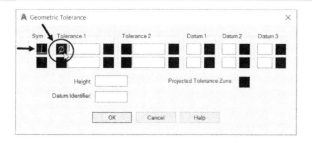
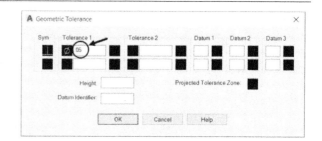

- Enter **A** in the upper box of the **Datum 1** group.

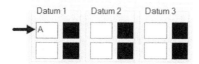

- Click **OK** and place the **Feature Control frame** as shown below.

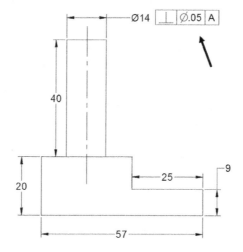

Next, you need to add the datum reference.

- Type **QLEADER** in the command line and press **ENTER**.
- Select **Settings** from the command line; the **Leader Settings** dialog box appears.
- In the **Leader Settings** dialog box, select the **Tolerance** option.

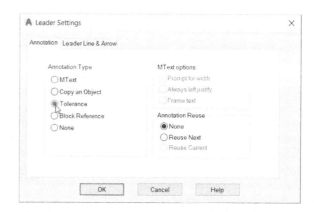

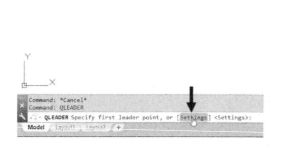

- Click the **Leader Line & Arrow** tab and set the **Arrowhead** type to **Datum triangle filled**.
- Set **Number of Points** to **3**.

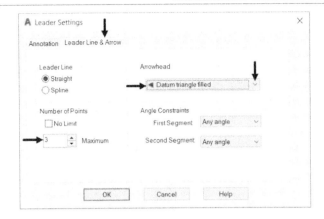

- Click **OK** and specify the first, second and third points of the datum reference as shown below; the **Geometric Tolerance** dialog box appears.
- In the **Geometric Tolerance** dialog box, set **Datum Identifier** to **A**.

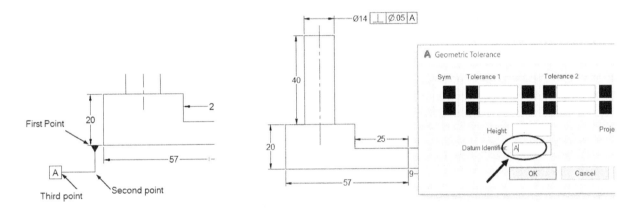

- Click **OK**.

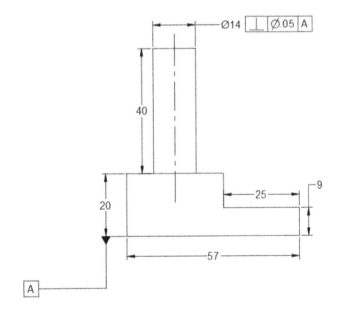

Editing Dimensions by Stretching

In AutoCAD, the dimensions are associative to the drawing. If you modify a drawing, the dimensions will be modified, automatically. In the following example, you will stretch the drawing to modify the dimensions.

Example:

Create the drawing as shown below and apply dimensions to it.

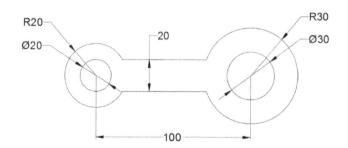

- Click **Home > Modify > Stretch** on the ribbon.
- Drag a window over the right-side circles and the horizontal lines to select them.

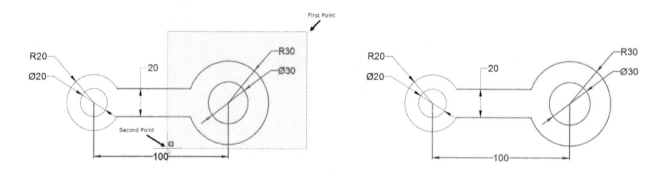

- Right-click and select the center point of the right-side circles.
- Move the cursor to stretch the drawing; you will notice that the horizontal dimension also changes.
- Type **40** and press **ENTER**; the horizontal dimension is updated to **140**.

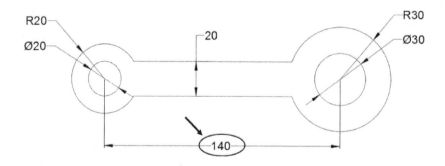

Modifying Dimensions by Trimming and Extending

In earlier chapters, you have learned to the modify drawings by trimming and extending objects. In the same way, you can modify dimensions by trimming and extending. The following example shows you how to modify dimensions by this method.

Example:

Create a drawing as shown below and add dimensions to it.

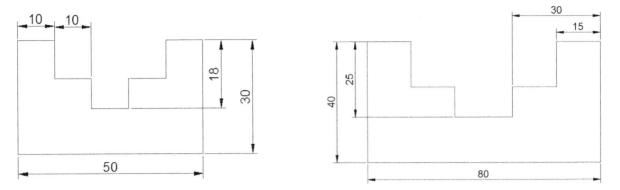

- Click **Home > Modify > Trim** from the ribbon.
- Select the horizontal edge as shown in figure and right-click to accept.

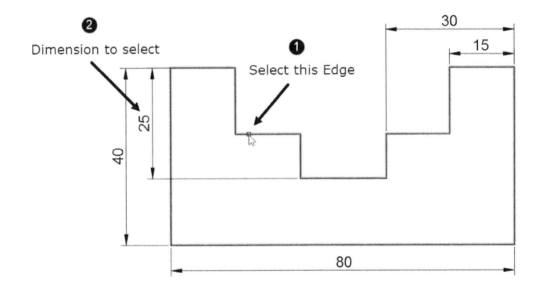

- Select the vertical dimension with the value **25**; it will be trimmed upto the selected edge.

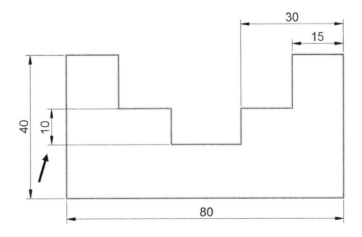

- Press ESC.
- Click **Home > Modify > Trim > Extend** from the ribbon.
- Select the vertical edge as the boundary, as shown below. Next, right-click to accept.

- Select the horizontal dimension with the value **30**; the dimension will be extended upto the selected boundary.

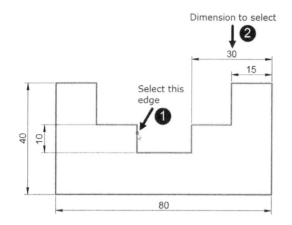
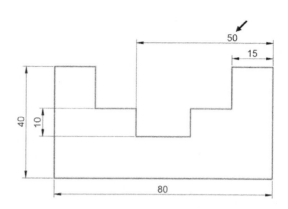

Using the DIMEDIT command

The **DIMEDIT** command can be used to modify dimension. Using this command, you can add text to a dimension, rotate the dimension text and extension lines or reset the position of the dimension text.

Example: (Adding Text to the dimension)

- Type **DED** in the command line and press **ENTER**.
- Select the **New** option from the command line; a text box appears.
- Enter **TYP** in the text box and press the **SPACEBAR**.

- Left-click and select the dimension with value **50**.
- Press **ENTER**; the dimension text will be changed.

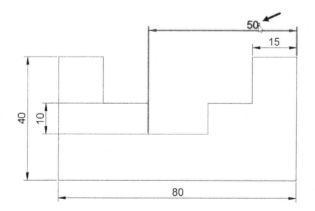
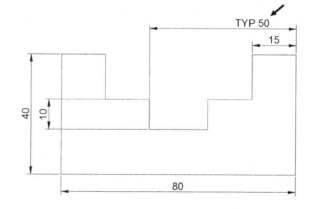

Example: (Rotating the dimension text)

- Enter **DED** in the command line and select the **Rotate** option; the message, "Specify angle for dimension text" appears in the command line.
- Type **45** and press **ENTER**.
- Select the dimension with the value **TYP 50** and right-click; the angle of the dimension text is changed to **45** degrees. Note that the angle is measured from the horizontal axis (X-axis).

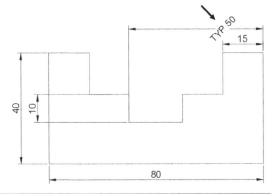

Using the Update tool

The **Update** tool is used to update a dimension with the currently active dimension style. For example, if you have created new dimension style, you can apply it an already existing dimension using the **Update** tool.

Example: (Update the dimension with current active style)

- Type **D** in the command line and press **ENTER**; the **Dimension Style Manager** dialog box appears.
- In the **Dimension Style Manager** dialog box, select **Standard** from the **Styles** list and click **Modify**.
- In the **Modify Dimension Style** dialog box, set the **Text height** to **2.5**.
- Click the **Text Style** button; the **Text Style** dialog box appears.
- In the **Text Style** dialog box, change the **Font Style** to **Italic**.

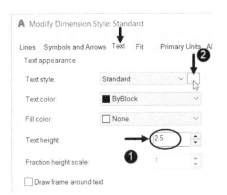 

- Click **Apply** and then **Close** from the **Text Style** dialog box.
- Click **OK** from the **Modify Dimension Style** dialog box.
- Next, click **Close** from the **Dimension Style Manager** dialog box to close it.
- In the **Dimensions** panel, set the dimension style to **Standard**.

- Click the **Update** button on the **Dimensions** panel.

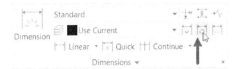

- Select the horizontal dimension with the value **30**. Next, right-click; the dimension will be updated with the current the dimension style.

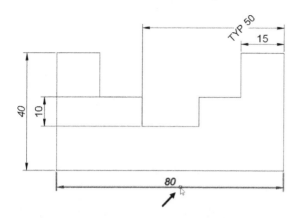 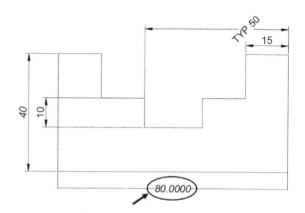

Using the Oblique tool

The **Oblique** tool is used to incline the extension lines of a dimension. This tool is very useful while dimensioning the isometric drawings. It can also be used in 2D drawings when the dimensions overlap with each other.

Example:

In this example, you will create an isometric drawing and add dimensions to it. Next, you will use the **Oblique** tool to change the angle of the dimensions lines.

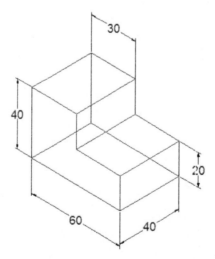

- Click on the down arrow next to the **SNAPMODE** button from the status bar and select **Snap Settings**; the **Drafting Settings** dialog box appears.

  Alternatively, you can enter **DS** in the command line to display the **Drafting Settings** dialog box.

- In the **Drafting Settings** dialog box, set **Snap type** to **Isometric snap** and click **OK**.

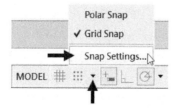 

- Turn on the **Snap Mode** [⊞], **Ortho Mode** [⌐], and the **Dynamic Input** [⊹].

  You can simply press **F9**, **F8**, and **F12** key to activate.

- Click **Zoom All** on the **Navigation Bar**.
- Type **L** in the command line and press **ENTER**.
- Click at a random point and move the cursor vertically upwards.
- Type **60** in the command line and press **ENTER**; a vertical line will be created.
- Move the cursor toward right; you will notice that an inclined line is attached to the cursor.
- Click when the tooltip shows **40 < 330**.

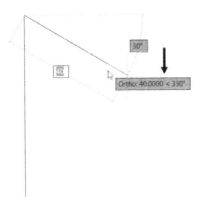

- Move the cursor toward downward and click when the tooltip shows **30 < 270**.
- Move the cursor toward right and click when the tooltip displays **40 < 330**.

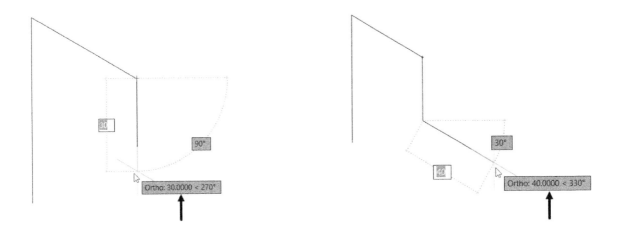

- Move downward and click when the tooltip shows **30 < 270**.
- Move the cursor toward left and click on the start point of the sketch.
- Right-click select **Enter**.

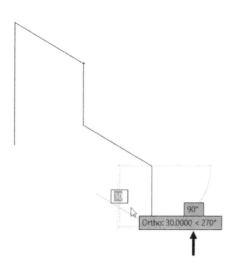
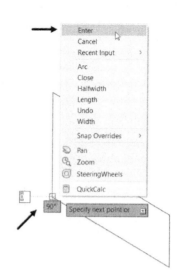

- Turn off the **Ortho Mode**.
- Drag a selection window and select all the objects of the sketch.
- Right-click and select **Copy-Selection** from the shortcut menu.
- Select the lower left corner point as the base point.
- Move the cursor toward right and click when the tooltip shows **70 < 30**.

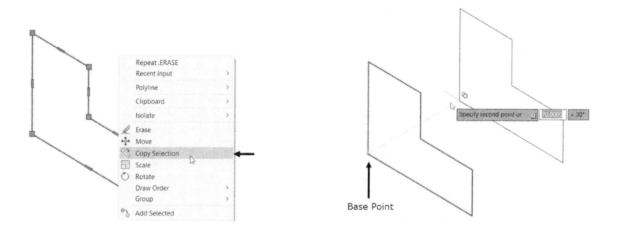

Base Point

- Right-click and select **Enter**.

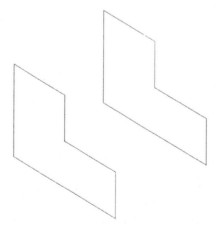

- Use the **Line** tool and connect the endpoints of the two sketches.

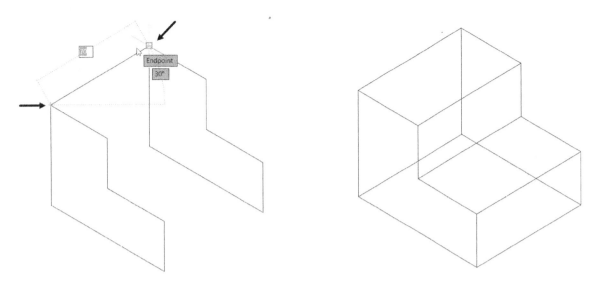

- Use the dimensioning tools and apply dimensions to the sketch.

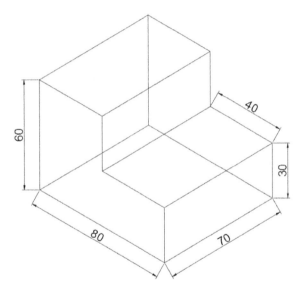

- Expand the **Dimensions** panel on the **Annotate** ribbon and click the **Oblique** button.
- Select the vertical dimensions and right-click to accept; the message, "**Enter obliquing angle**" appears in the command line.

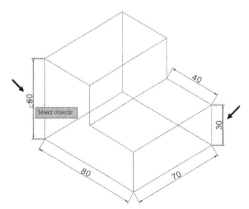

S

- Type **150** as the oblique angle and press **ENTER**; the dimensions are oblique as shown below.

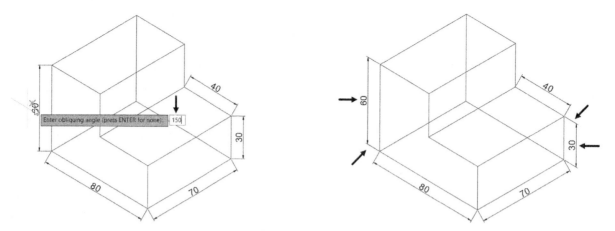

- Again, click the **Oblique** tool from the **Dimensions** panel and select the aligned dimensions. Next, right-click to accept.

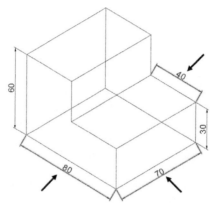

- Type **90** as the oblique angle and press **ENTER**; the dimensions will be oblique as shown below.

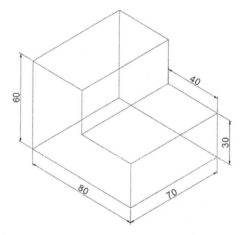

Editing Dimensions using Grips

In Chapter 4, you have learned to edit objects using grips. In the same away, you can edit dimensions using grips. The editing operations using grips are discussed next.

Example: (Stretching the Dimension)

- Select the dimension to display grips on it.
- Select the endpoint grip of the dimension.
- Next, move the cursor and select a new point; the dimension value will be updated, automatically.

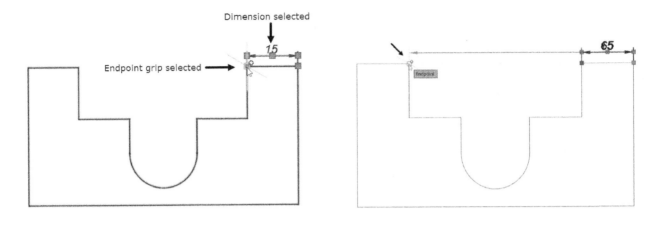

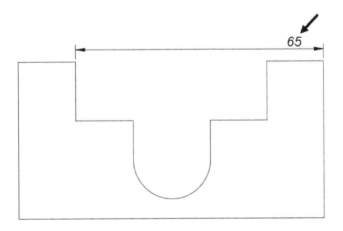

- You can also stretch angular or radial dimensions.

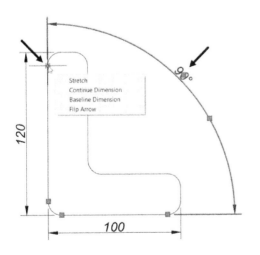

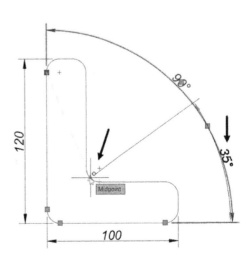

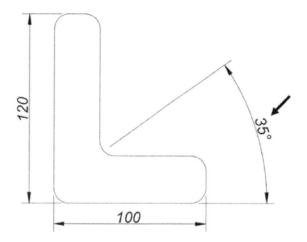

Example: (Moving the Dimension)

- To move a linear dimension, select the middle grip and move the cursor.

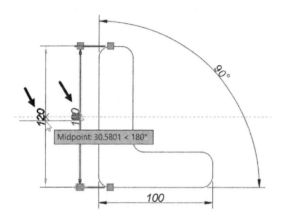

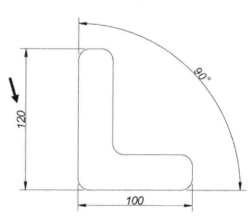

- Similarly, you can move the angular and radial dimensions.

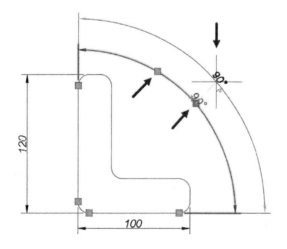

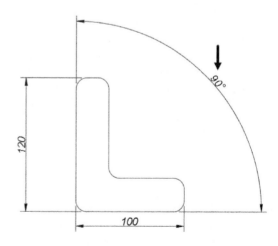

Example: (Modifying the Dimension text)

- Select the dimension and place the cursor on the middle grip; a shortcut menu appears as shown below.

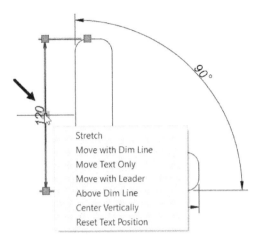

The options in the menu are self-explanatory. You can perform the required operation by selecting the corresponding option.

- Similarly, place the cursor on the endpoint of the dimension line and select the required option from the menu.

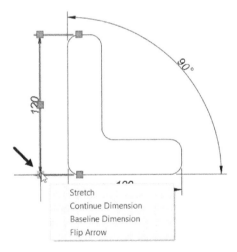

Modifying Dimensions using the Properties palette

Using the **Properties** palette, you can modify the dimensional properties such as text, arrow size, precision, linetype, lineweight, and so on. The **Properties** palette comes in handy when you want to modify the properties of a particular dimension only.

Example:

Create the drawing shown in figure and apply dimensions to it.

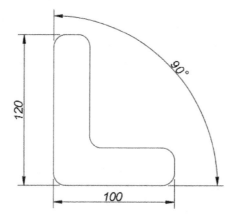

- Select the vertical dimension and right-click.
- Select **Properties** from the shortcut menu; the **Properties** palette appears.
- In the **Properties** palette, under the **Lines & Arrows** section, set the **Arrow size** to **4**.

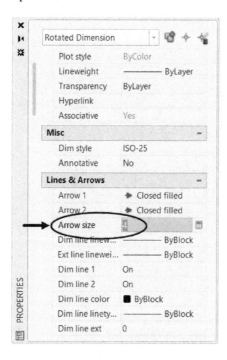

- Under the **General** section, set **Color** to **Blue**.

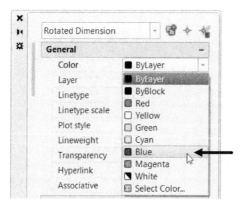

- Set the **Ext line offset** value to **2**.
- Scroll down to the **Text** section and set **Text height** to **4**.

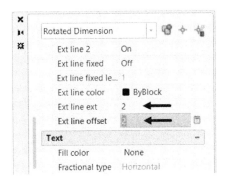 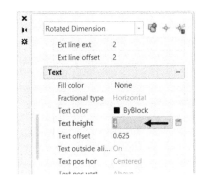

- Close the **Properties** palette; you will notice that the properties of the dimension are updated as per the changes made.

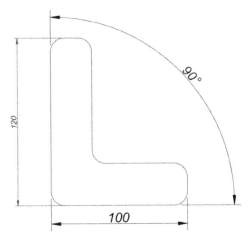

Matching Properties of Dimensions or Objects

In the previous section, you have learned to change the properties of a dimension. Now, you can apply these properties to other dimensions by using the **Match Properties** tool.

- Click **Home > Properties > Match Properties** from the ribbon or type **MA** and press **ENTER**; the message, "Select source object" appears in the command line.
- Select the vertical dimension from the drawing; the message, "Select destination object(s) or [Settings]:" appears in the command line.

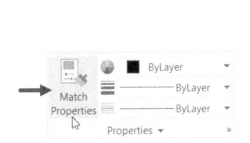 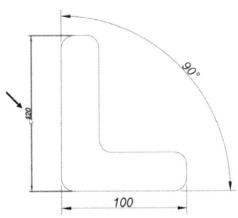

- Select the **Settings** option from the command line; the **Property Settings** dialog box appears.

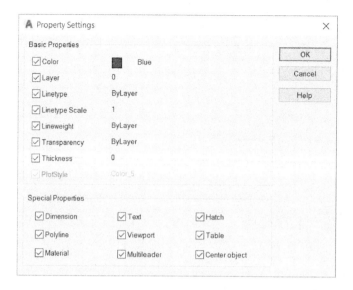

In this dialog box, you can select the settings that can be applied to the destination dimensions or objects. By default, all the options are selected in this dialog box.

- Click **OK** from the **Property Settings** dialog box. Next, you need to select the destination objects.
- Select the other dimensions from the drawing; the properties of the source dimension are applied to other dimensions.
- Right-click and select **Enter**.

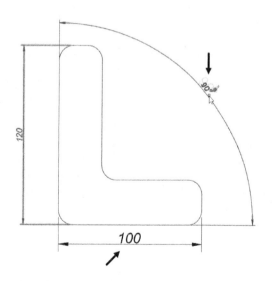

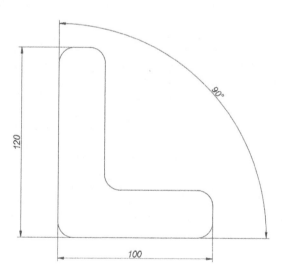

Questions:

1. Which tool is used to create vertical or horizontal dimensions?
2. Which tool is used to create total length of an arc?
3. Which tool is used to create radial dimension?
4. Which tool is used to dimension one or more dimensions at the same time?
5. Which command is used to modify dimensions?
6. Which tool is used to incline the extension lines of a dimension?
7. Which tool is used to match properties of dimensions or objects?

Exercises

Exercise 1:

Create the drawing shown below and create hole callouts for different types of holes. Assume missing dimensions.

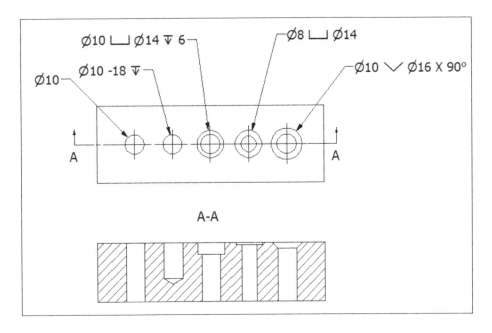

Exercise 2:

Create the drawing shown below. The Grid spacing is 10 mm. After creating the drawing, apply dimensional tolerances to it. The tolerance specifications are given below.

Method: Limits

Precision: 0.00

Upper Value: 0.05

Lower Value: 0.05

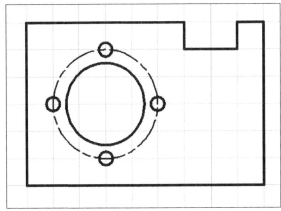

Exercise 3:

Create the following drawings and apply dimensions and annotations. The Grid Spacing X= 10 and Grid Spacing Y=10.

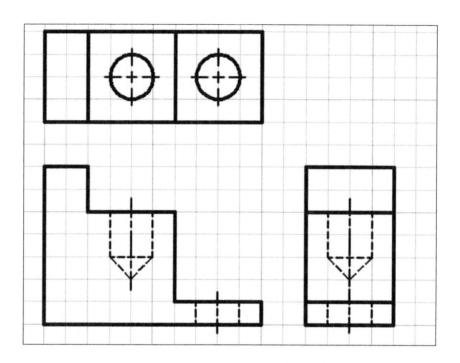

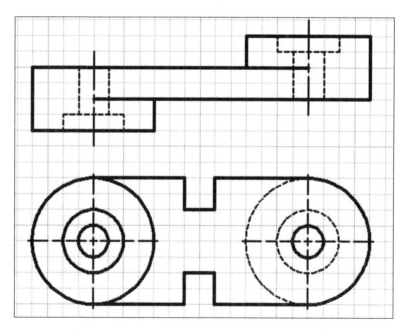

Chapter 7: Parametric Tools in AutoCAD

In this chapter, you will learn to do the following:

- ❖ **Apply Geometric and Dimensional Constraints**
- ❖ **Create Equations using the Parameter Manager**
- ❖ **Create Inferred Constraints**

Parametric Tools

Parametric tools are one of the main advancements in CAD/CAM/CAE. Using the parametric tools, you can define the shape and size of a drawing by applying relations and dimensions between the objects. You can also use equations in place of dimensions. Changing one parameter of an equation would change the entire shape and size of the drawing. This makes it easy to modify the design.

The parametric tools can be accessed from the **Ribbon**, **Menu Bar**, and **Command line**.

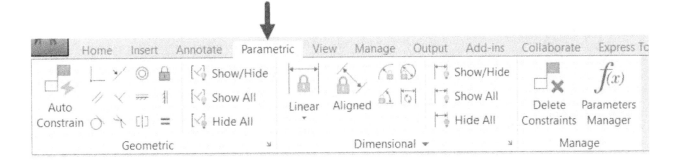

Ribbon

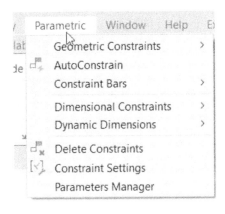

Menu Bar

Geometric Constraints

Geometric Constraints are used to control the shape of a drawing by applying geometric relationships between the objects. For example, you can apply the **Tangent** constraint to make a line tangent to a circle. You can use the **Equal** constraint to make two lines equal in length.

The following table shows various geometric constraints and their functions

Constraint	Function
Coincident	It is used to constraint a point to lie on another point or an object. • Click **Parametric > Geometric > Coincident** on the ribbon. • Select a point on a line or arc. • Select a point on another object; the two points will coincide with each other.
Collinear	It is used to constraint a line along another line. The lines are not required to touch each other. • Click **Parametric > Geometric > Collinear** on the ribbon. • Select the first line and the second line; the first line will be made collinear with the second line.
Concentric	It is used to make the center points of arcs, circles or ellipses coincident. • Click **Parametric > Geometric > Concentric** on the ribbon. • Select a circle or arc from the drawing. • Select another circle or arc; the second circle will be concentric with the first circle.

Fix	It is used to fix a point or an object at a particular location.
	• Click **Parametric > Geometric > Fix** on the ribbon.
	• Select a point to make it fixed at its location.
	• After you fix it, you can change its shape and size but can't move it.
	• You can also use the Objects option to select objects from the drawing.
	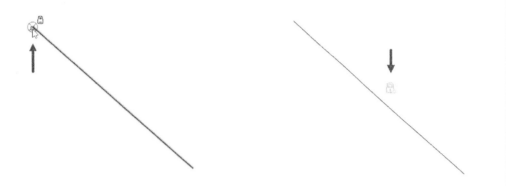
Parallel	It is used to make two lines parallel to each other.
	• Click **Parametric > Geometric > Parallel** on the ribbon.
	• Select two lines from the drawing; the second line is made parallel to the first line.

Perpendicular	It is used to make two lines perpendicular to each other.
	• Click **Parametric > Geometric > Perpendicular** on the ribbon.
	• Select two lines from the drawing; the second line is made perpendicular to the first line.
	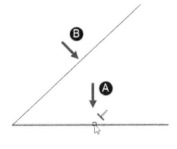 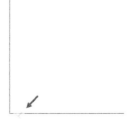

Horizontal	It is used to make a line horizontal. You can also make two points lie along the horizontal axis.

- Click **Parametric > Geometric > Horizontal** on the ribbon.
- Select a line/lines to make them horizontal.

- If you want to make points horizontal, select the **2Points** option from the command line and select the two points.

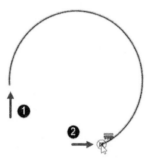

Vertical	It is used to make a line vertical. You can also make two points vertical.

- Click **Parametric > Geometric > Vertical** on the ribbon.
- Select a line to make it vertical.
- You can also use the **2Points** option to make two lines vertical.

Tangent	It is used to make an arc, circle, or line tangent to another arc or circle. 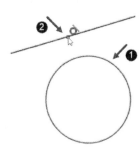 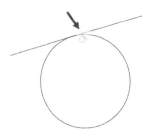 <ul><li>Click **Parametric > Geometric > Tangent** on the ribbon.</li><li>Select a circle, arc, or line.</li><li>Select another circle, arc, or line; the second object will be tangent to the first object.</li></ul>
Smooth	It is used to make a spline continuous with another spline or arc. <ul><li>Click **Parametric > Geometric > Smooth** on the ribbon.</li><li>Select a spline curve.</li><li>Select another spline or arc; the first curve will become continuous with the second curve.</li></ul> 
Symmetric	It is used to make two objects symmetric about a line. The objects will have same size, position and orientation about a line. <ul><li>Click **Parametric > Geometric > Symmetric** on the ribbon.</li><li>Select two objects from the drawing.</li><li>Select the symmetry line; the objects will be made symmetric about the selected line.</li></ul> 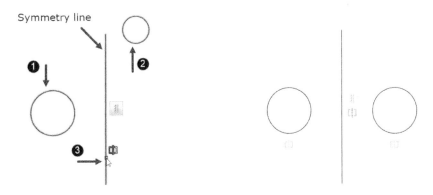 <ul><li>You can also use the **2Points** option to make two points symmetric about a line.</li></ul>

Equal	It is used to make two objects equal. For example, if you select two circles, the diameter of the two circles will become equal. If you select two lines, the length of the two lines will be equal. • Click **Parametric > Geometric > Equal** on the ribbon. • Select two objects from the drawing; the second object will be made equal to the first object. 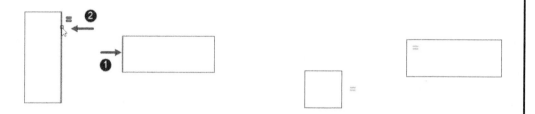
Auto Constrain	The **Auto Constraint** tool is used to apply constraints to the objects, automatically. • Click **Parametric > Geometric > Auto Constrain** on the ribbon. • Select the **Settings** option from the command line; the **Constraint Settings** dialog box appears.  • In this dialog box, select the constraints that you want to apply. You can also select the **Tangent objects must share an intersection point** and **Perpendicular objects must share an intersection point** options. • Click **OK**. • Select multiple objects by clicking on them or by dragging a selection window. • Right-click and select **Enter**; geometric constraints are applied to the objects based on their geometric condition.

Example:

In this example, you will create the following drawing by using the drawing tools and parametric tools.

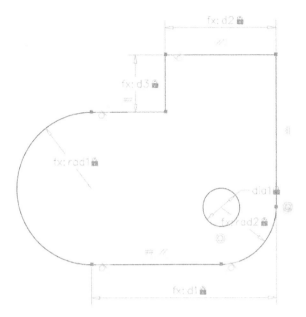

- Open a new AutoCAD file.
- Create two circles and a line as shown in figure.

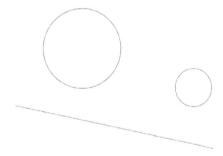

- Click **Parametric > Geometric > Horizontal** from the ribbon.
- Select the line to make it horizontal, as shown.

- Press the **SPACEBAR** and select the **2Points** option from the command line.
- Select the large circle and the small circle; the center points of the two circles will be horizontal.

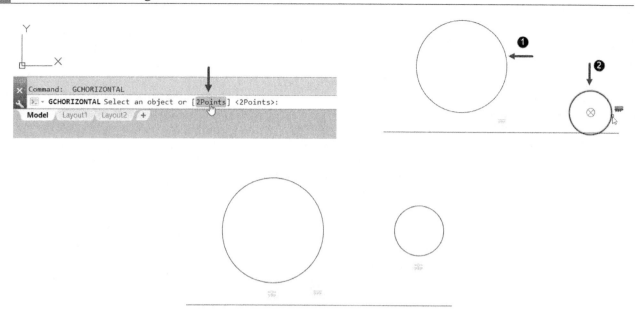

- Create four lines as shown below.

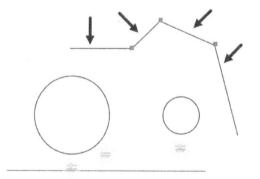

- Click the **Coincident** button on the **Geometric** panel and select the two endpoints of the lines as shown below; the endpoints will be made coincident.

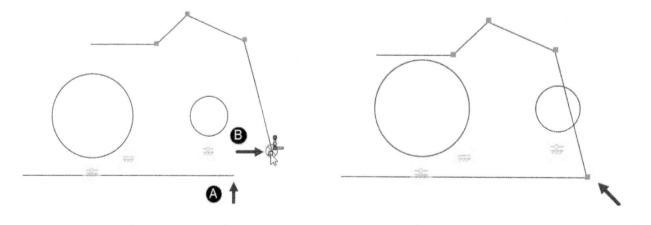

- Click the **Auto Constrain** [Auto Constrain] button from the **Geometric** panel and select the four lines as shown below.
- Right-click and select **Enter**; constraints are applied to the selected objects, automatically.

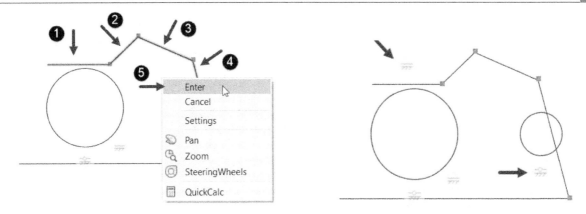

- Click the **Vertical** button on the **Geometric** panel and select the line as shown below; the line will become vertical.

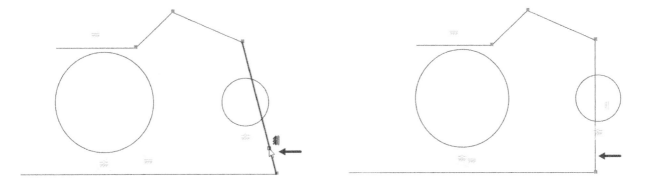

- Use the **Parallel** tool and make the two lines parallel, as shown below.

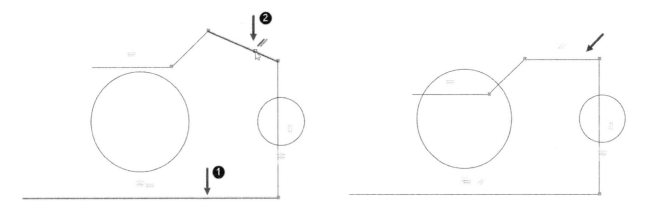

- Use the **Perpendicular** tool and make the two lines perpendicular, as shown below.

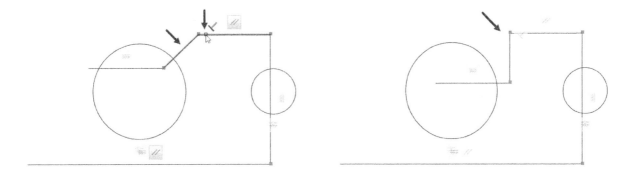

- Use the **Tangent** tool and make the two horizontal lines tangent to the large circle, as shown below.

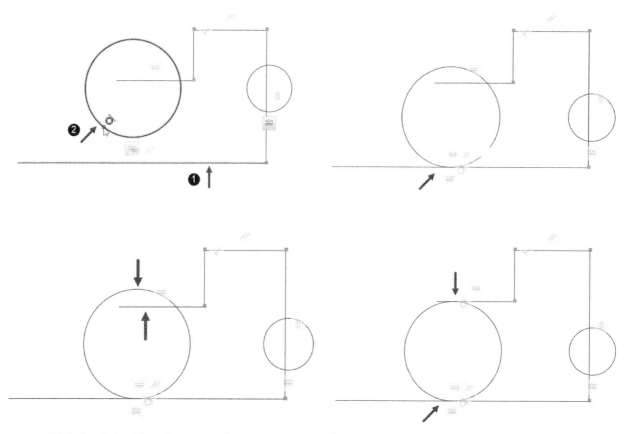

- Click the **Coincident** button on the **Geometric** panel.
- Select the **Object** option from the command line and select the large circle.

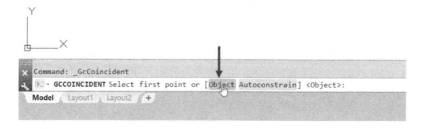

- Select the endpoint of the lower horizontal line to make it coincident with the circle.

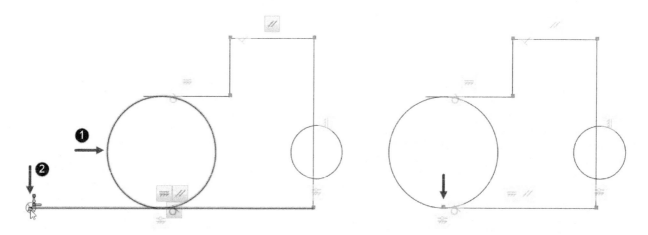

- Similarly, apply the **Coincident** constraint between the large circle and the upper horizontal line.

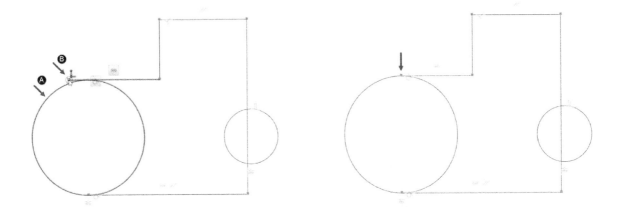

- Use the **Trim** tool and trim the unwanted portion of the circle.

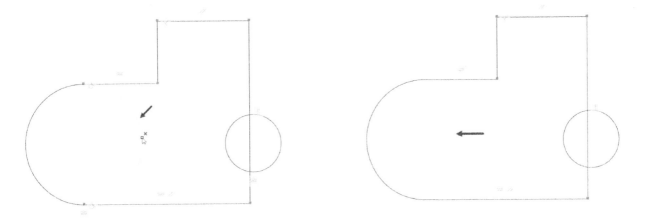

Also, you will notice the **Tangent** and **Coincident** constraints have been deleted. These constraints were the properties of the trimmed portion of the circle. As a result, constraints are also deleted along with the trimmed portion.

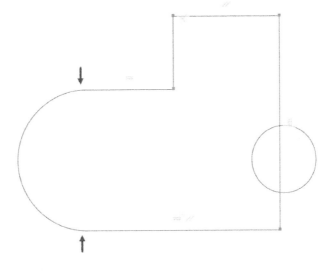

- Click the **Auto Constrain** button from the **Geometric** panel.
- Drag a window around the arc and horizontal lines.

- Right-click and select **Enter**; the **Tangent** and **Coincident** constraints are applied between the arc and the horizontal lines.

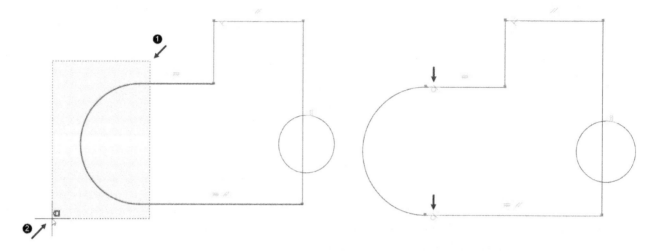

Dimensional Constraints

Dimensional constraints are applied to a drawing after applying the Geometric constraints. They are used to control the size and position of the objects in a drawing. You can apply the dimensional constraints using the tools available in the **Dimensional** panel of the **Parametric** ribbon.

- Click the inclined arrow on the **Dimensional** panel; the **Constraint Settings** dialog box appears.
- In the **Constraints Settings** dialog box, set **Dimension name format** to **Name**.

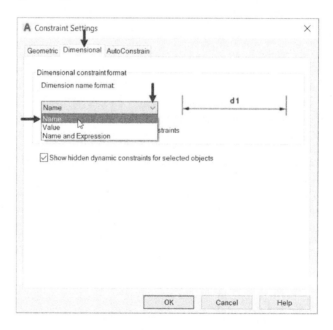

- Click the **OK** button.
- Click **Parametric > Dimensional > Linear** on the ribbon.

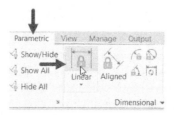

- Select the two endpoints of the lower horizontal line; the dimensional constraint is attached to the cursor.
- Place the dimension constraint and left click.

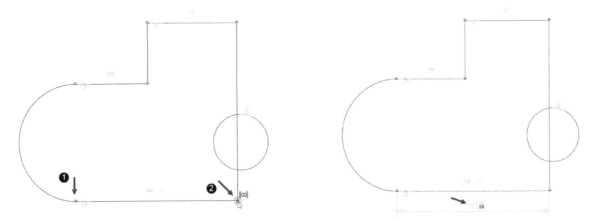

- Similarly, apply linear dimensions to other lines as shown below.

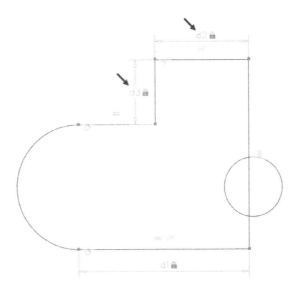

You will notice that when you try to apply dimensional constraint to the horizontal line connected to the arc, the **Dimensional Constraints** message box appears. It shows that the dimension will over-constrain the geometry. In an over-constrained geometry, there are conflicting dimensions or relations or both. Click the **Cancel** button on the **Dimensional Constraints** message box.

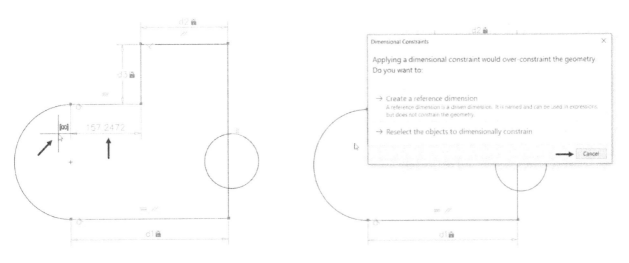

- Click the **Diameter** 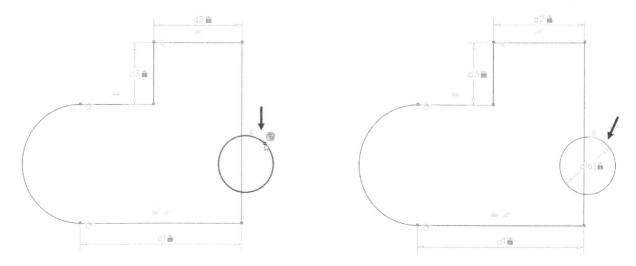 button on the **Dimensional** panel and apply the diameter dimension to the circle located on the left side.

- Click the **Radius** button on the **Dimensional** panel and apply radial dimension to the arc.

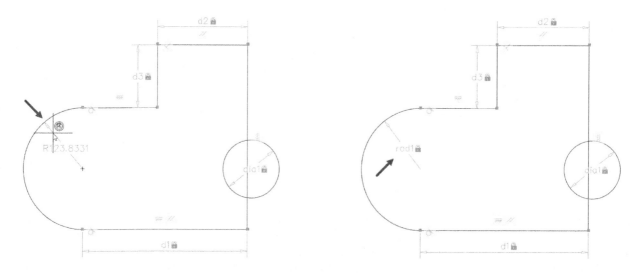

Creating equations using the Parameters Manager

Equations are relations between the dimensional constraints. Look at the drawing given below. In this drawing, all the dimensions are controlled by the diameter of the hole. In AutoCAD, you can create this type of relations between dimensions very easily using the **Parameter Manager** palette.

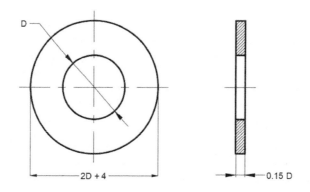

- Click the **Parameters Manager** button on the **Manage** panel; the **PARAMETERS MANAGER** palette appears.

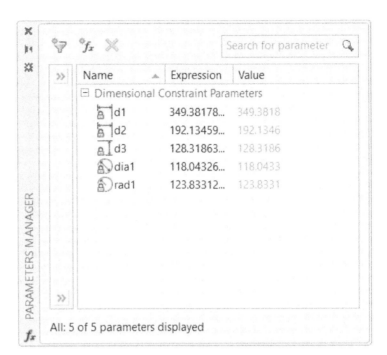

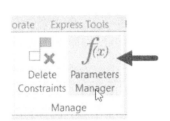

- Double-click in the box next to the **dia1** and enter **50**.

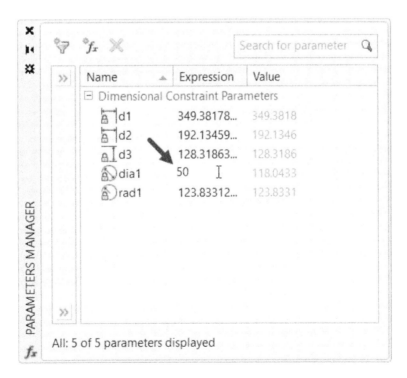

- Similarly, change the values of the other dimensions as shown below.

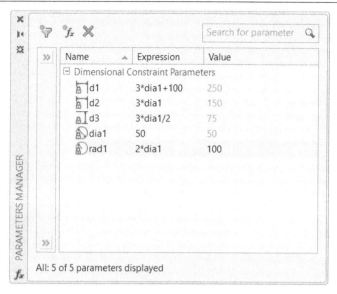

You will notice that the circle is placed outside the loop.

- Click **Zoom All** on the **Navigation Bar** to view the circle.

Creating Inferred Constraints

With the **Infer Constraints** button active at the status bar, you can automatically create constraints while drawing a sketch.

- Activate the **Infer Constraints** button at the status bar.

- Click the **Fillet** button on the **Modify** panel of the **Home** ribbon.
- Select the **Radius** option from the command line and enter **50** as the radius.
- Create a fillet at the lower left corner of the sketch.

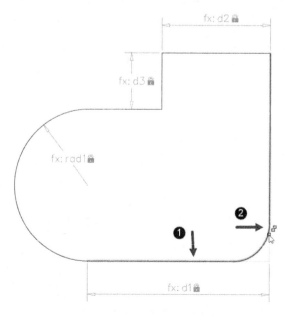
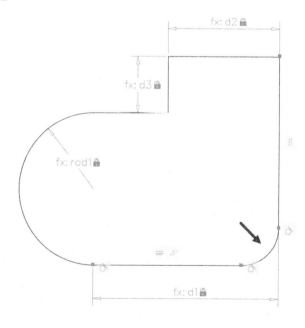

You will notice that **Tangent** and **Coincident** constraints are applied, automatically.

- Click the **Concentric** button on the **Geometric** panel.
- Select the circle located outside the loop and the fillet; they both will be concentric.

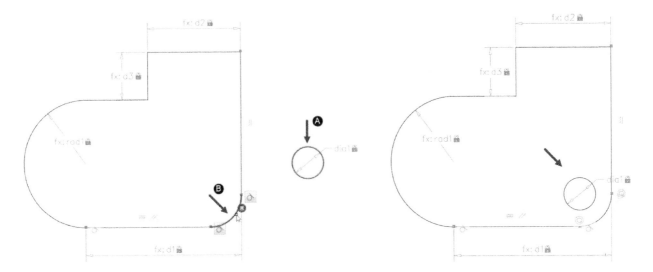

- Use the **Radius** tool from the **Dimensional** panel and apply the radius dimensional constraint to the fillet.

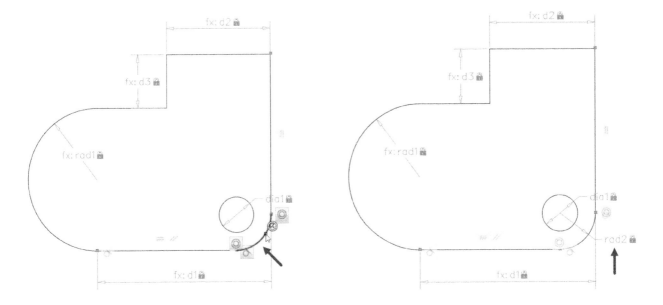

- Open the **Parameters Manager** palette and modify the **rad2** value to **3/2*dia1,** as shown.

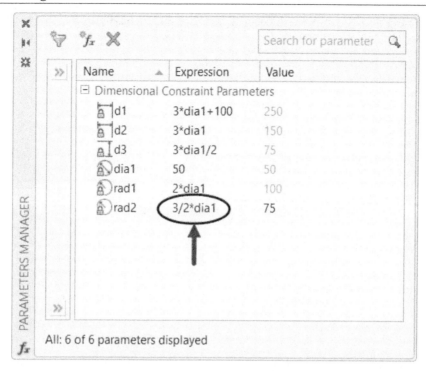

- To hide all the Geometric Constraints, click the **Hide All** button on the **Geometric** panel.
- Similarly, click **Hide All** on the **Dimensional** panel to hide all the dimensional constraints.

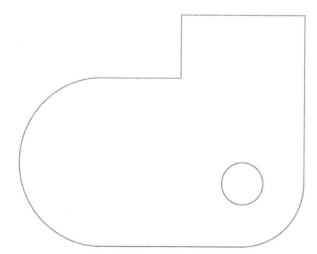

- To modify the size of the drawing, change the value of **dia1** in the **Parameters Manager** window; you will notice that all the values will be changed, automatically.
- Save and close the file.

Questions:

1. Which tool is used to make a spline continuous with another spline?
2. Which tool is used to apply constraints to the objects, automatically?
3. Which tool is used to constraint a line along another line?
4. Which tool is used to constraint a point to lie on another point or an object?
5. Where are Geometric Constraints available in AutoCAD?

Exercises

Exercise 1:

In this exercise, you need to create the drawing shown in figure and apply geometric and dimensional constraints to it.

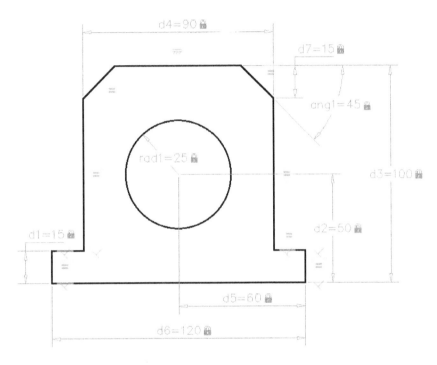

Exercise 2:

In this exercise, you need create the drawing as shown below and apply geometric and dimensional constraints to it. Also, create relations between dimensions in the **Parameter Manager**.

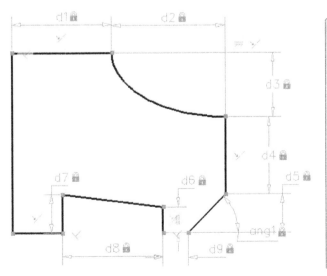

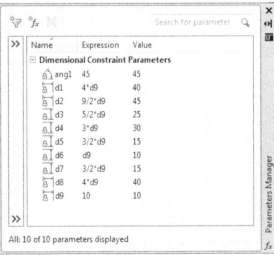

Chapter 8: Section Views in AutoCAD

In this chapter, you will learn the following tools:

- **Create Section Views**
- **Set Hatch Properties**
- **Use Island Detection tools**
- **Create text in Hatching**
- **Edit Hatching**

Section Views

In this chapter, you will learn to create section views, which are created by cutting an object along an imaginary cutting plane in order to view its interiors that cannot be shown clearly by means of hidden lines. In a section view, section lines, or cross-hatch lines, are added to indicate the surfaces that are cut by the imaginary cutting plane. In AutoCAD, you can add these section lines or cross-hatch lines using the **Hatch** tool.

The Hatch tool

The **Hatch** tool is used to generate hatch lines by clicking inside a closed area. When you click inside a closed area, a temporary closed boundary will be created using the **PLINE** command. The closed boundary will be filled with hatch lines, and then it will be deleted.

Example 1:

In this example, you will apply hatch lines to the drawing as shown in figure below.

- ➢ Open a new AutoCAD file.
- ➢ Create four layers with the following properties.

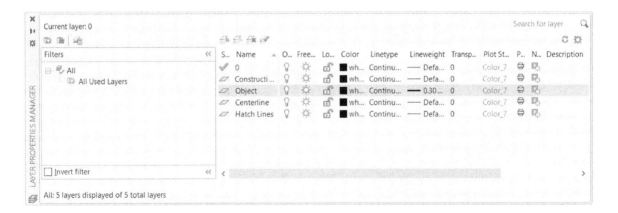

- ➢ Create the drawing as shown below. Do not apply dimensions.

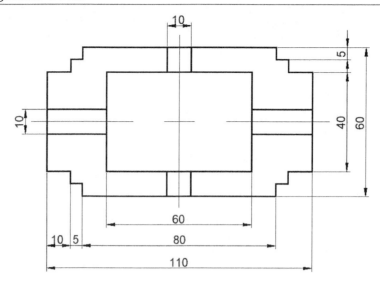

> ➤ Select the **Hatch lines** layer from the **Layer** drop-down.

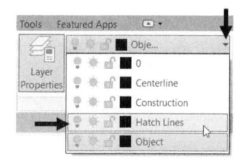

> ➤ Click **Home > Draw > Hatch** on the ribbon or enter **H** in the command line; the **Hatch Creation** tab appears in the ribbon.

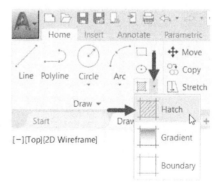

> ➤ Select **ANSI31** from the **Pattern** panel of the **Hatch Creation** ribbon.

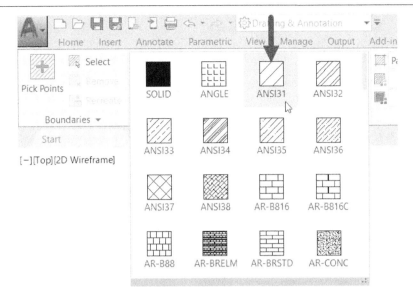

> ➤ Click in the four areas of the drawing, as shown below.

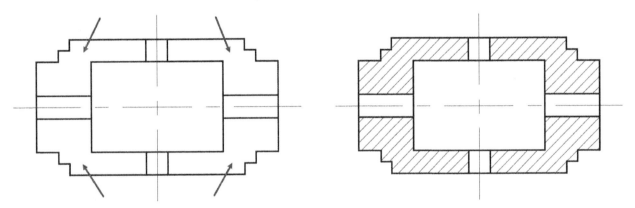

> ➤ Right-click and select **Enter**.

Example 2:

In this example, you will create the front view and section view of a crank.

> ➤ Create five layers with the following settings:

Layer	Linetype	Lineweight
Construction	Continuous	0.00 mm
Object	Continuous	0.30 mm
Centerline	CENTER	0.00 mm
Hatch lines	Continuous	0.00 mm
Cutting Plane	PHANTOM	0.30 mm

> ➤ Set the **Construction** layer as the current and create construction lines as shown.

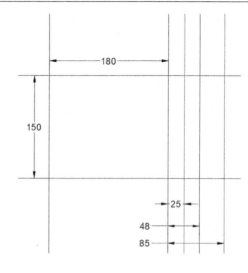

➤ Set the **Object** layer as the current and create draw circles as shown.

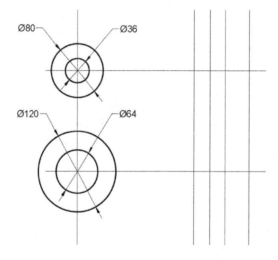

➤ Switch to **Construction** layer and create construction lines as shown.

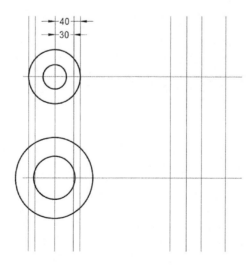

➤ Switch to **Object** layer and create two lines as shown.

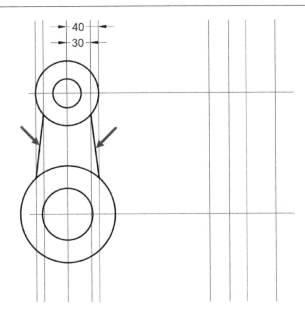

➤ On your own, create other objects on the front view as shown.

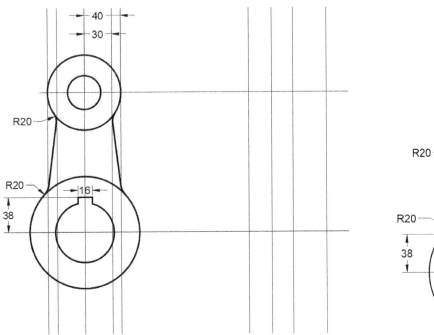

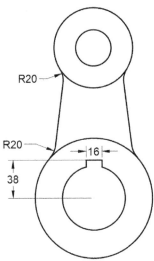

➤ On your own, create the objects of the section view as shown.

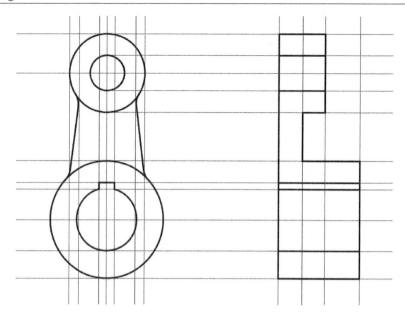

> ➤ Set the **Centerlines** layer as current and create center marks and centrelines.

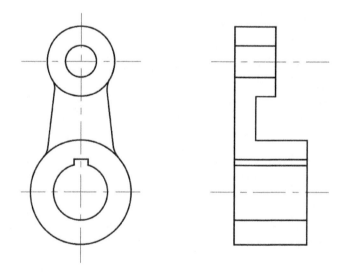

> ➤ Set the **Cutting Plane** layer as current.
> ➤ Click the **Polyline** button on the **Draw** panel and pick a point below the front view as shown.

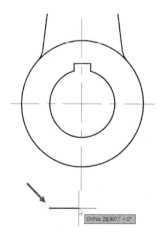

➢ Select the **Width** option from the command line.

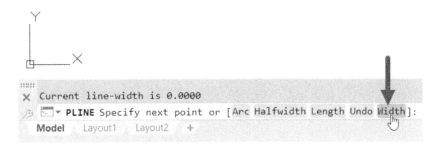

➢ Type **0** as the starting width and press **ENTER**.
➢ Type **10** as the ending width and press **ENTER**.
➢ Move the cursor horizontally toward right and enter **20**.
➢ Again, select the **Width** option from the command line.
➢ Set the starting and ending width to **0**.
➢ Move the cursor horizontally and click when trace lines are displayed as shown below.

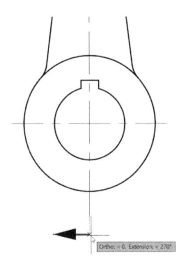

➢ Move the cursor vertically up and click.
➢ Move the cursor toward left and click when trace lines are displayed from the endpoint of the lower horizontal line.
➢ Create another arrow by changing the width of the polyline.

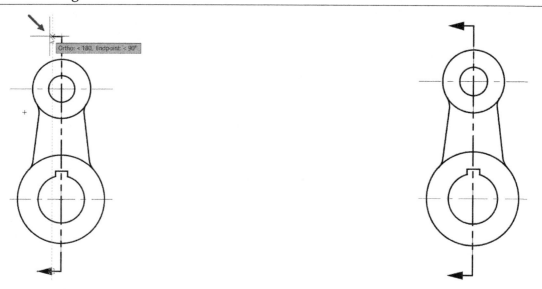

> ➢ Set the **Hatch Lines** layer as current.
> ➢ Type **H** in the command line and press **ENTER**.
> ➢ Select the **SeTtings** option from the command line; the **Hatch and Gradient** dialog box appears.
> ➢ Click on the **Swatch** box under the **Type and pattern** group; the **Hatch Pattern Palette** dialog box appears.
> ➢ Select **ANSI31** from the dialog box and click **OK**.

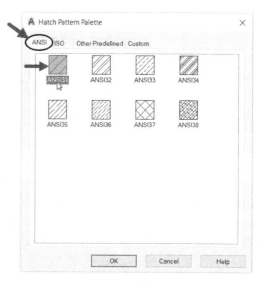

Note: You can also select the required pattern type, directly from the **Pattern** drop-down of the **Hatch and Gradient** dialog box, as shown below.

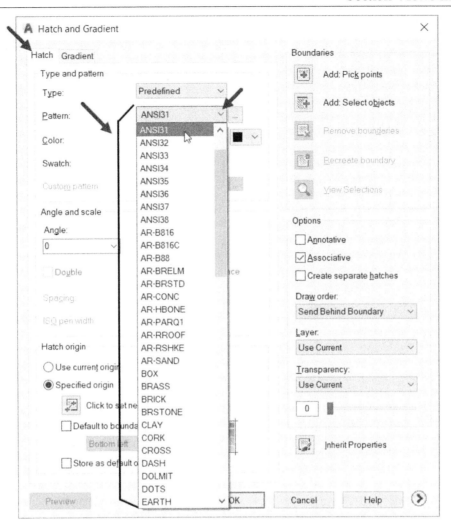

> Set the **Scale** value to **2** under **Angle and Scale** area of the **Hatch and Gradient** dialog box.

> Click the **Add Pick Points** button from the Boundaries group and click in Region 1, Region 2 and Region 3.

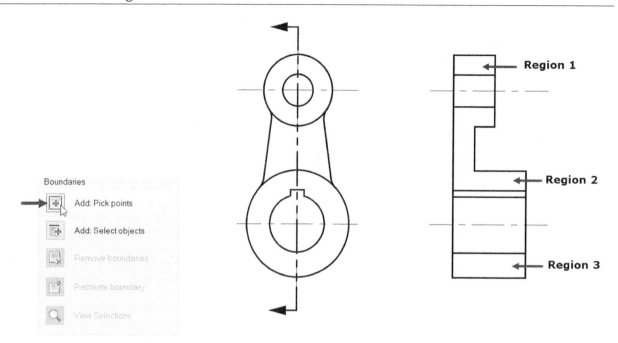

> ➢ Press **ENTER** to create hatch lines.

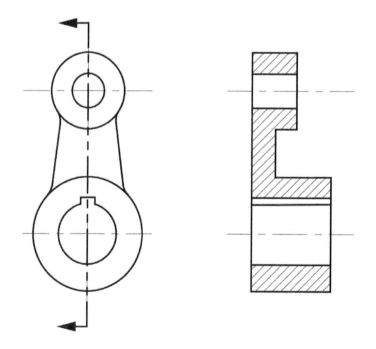

> ➢ Save the drawing as **Crank.dwg** and close.

Setting the Properties of Hatch lines

You can set the properties of the hatch lines such as angle, scale, transparency in the **Properties** panel of the **Hatch Creation** ribbon.

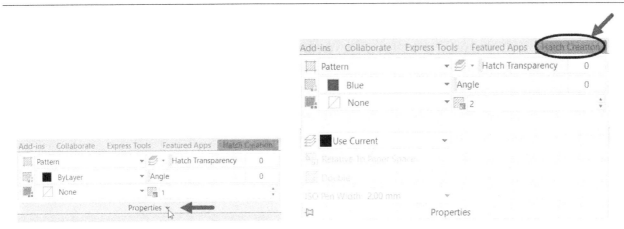

Example:

Create four layers with the following settings.

Layer	Linetype	Lineweight
Construction	Continuous	0.00 mm
Object	Continuous	0.30 mm
Centerline	CENTER2	0.00 mm
Hatch lines	Continuous	0.00 mm

➢ Create the following drawing in different layers. Do not apply dimensions.

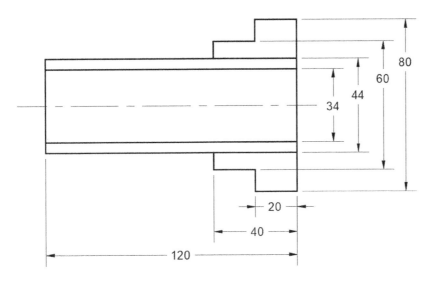

➢ Type **H** and press **ENTER**; the **Hatch Creation** tab appears in the ribbon.
➢ Select the **Pattern** option from the **Hatch Type** drop-down in the **Properties** panel.

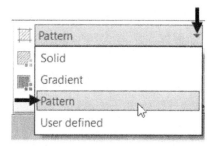

You can also select different hatch type such as Solid, Gradient, and User defined.

➢ Select **ANSI31** from the **Pattern** panel.
➢ Select **Blue** from the **Hatch Color** drop-down.

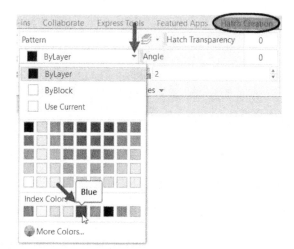

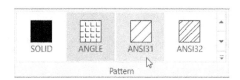

➢ Expand the **Properties** panel and set the **Hatch Layer Override** to **Hatch lines**.

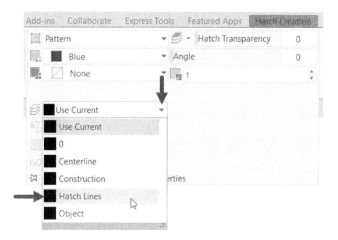

➢ Click the **Pick Points** button from the **Boundaries** panel.

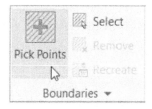

➢ Pick points in the outer areas of the drawing as shown below.

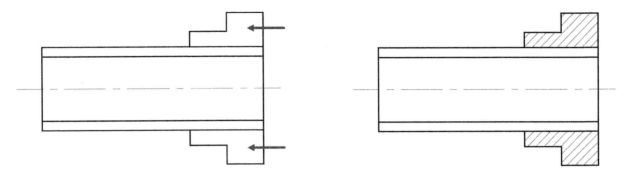

> ➢ Adjust the **Hatch Pattern Scale** to **1.5**; you will notice that the distance between the hatch lines is increased.

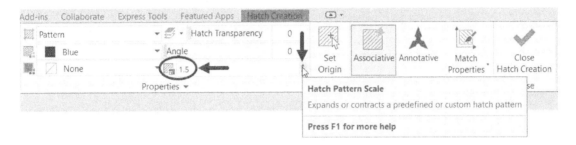

> ➢ Click **Close Hatch Creation** button on the **Close** panel.

> ➢ Press the **SPACEBAR** to invoke the **HATCH** command again.
> ➢ Change the **Hatch Angle** value to **90** in the **Properties** panel, as shown.

> ➢ Pick points in the area as shown below.

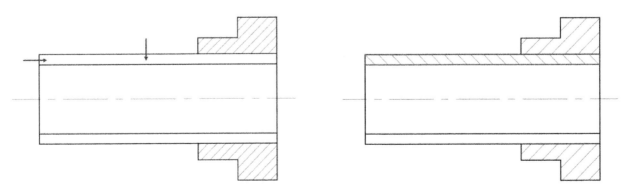

On zooming into the hatch lines, you may notice that they are not aligned properly. This is because the **Use Current Origin** button activated in the **Origin** panel. As a result, the origin of the drawing will act as the origin of the hatch pattern. However, you can change the origin of the hatch pattern.

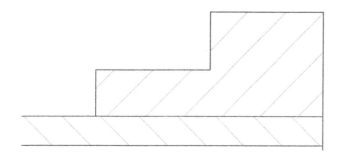 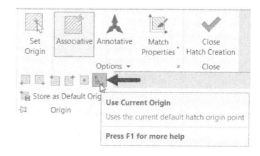

> ➤ Click **Set Origin** button on the **Origin** panel.
> ➤ Click to set the origin point as shown below.

 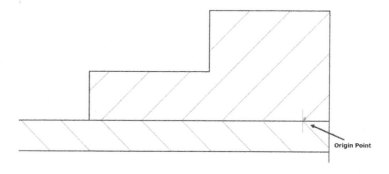

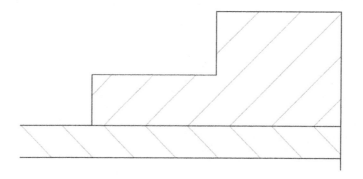

> ➤ Invoke the **Hatch** tool and click **Match Properties > Use source hatch origin** on the **Options** panel.

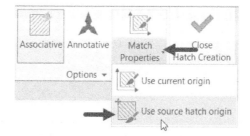

The **Match Properties** tools are used to create new hatch lines by using the properties of an existing one. The **Use source hatch origin** tool will create a new hatching using the origin of the source.

- Select the source hatching, as shown in figure.

- Pick a point in the empty area as shown below.

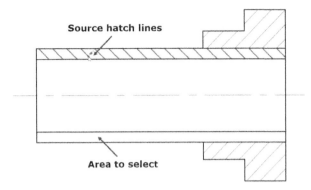

New hatch lines are created using the properties and origin of the source hatching.

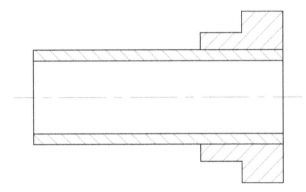

- Save and close the file.

Island Detection tools

While creating hatch lines, the island detection tools help you detect the internal areas of a drawing.

Example:

Create the drawing as shown below. Do not apply dimensions.

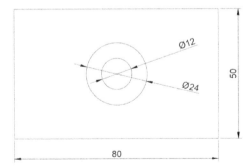

- ➤ Click **Home > Draw > Hatch** on the ribbon.
- ➤ Select **ANSI31** from the **Pattern** panel.
- ➤ Expand the **Options** panel and select the **Normal Island Detection** tool.

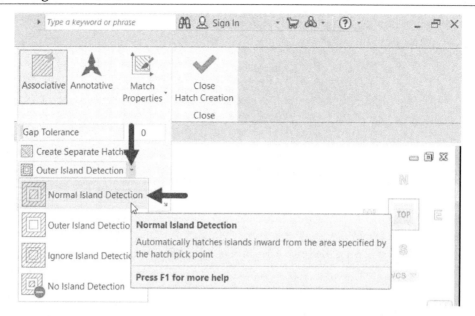

> ➤ Pick a point in the area outside the large circle; you will notice that the area inside the small circle is detected automatically. Also hatch lines are created inside the small circle.

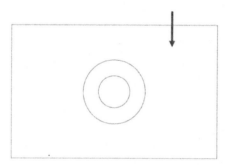

> ➤ Right-click and select **Enter**.

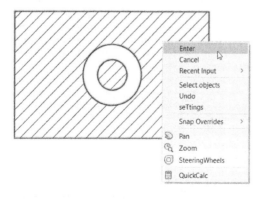

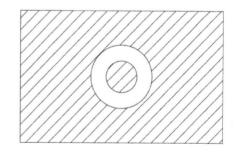

> ➤ Click **Undo** on the **Quick Access Toolbar**.

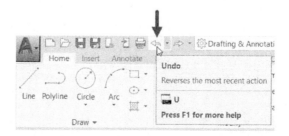

➢ Invoke the **Hatch** tool and select **ANSI31** from the **Pattern** panel.
➢ Expand the **Options** panel and select **Outer Island Detection** option.

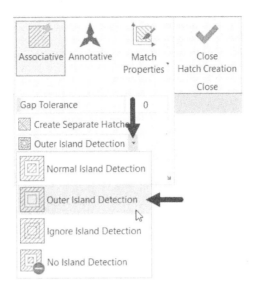

➢ Pick a point in the area outside the large circle and press **ENTER**; you will notice that hatch lines are created only outside the large circle. The **Outer Island Detection** tool will enable you create hatch lines only in the outermost level of the drawing.

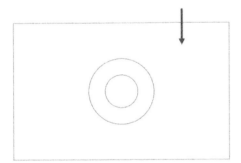
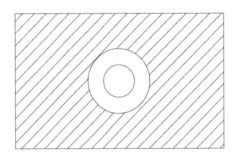

➢ Repeat the process using the **Ignore Island Detection** tool. You will notice that the internal loops are ignored while creating the hatch lines.

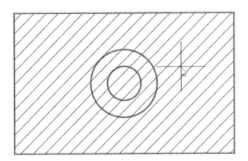
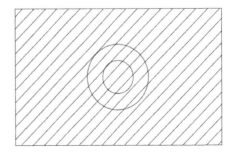

Text in Hatching

You can create hatching without passing through the text and dimensions.

➢ Create a drawing as shown in figure.

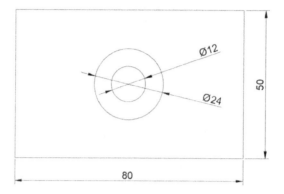

➢ Click **Home > Annotation > Multiline Text** on the ribbon.
➢ Specify the first and second corner of the text editor, as shown.

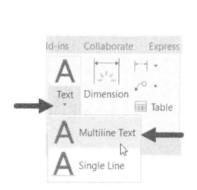

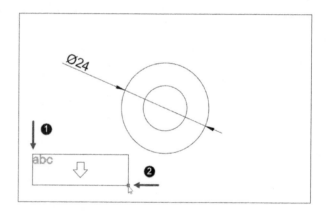

➢ Select **Arial** from the **Font** drop-down of the **Formatting** panel.

- Ensure that **Text Height** is set to **3.5**.
- Type **AutoCAD** in the text editor. Left-click in the empty space of the drawing window.

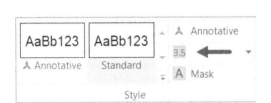

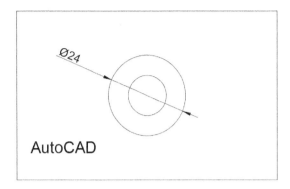

- Invoke the **Hatch** tool and select the **Normal Island Detection** option from the **Options** panel.
- Pick a point in the area covered by the outside boundary and press **ENTER**; hatch lines are created.

You will notice that hatch lines do not pass through the text and dimension.

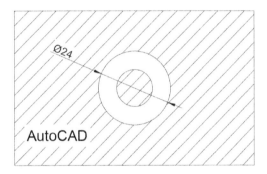

Editing Hatch lines

You can edit a hatch by using the **Edit Hatch** tool or simply selecting the hatch.

- To edit a hatch using the **Edit Hatch** tool, expand the **Modify** panel of the **Home** ribbon and select the **Edit Hatch** tool.

- Select the hatch from the drawing, the **Hatch Edit** dialog box appears. The options in this dialog box as same as that available in the **Hatch Creation** ribbon. Expand this dialog box by clicking the **More Options** button located at the bottom right corner.

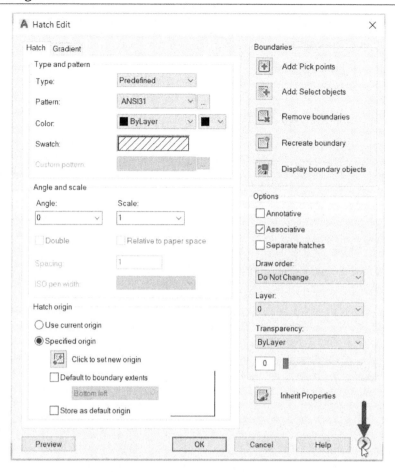

The expanded dialog box will display more options as shown below. The options in this dialog box are same as that available in the **Hatch Creation** tab.

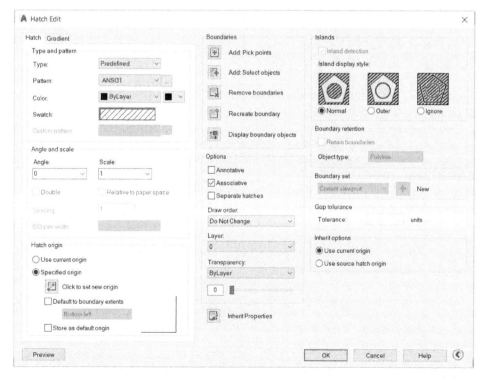

➢ Specify the options in the **Hatch Edit** dialog box and click the **OK** button; the hatch pattern will be modified.

Questions:

1. Which tools are used to detect the internal areas of a drawing?
2. Which tool is used to create section lines in AutoCAD?
3. Which tool is used to edit hatch?
4. Where is **Outer Island Detection** option available?
5. After activating the **Hatch** tool, which tab get visible?

Exercises

Exercise 1:

Create the half section view of the object shown below.

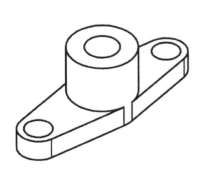

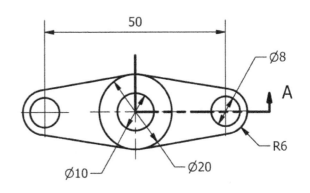

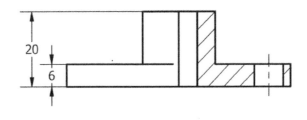

A-A

Exercise 2:

In this exercise, the top, front, and right-side views of an object are given. Replace the front view with a section view. The section plane is given in the top view.

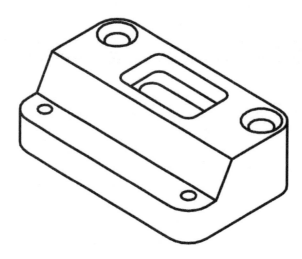

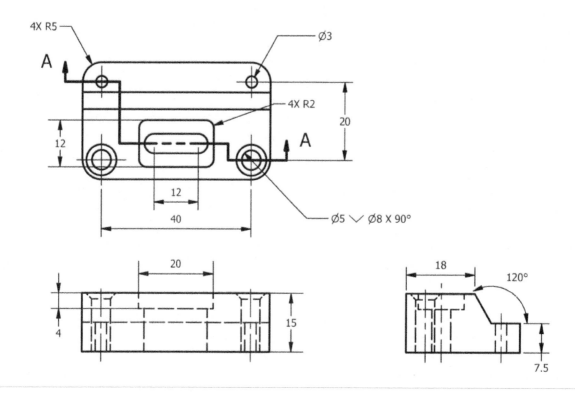

Chapter 9: Blocks, Attributes and Xrefs in AutoCAD

In this chapter, you will learn to do the following:

- ❖ **Create and insert Blocks**

- ❖ **Create Annotative Blocks**

- ❖ **Explode, purge Blocks**

- ❖ **Use the Divide tool**

- ❖ **Use the DesignCenter and Tool Palettes to insert Blocks**

- ❖ **Insert Multiple Blocks**

- ❖ **Edit Blocks**

- ❖ **Create Blocks using the Write Block tool**

- ❖ **Define and insert Attributes**

- ❖ **Work with Xrefs**

Introduction

In this chapter, you will learn to create and insert Blocks and Attributes in a drawing. You will also learn to attach external references to a drawing. The first part of this chapter deals with Blocks. A Block is a group of objects combined and saved together. You can later insert it in drawings. The second part of this chapter deals with Attributes. An Attribute is an intelligent text attached to a block. It can be any information related to the block such as description, part name, and value and so on. The third part of the chapter deals with the Xrefs (external references). External references are drawing files, images, PDF files attached to a drawing.

Creating Blocks

To create a block, first you need to create shapes using the drawing tools and use the **BLOCK** command to convert all the objects into a single object. The following example shows the procedure to create a block.

Example:

Create the drawing as shown below. Do not apply dimensions. Assume the missing dimensions.

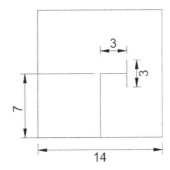

- ➤ Click **Insert > Block Definition > Create Block** on the ribbon; the **Block Definition** dialog box appears.

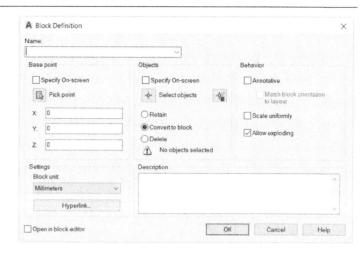

> ➤ Enter **Target** in the **Name** field of dialog box.
> ➤ Click the **Select Objects** button of the dialog box. Drag a window and select all the objects of the drawing, as shown.
> ➤ Right-click to accept; the dialog appears again.

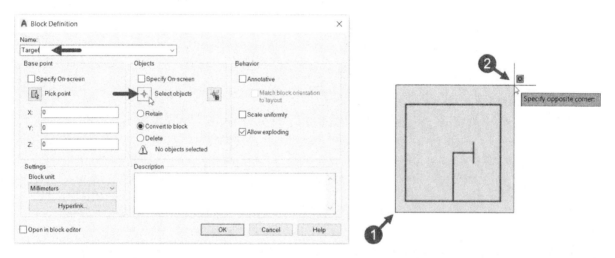

You can choose to retain or delete the objects after defining the block. The **Retain** option under the **Objects** section retains the objects in the drawing window after defining the block. The **Convert to Block** option deletes the objects and displays the block in place of them. The **Delete** option completely deletes the objects from the drawing window.

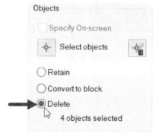

> ➤ Select the **Delete** option under the **Objects** section.
> ➤ Click the **Pick point** button on the dialog box.
> ➤ Select the midpoint of the left vertical line. The selected point will be the insertion point when you insert this block into a drawing.

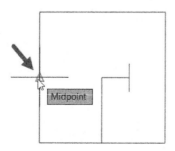

You can also add description to the block in the **Description** box. In addition to that, you can set the behaviour of the block such as scalability, annotative and so on using the options in the **Behavior** section. The options in the **Settings** area can be used to set the units of the block and link a website or other files with the block.

➤ Click **OK** on the dialog box; the block will be created and saved in the database.

Inserting Blocks

After creating a block, you can insert it at the desired location inside the drawing using the **INSERT** command. The procedures to insert blocks are explained in following examples.

Example:

➤ Click **View > Palettes > Blocks** from the ribbon to display the **BLOCKS** dialog box, as shown.

➤ Next, select the block and drag the cursor to place it in the drawing area, as shown.

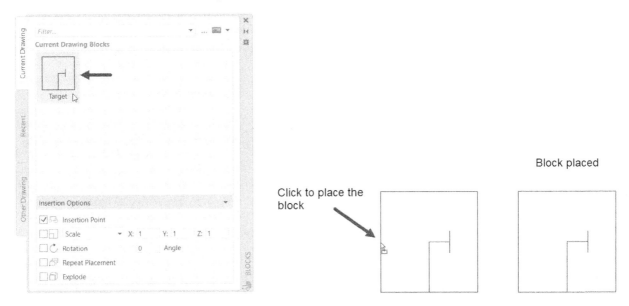

The **Insertion Point** check box and its edit boxes are used to define the insertion point while inserting the block. You can either place the block using the mouse or by entering the required coordinates in their respective edit boxes on the right side, as shown. If the checkbox is selected, the system will define previously applied coordinates.

Various tabs of this dialog box are discussed below:

CurrentDrawing – This tab displays the blocks that you create in the current drawing.

Recent – This tab displays the block that you created and inserted recently in the current & other drawings.

Other Drawing – This tab is used to display the blocks that you created in different drawings by browsing and importing them, as shown.

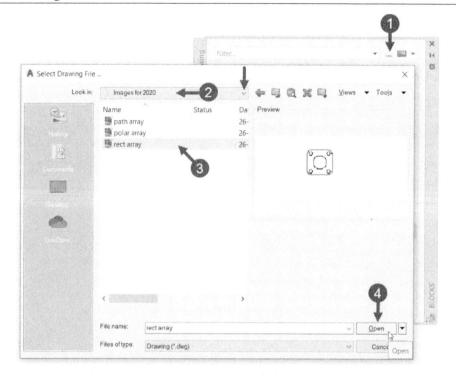

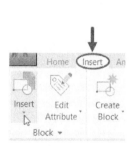

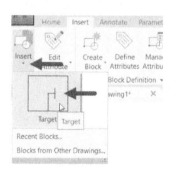

Example (Scaling the block):

➢ Activate the **Block** tool to display the **BLOCKS** dialog box, as discussed above.
➢ Enter the required scale values in the **X**, **Y**, and **Z** edit boxes of the **BLOCKS** dialog box, as shown.
➢ Next double click on the block displayed in the dialog box and click to place the scaled block in the drawing area, as shown.

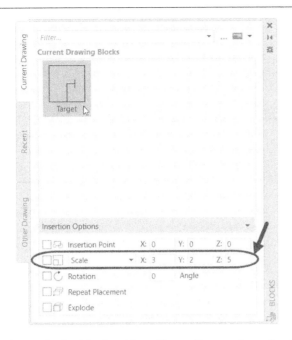
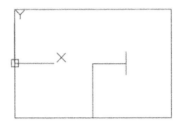

You can also scale the block with uniform distance by selecting the **Uniform** option, as shown. And by selecting the check box on its left, the system will scale the block with default scale value.

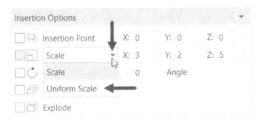
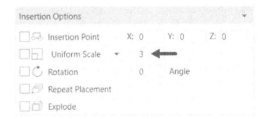

You can also scale the block by enter the **CLASSICINSERT** in the **Command Bar** to display the **Insert** dialog box. And then enter the required scale value in their respective boxes and place the scaled block anywhere in the drawing area, as shown.

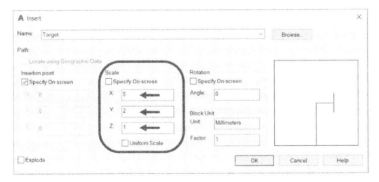

Example (Rotating the block):

> ➤ Activate the **Block** tool to display the **BLOCKS** dialog box.
> ➤ Enter the required rotation angle values in its respective edit box of the **BLOCKS** dialog box, as shown.
> ➤ Next click on the block displayed in the dialog box and click in the drawing area to place the block with angle value entered, as shown.

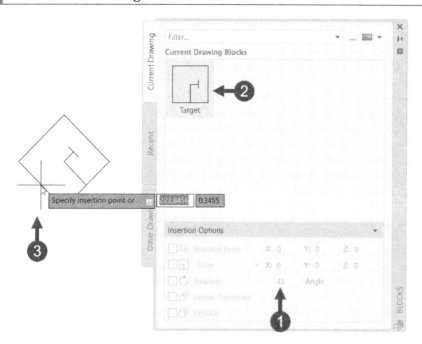

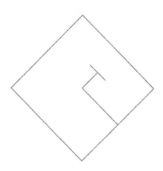

You can also rotate the block by enter the **CLASSICINSERT** in the **Command Bar** to display the **Insert** dialog box. And then enter the required rotation angle value in the respective edit box and place the block in the drawing area with angle value entered, as shown.

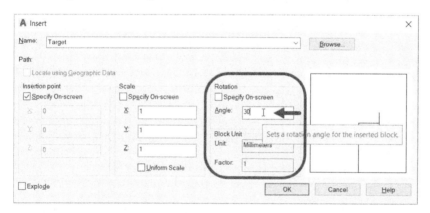

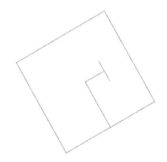

> Save and close the drawing file.

Creating Annotative Blocks

Annotative blocks possess the annotative properties. They will be scaled automatically depending upon the scale of the drawing sheet. The procedure to create and insert annotative blocks is explained in the following example.

Example:

> Start a new drawing file.
> Create the drawing a shown in figure. Assume the missing dimensions.
> Click **Insert > Block Definition > Create Block** on the ribbon; the **Block Definition** dialog box appears.
> Enter **Turbine Driver** in the **Name** field.
> Click the **Select Objects** button on the dialog box. Drag a window and select all the objects of the drawing. Right-click to accept the selection.

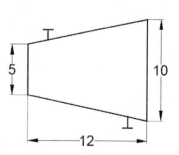

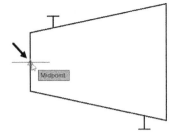

- ➢ Select the **Delete** option under the **Objects** section, if it is not selected.
- ➢ Click the **Pick Point** button and select the midpoint of the left vertical line, as shown.
- ➢ Select the **Annotative** check box under the **Behavior** section of the dialog box. Click the **OK** button on the dialog box.
- ➢ Activate the 🏃 button located at the right-side of the Status Bar, as shown.

- ➢ Set the **Annotation Scale** to **1:10**.

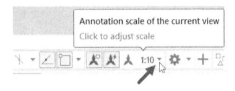

- ➢ Activate the **Block** tool to display the **BLOCKS** dialog box, as discussed earlier in this chapter.
- ➢ Select the **Turbine Driver** block from the dialog box to display the preview of block with scale factor 1:10, as shown.
- ➢ Click in the drawing area to place it.
- ➢ Click **Zoom All** on the **Navigation Bar** to view the block.
- ➢ Change the **Annotation Scale** to **1:2**; you will notice that the block is automatically scaled to **1:2**, as shown.

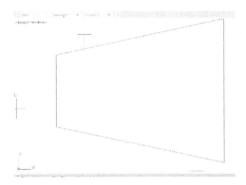

Exploding Blocks

When you insert a block in a drawing, it will be considered as a single object even though it consists of numerous individual objects. At many times, you may require to break a block into its individual parts. You can do so by using the **Explode** tool.

- ➢ To explode a block, click **Home > Modify > Explode** ⬜ on the ribbon or type **EXPLODE** in the command line and press **ENTER**.
- ➢ Select the block and press **ENTER**; the block will be broken into individual objects. You can select the individual objects by clicking on them.

Using the Purge tool

You can remove the unused blocks and other unwanted drawing data from the database using the **Purge** tool.

- To delete the unused data, click **Application Menu > Drawing Utilities > Purge**; the **Purge** dialog box appears, as shown.
- Expand the **Blocks** tree and select the required block to purge, as shown.
- Click on the **Purge Checked Items** button of the dialog box; the **Purge – Confirm Purge** message box appears, as shown.

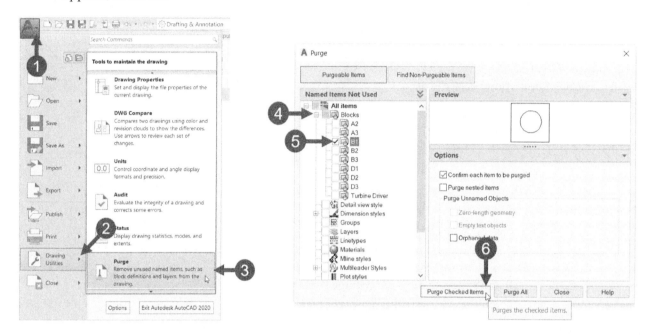

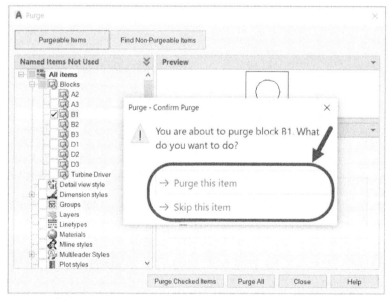

- Click **Purge this item** from the **Purge – Confirm Purge** message box to delete the item from the database.

  Note that if you want to purge all items then you can simply select the **Purge all checked items** from the message box, as shown above. And if you select the **Purge this item** or **Skip this item** then the message box will display again and again for the confirmation for other items.

- Click on the **Cancel** button of the message box and **Close** button of the dialog box to close it.

Note that if you want to purge all items then you can select the **Purge All** button of the dialog box. The **Purge – Confirm Purge** message box get visible, as shown. The you can simply select the **Purge all checked items** from the message box, as shown.

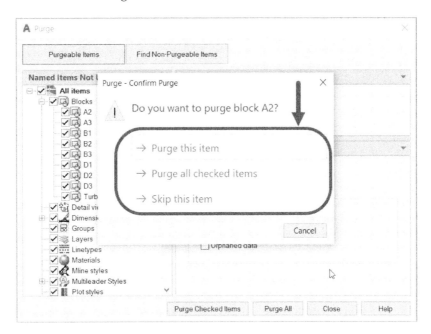

The options in the **Find Non-Purgeable Items** tab are used to display the items that cannot be purge with the reason also displayed in the dialog box, as shown.

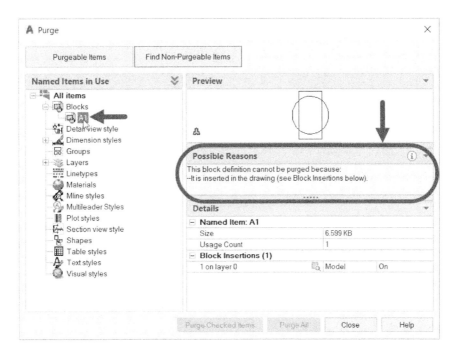

Using the Divide tool

The **Divide** tool is used to place number of instances of an object equally spaced on a line segment. You can also place blocks on a line segment. The following example shows you to divide a line using the **Divide** tool.

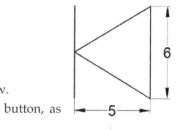

Example:

- Create the object as shown in figure.
- Create a block with the name **DIODE**.
- Specify the midpoint of the left vertical line as the base point.
- Create a line of **60** mm length and **15** degrees inclination, as shown below.
- Expand the **Draw** panel in the **Home** tab and click the **Divide** button, as shown.

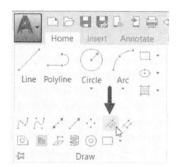

- Select the line segment; the message, "**Enter the number of segments or [Block]:**" appears.
- Select the **Block** option from the command line; the message, "**Enter name of block to insert**" appears.
- Type **Diode** and press **ENTER**; the message, "**Align block with object? [Yes No] <Y>:**" appears.
- Select the **Yes** option; the message, "**Enter the number of segments:**" appears.
- Type **6** and press **ENTER**; the line segment will be divided into six segments and four instances of blocks will be placed, as shown.
- Trim the unwanted portions as shown below.

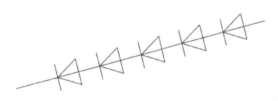

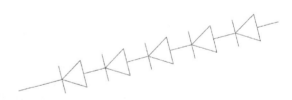

Renaming Blocks

You can rename blocks to suit with your requirements and to make their meaning clearer. The procedure to rename blocks is discussed next.

- On Menu bar, click **Format > Rename** or type **RENAME** in the command line and press **ENTER**; the **Rename** dialog box appears.
- In the **Rename** dialog box, select **Blocks** from the **Name Objects** list.
- Select the block to be named from the **Items** list and enter a new name in the **Rename To** box.
- Click **OK**; the block will be renamed.

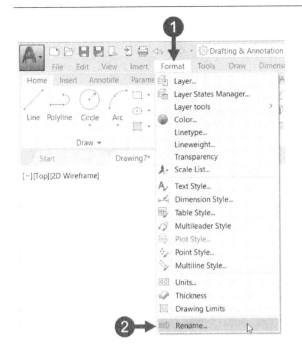

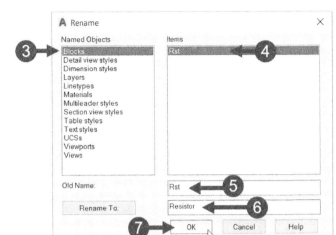

Inserting Blocks in a Table

You can insert blocks in a table and fit inside the table cells. Note that you cannot insert Annotative blocks in a table. The following example shows you to insert a block in a table.

Example:

Create three blocks as shown below.

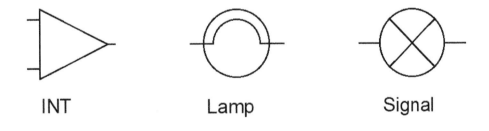

INT   Lamp   Signal

- Click on **Annotate > Table > Table** Table from the Ribbon to display **Insert Table** dialog box.
- Insert the values in the dialog box, as shown below.

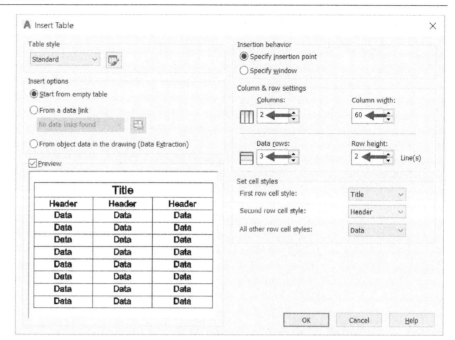

- Click **OK** and click anywhere in the drawing area to define the insertion point of the table, as shown.
- After inserting the table, you can change its size (width and height) uniformly by dragging its corner grip, as shown below.

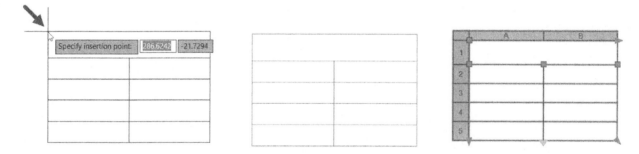

- Enter the names in the table cells, as shown below.

Electronic/Electrical Symbol	
Symbol	**Name**
	INT
	Lamp
	Signal

- Select the first cell in the **Symbol** row and right-click, as shown.
- Select **Insert > Block** from the shortcut menu; the **Insert a Block in a Table Cell** dialog box appears.

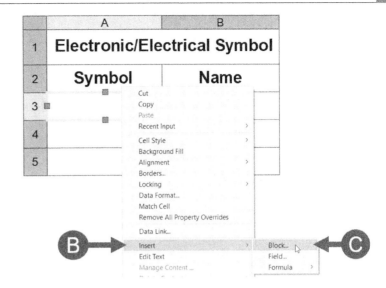

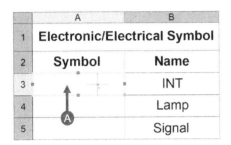

- In the **Insert a Block in a Table Cell** dialog box, select **INT** from the **Name** drop-down.
- Set **Overall cell alignment** to **Middle Center**.
- Click **OK**; the **INT** symbol will be placed in the selected cell.

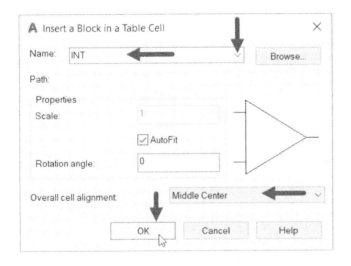

Electronic/Electrical Symbol	
Symbol	**Name**
▷	INT
	Lamp
	Signal

- Similarly, insert the other symbols in the respected cells.

Electronic/Electrical Symbol	
Symbol	**Name**
▷	INT
⊖	Lamp
⊗	Signal

Using the DesignCenter

DesignCenter is one of the additional means by which you can insert blocks and drawing in an effective way. Using the DesignCenter, you can insert blocks created in one drawing into another drawing. You can display the DesignCenter by clicking **View > Palettes > DesignCenter** on the ribbon or entering **DC** in the command line, as shown.

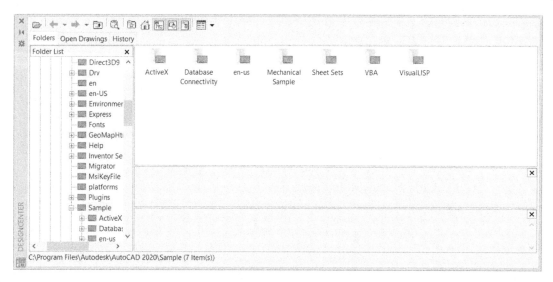

The following example shows you insert blocks using the DesignCenter.

- Open a new drawing file.
- Create the following symbols and convert them into blocks.

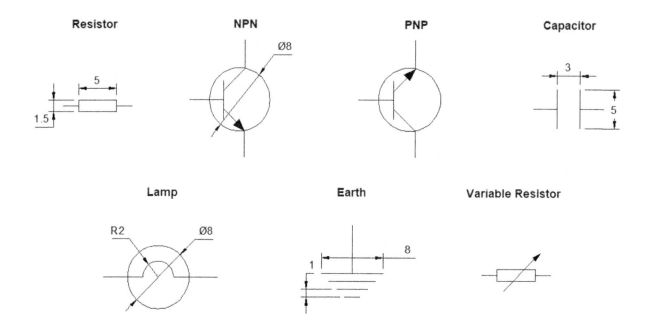

- Save the file as **Electronic Symbols.dwg**. Close the file.

- Open a new drawing file.
- Set the maximum limit of the drawing to **100,100**. Click **Zoom All** on the Navigation Bar.
- Click **View > Palettes > DesignCenter** on the ribbon; the **DesignCenter** palette appears.
- In the **DesignCenter** palette, browse to the location of the **Electronic Symbols.dwg** file using the **Folder List**, as shown.
- Select the file and double-click on the **Blocks** icon; all the blocks present in the file will be displayed, as shown.
- Drag and place the blocks in the drawing window.

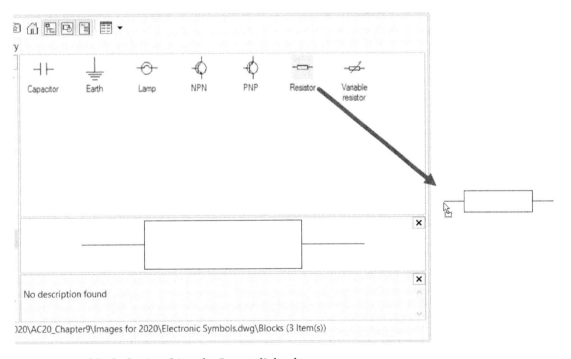

You can also insert blocks by invoking the **Insert** dialog box.

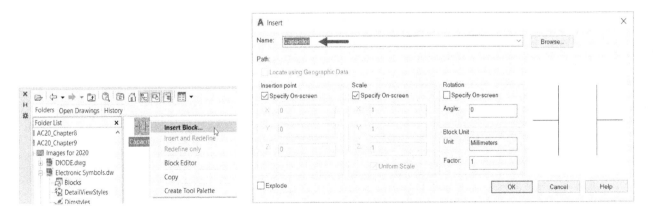

- Use the **Move** and **Rotate** tools and arrange the blocks as shown below.

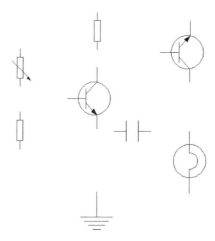

- Close the **DesignCenter** palette, as shown.
- Use the **Line** tool and complete the drawing as shown below.

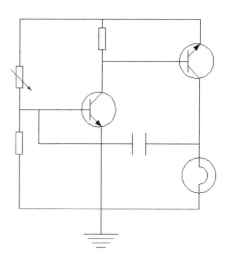

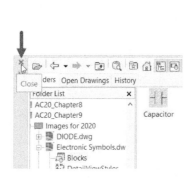

Using Tool Palettes

You can arrange blocks, dimensions, hatch patterns and other frequently used tools in Tool Palettes. Similar to the **DesignCenter** palette, you can drag and place various features from Tool Palettes into the drawing. You can display the Tool Palettes by the clicking **View > Palettes > Tool Palettes** on the ribbon or entering **TOOLPALETTES** in the command line.

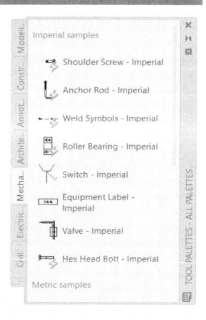

There are many palettes arranged in the **TOOL PALETTES** window. You can display more palettes by clicking the lower left corner of the Tool Palettes and selecting the required palettes.

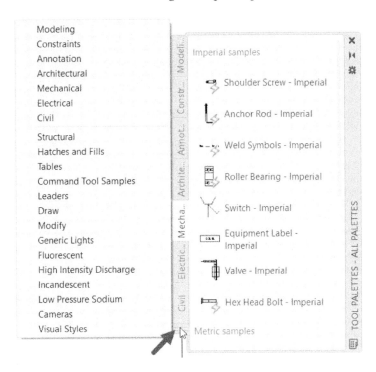

There are many blocks available in the **Architectural**, **Mechanical**, **Electrical**, **Civil**, and **Structural** palettes. You can drag and place blocks from these palettes. You can also right-click on a block and perform various operations using the shortcut menu displayed as shown below.

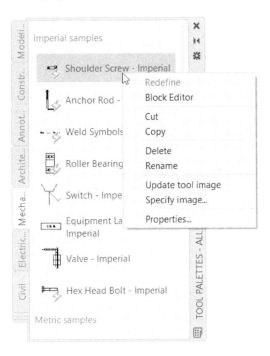

Creating a New Tool Palette

- Right-click on the Tool Palette and select **New Palette** from the shortcut menu; a new palette is added to Tool Palettes.
- Enter **Electronic Symbols** as the name. The newly created Tool Palette get added, as shown.

- Also you can right click and select the Move Up and Move Down to change its location in the **TOOL PALETTES** window, as shown.

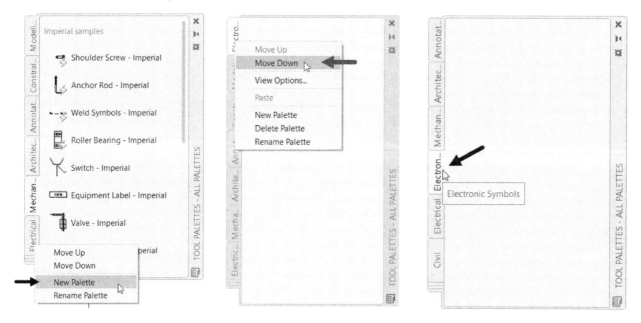

You can also create a new tool palette using the **Customize** dialog box.

- Right-click on Tool Palettes and select **Customize Palettes**; the **Customize** dialog box appears, as shown.
- In the **Customize** dialog box, right-click in the **Palettes** list and select **New Palette**.

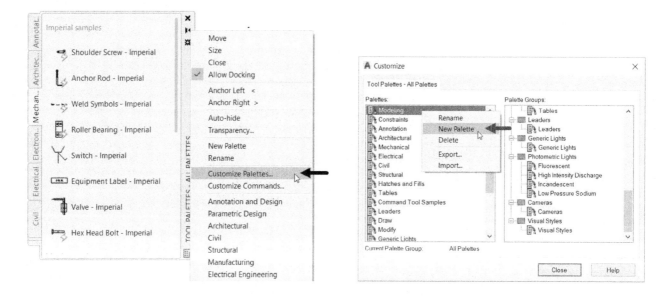

- Enter the name of the palette and click the **Close** button.

Adding Blocks to a Tool Palette

- Open the **DesignCenter** palette and select the **Electronic Symbols.dwg** file from the **Folders** list; the blocks available in the selected file are displayed.
- Drag the blocks from the **DesignCenter** and place them in the Tool Palette.

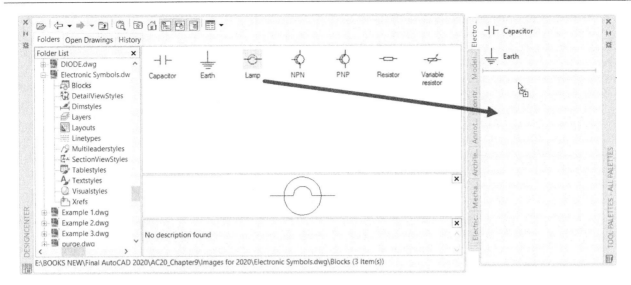

You can also create a new tool palette from a drawing consisting of blocks.

- In the **DesignCenter** palette, select the **Electronic symbols.dwg** file from **Folder List**.
- Right-click and select **Create Tool Palette**; a new palette will be created from the drawing file.

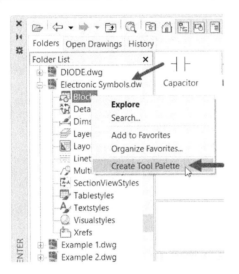
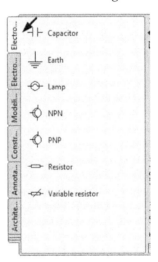

In the Tool Palette, you can group blocks depending on their function.

- Right-click on the **Tool Palette** and select **Add Separator**; a separator will be added.

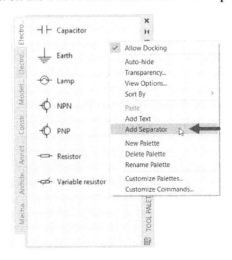
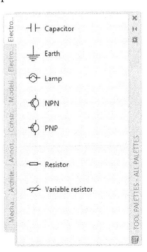

- Right-click and select **Add Text**. Enter the name of the group.

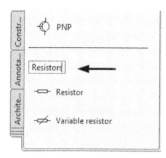

Inserting Multiple Blocks

You can insert multiple instances of a block at a time by using the **MINSERT** command. This command is similar to the **ARRAY** command. The following example explains the procedure to insert multiple blocks at a time.

Example:

Create two blocks as shown below.

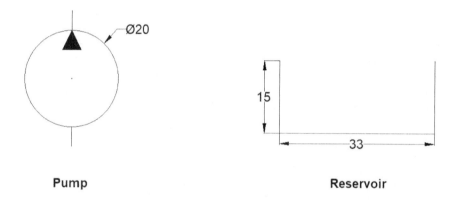

Pump   Reservoir

- Type **MINSERT** in the command line and press **ENTER**; the message, "**Enter block name or [?]:**" appears.
- Type **Pump** and press **ENTER**; the Pump is attached to the cursor.
- Pick a point in the drawing window.
- Enter **1** as the scale factor.
- Enter **0** as the rotation angle; the message, "**Enter number of rows (---) <1>:**" appears.
- Enter **1** as the row value; the message, "**Enter number of columns (| | |) <1>:**" appears.
- Enter **4** as the column value; the message, "**Specify distance between columns (| | |):**" appears.
- Type **60** and press **ENTER**; the pumps will be inserted as shown below.

- Similarly, insert the reservoirs and create lines as shown below.

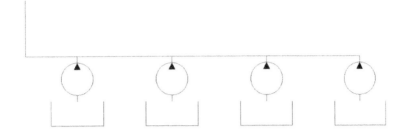

Editing Blocks

During the design process, you may need to edit blocks. You can easily edit a block using the **Block Editor** window. As you edit a block, all the instances of it will be automatically updated. The procedure to edit a block is discussed next.

- Click **Insert > Block Definition > Block Editor** on the ribbon; the **Edit Block Definition** dialog box appears.

- In the **Edit Block Definition** dialog box, select **Pump** from the list and click **OK**; the **Block Editor** window appears.

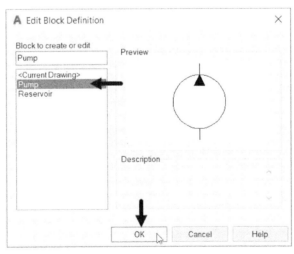

- Click **Home > Draw > Polyline** on the ribbon and draw a polyline as shown below.

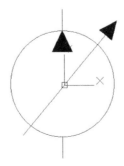

- Click **Close Block Editor** on the **Close** panel.

- In the **Block – Changes Not Saved** dialog box, click **Save the changes to Pump**.

All the instances of the block will be updated automatically.

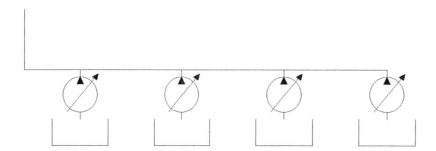

Using the Write Block tool

Using the **Write Block** tool, you can create a drawing file from a block or objects. You can later insert this drawing file as a block into another drawing. The procedure to create a drawing file using blocks is discussed in the following example.

Example:

Start a new drawing file and create two blocks, as shown below.

Gate Valve   Orifice

- Insert the blocks and create the drawing as shown below.

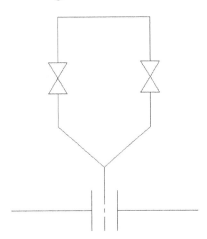

- Expand the **Block Definition** panel and select the **Set Base Point** button.
- Select the endpoint of the lower horizontal line as shown.

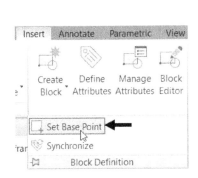

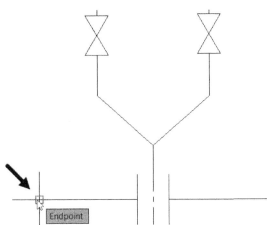

- Click **Insert > Block Definition > Write Block** on the ribbon; the **Write Block** dialog box appears.

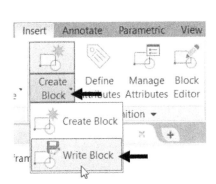

In the **Write Block** dialog box, you can select three different types of sources (Block, Entire drawing, or Objects) to create a block. If you select the **Block** option, you can select blocks present in the drawing from the drop-down.

- Select the **Entire drawing** option.
- Specify the location of the file and name it as **Tap-in line**.

- Click the **OK** button.
- Close the drawing file.
- Open a new drawing file, and then type **I** in the command line and press **ENTER**; the **Insert** dialog box appears.
- Select **Tap-in line** from the **Name** drop-down and click **OK**.
- Pick a point in the drawing window to insert the block.

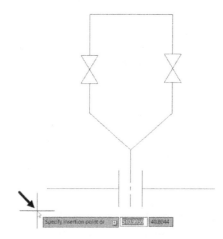

Defining Attributes

An attribute is a line of text attached to a block. It may contain any type of information related to a block. For example, the following image shows a Compressor symbol with an equipment tag. The procedure to create an attribute is discussed in the following example.

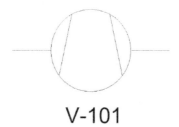

V-101

Example:
- Open a new drawing file.
- Create the symbols as shown below.

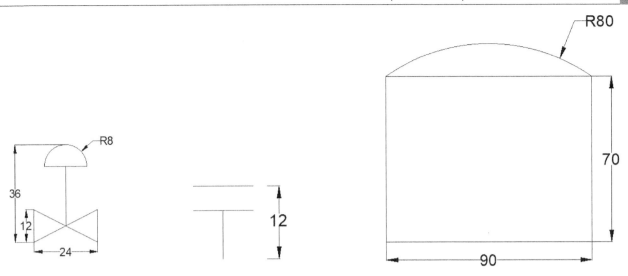

- Click **Insert > Block Definition > Define Attributes** on the ribbon; the **Attribute Definition** dialog box appears.

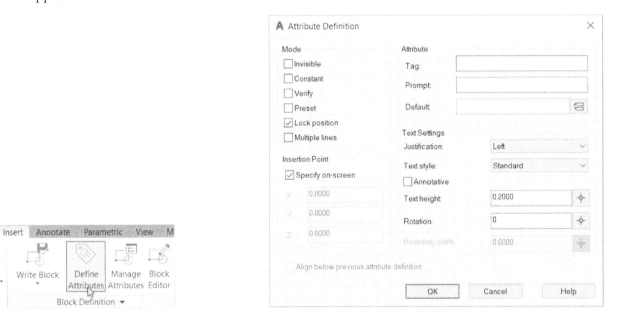

The options in the **Mode** group of the **Attribute Definition** dialog box are used to set the display mode of the attribute. If you select the **Invisible** option, the attribute will be invisible. The **Constant** option makes the value of the attribute constant. You cannot change the value. The **Verify** option prompts you to verify after you enter a value. The **Preset** option allows you to set a predefined value for the attribute. The **Lock position** option fixes the position of the attribute to a selected point. The **Multiple lines** option allows typing the attribute value in single or multiple lines.

- Ensure that the **Lock position** option is selected.

The options in the **Attribute** group are used to specify the values of the attribute. The **Tag** box is used to enter the label of the attribute. For example, if you want to create an attribute called RESISTANCE, you need to type **Resistance** in the **Tag** box. The **Prompt** box is used to specify the prompt message that appears after placing the block. The **Default** box is used to specify the default value of the attribute.

- In the **Attribute Definition** dialog box, enter **Valvetag** in the **Tag** box.

The **Text Settings** options are used to specify the display properties of the text such as style, height and so on. Observe the other options in this dialog box. Most of them are self-explanatory.

- Enter **4** in the **Text Height** box.
- Set the **Justification** to **Middle** and click **OK.**
- Specify the location of the attribute as shown below.

- Click the **Create Block** button on the **Block Definition** panel; the **Block Definition** dialog box appears.
- Click on the **Select Object** ⊕ button from the dialog box.
- Drag a window and select the control valve symbol and attribute. Press **ENTER**.
- Select the **Delete** option from the **Objects** group.
- Click the **Pick Point** button under the base point group and select the point as shown below.

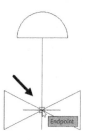

VALVETAG

- Enter **Control Valve** in the **Name** box and click **OK**.
- Similarly, create **Equipmenttag** and place inside the tank symbol.
- Create a block and name it as **Tank**, as shown.
- Also, create a block of the nozzle symbol and name it **Nozzle**, as shown.

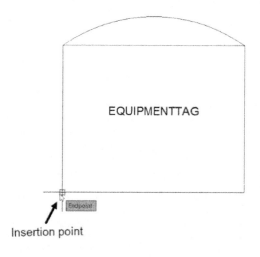

EQUIPMENTTAG

Insertion point

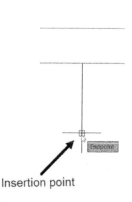

Insertion point

Note: If you want to use these blocks in any other drawings then instead of using **Create Block** tool, you need to use **Write Block** tool, as discussed earlier.

Inserting Attributed Blocks

You can use the **INSERT** command to insert the attributed blocks into a drawing. The procedure to insert attributed blocks is discussed next.

- Click the **Insert** button with drop-down from the **Block** panel to expand it.
- Click on the **Tank** block and click anywhere in the drawing area to specify the insertion point, as shown.

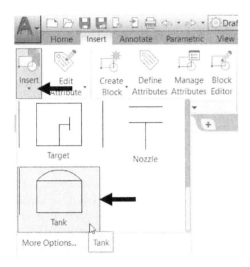

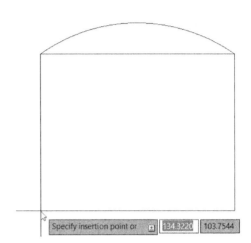

- Enter **TK-001** in the **EQUIPMENTTAG** field of the **Edit Attributes** dialog box displayed, as shown.
- Click **OK** from the dialog box; the block will be placed along with the attribute.

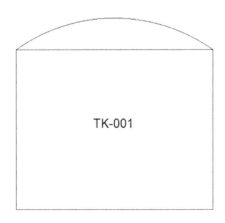

- Similarly, place control valves as shown below.

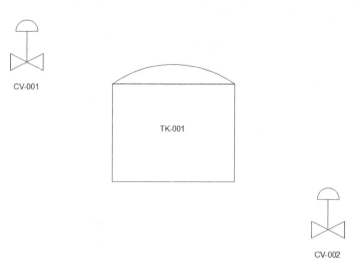

- Now, place the nozzles on the tank as shown below.

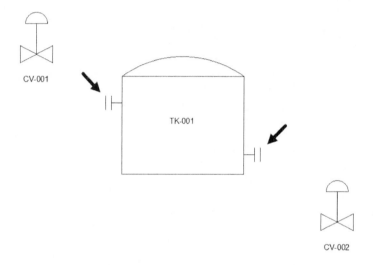

- Use the **Polyline** tool and connect the control valve and tank.

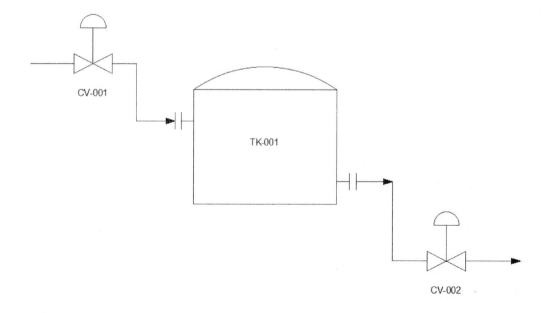

Working with External references

 In AutoCAD, you can attach a drawing file, image or a pdf file to another drawing. These attachments are called External References (Xrefs). They are dynamic in nature and update automatically when changes are made to them. The following example, you will learn to attach drawing files to a drawing.

Example:
Create the drawing shown below.

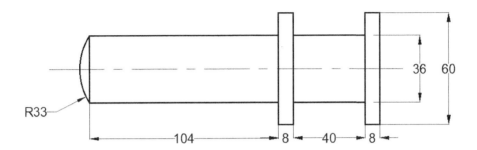

- Type **BASE** in the command line and press **ENTER**.
- Select the midpoint of the vertical line as the base point, as shown.

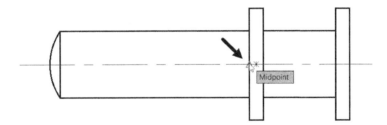

- Save the drawing as **Crank pin.dwg**
- Create another drawing as shown below.

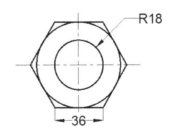

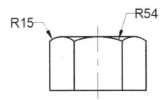

- Use the **Set Base Point** 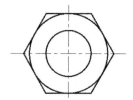 tool and specify the base point as shown below.

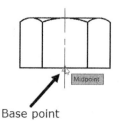

Base point

- Save the drawing as **Nut.dwg** and close it.
- Open the **Crank.dwg** file created in Chapter 8.
- Click **Insert > Reference > Attach** on the ribbon; the **Select Reference file** dialog box appears.
- Browse to the location of the **Crankpin.dwg** and double-click on it; the **Attach External Reference** dialog box appears.

Some of the options available in this dialog box are similar to that in the **Insert** dialog box, such as the insertion point, scale, and rotation angle of the external reference.

- Accept the default settings in this dialog box and click **OK**; the crank pin will be attached to the cursor.
- Select the point on the section view as shown below.

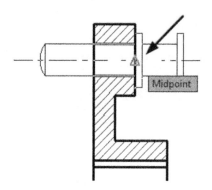
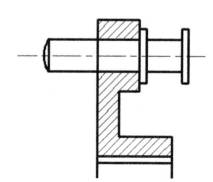

- Click **View > Palettes > External References Palette** on the ribbon; the **External References Palette** appears. This palette displays the Xrefs attached to the drawing.

- In the **External References** palette, open the **Attach** drop-down and select the **Attach DWG** option; the **Select References file** dialog box appears.

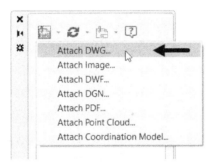

- Browse to the location of the **Nut.dwg** and double-click on it; the **Attach External Reference** dialog box appears.
- In the **Attach External Reference** dialog box, enter **90** in the **Angle** box under the **Rotation** group and click **OK**.
- Select the insertion point on the section view as shown below.

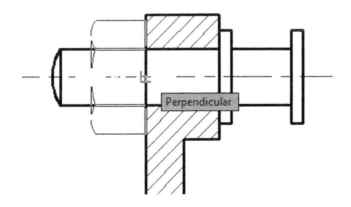

Fading an Xref

You can change the fading of Xref by using the Xref fading slider available in the expanded **Reference** panel.

- Expand the **Reference** panel of the **Insert** ribbon and use the **Xref fading** slider to adjust the fading.

Clipping External References

You can hide the unwanted portion of an external reference by using the **Clip** tool.

- Click **Insert > Reference > Clip** on the ribbon; the message, "**Select Object to clip**" appears in the command line.
- Select the **Nut.dwg** from the drawing window.
- Select the **New boundary** option from the command line.
- Select the **Rectangular** option from the command line.
- Draw a rectangle as shown below; only the front view of the nut is visible and the top view is hidden. Also, the clipping frame is visible.

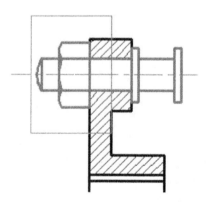

- To hide the clipping frame, type **XCLIPFRAME** in the command line
- Type **0** and press **ENTER**.
- You can also hide the frame by clicking **Modify > Object > External Reference > Frame** on the Menu Bar.

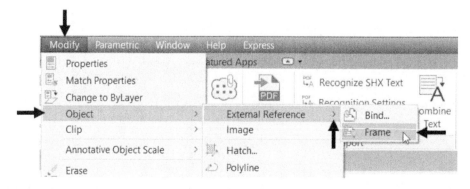

- Attach another instance of the **Nut.dwg** file.
- Use the **Rotate** and **Move** tools to position the top view as shown below.

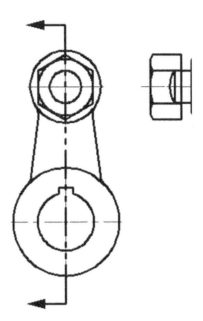

- Use the **Clip** tool and clip the Xref.

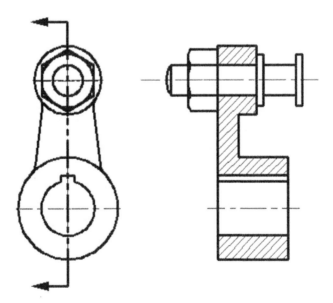

Editing the External References

AutoCAD allows you to edit the external references in the file to which they are attached. You can also edit them by opening their drawing file. The procedure to edit an external reference is discussed next.

- To edit an external reference, expand the **Reference** panel and click the **Edit Reference** button.

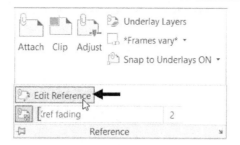

- Select **Nut** from the drawing; the **Reference Edit** dialog box appears
- Click **OK** to get into the reference editing mode.
- In the drawing, you will notice that the centerlines of the nut are overlapping on the centerlines of the crank. Delete the centerlines and center marks of the nut.
- Click **Save changes** on the **Edit Reference** panel; the **AutoCAD** message box appears.

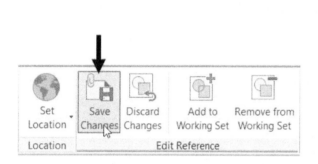

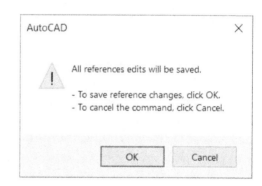

- Click **OK**.

Adding Balloons

- Click **Annotate > Leader > Multileader Style Manager** (inclined arrow) button on the ribbon; the **Multileader Style Manager** dialog box appears.
- Click the **New** button on the dialog box.
- In the **Create New Multileader Style** dialog box, enter **Balloon Callout** in the **New Style name** box and click **Continue**.

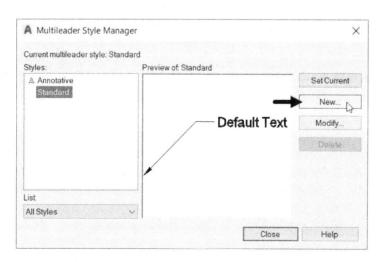

- In the **Modify Multileader Style** dialog box, click the **Content** tab and set the **Multileader type** to **Block**.

- Under **Block Options**, set the **Source block** to **Circle**.
- Set the **Scale** to **3**.

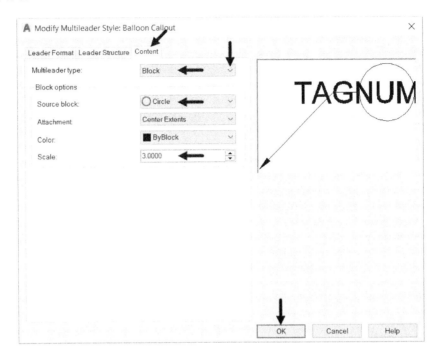

- Click **Leader Format** tab and set the Arrowhead **Size** to **8**.
- Click **OK** and set the **Balloon Callout** style as current, as shown.

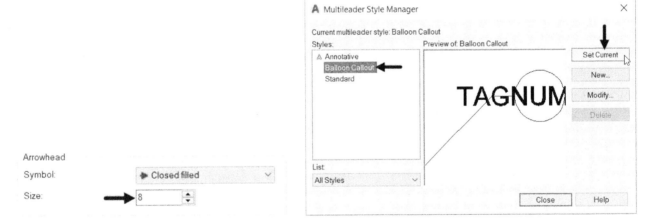

- Click **Close**.
- Click **Annotate > Leader > Multileader** on the ribbon.
- Click the down arrow next to the **Polar Tracking** button on the status bar and select **45** from the menu.
- Activate the **Polar Tracking**.
- Select a point on the section view of the crank.
- Move the cursor along the polar trace lines and click; the **Edit Attributes** dialog box appears.

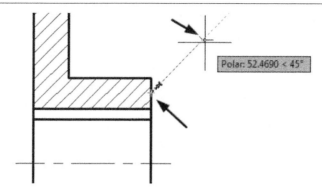

- In the **Edit Attributes** dialog box, enter **1** in the **Enter tag number** field.

- Click **OK**; the balloon will be created.

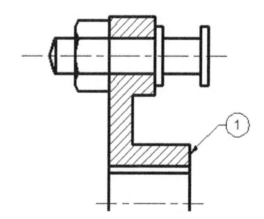

- Similarly, create other balloons.

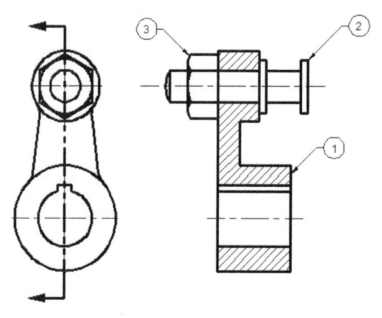

Creating Part List

- Click **Annotate > Table > Table Style** on the ribbon; the **Table Style** dialog box appears.

- In the **Table Style** dialog box, click the **New** button; the **Create New Table Style** dialog box appears.
- In the **Create New Table Style** dialog, enter **Part List** in the **Name** box. Click **Continue**; the **New Table Style** dialog box appears.
- Click the **Text** tab and set the **Text height** to 10, as shown.

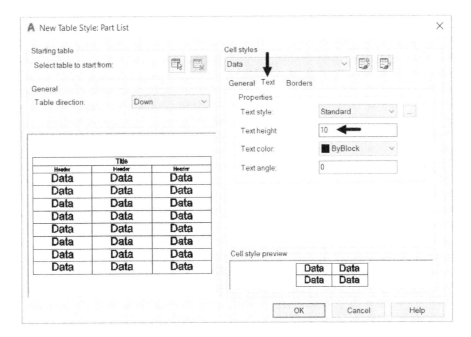

- Select the **Header** option from the **Cell Styles** drop-down and set the **Text height** to **10**.

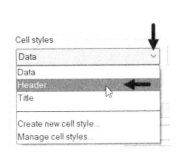

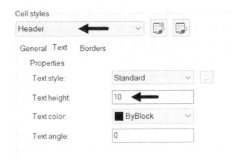

- Click **OK**.
- In the **Table Style** dialog box, select the **Part List** style and click **Set current**.
- Close the dialog box.
- Click the **Table** button on the **Tables** panel; the **Insert table** dialog box appears.

- Ensure that the **Table style** is set **Part List**.

- Under the **Set cell styles** group, set the **First row cell style** to **Header**.
- Set the **Second row cell style** and **All other row cell styles** to **Data**.

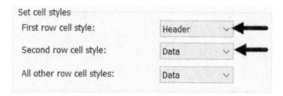

- Set the number of **Columns** to **4** and **Column width** to **65** and fill other entries, as shown.

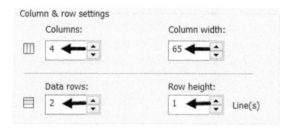

- Click **OK** and place the table at the lower right corner of the drawing window.
- Enter **PART No.**, **NAME**, **MATERIAL**, **QTY** in the first row of the **Part list** table. Use the **TAB** key to navigate between the cells.
- Click **Close Text Editor** button on the ribbon.

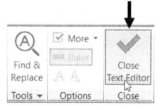

- Click on anyone of the edges of the table; you will notice that grips are displayed on it. You can edit the table using these grips.

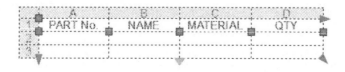

- Click and drag the square grip below the MATERIAL; the width of the cell will be changed.

- Click and drag the triangular grip located at the bottom left corner of the table; the height of the rows will be increased uniformly.

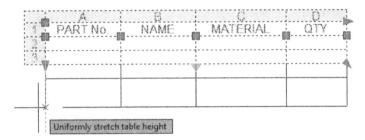

- Click in the second cell of the first column; the **Table Cell** ribbon appears. You can use this ribbon to modify the properties of the table cell.

- Click the **Insert Below** button on the **Rows** panel; a new row will be added to the cell.

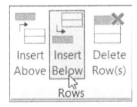

- Click in the top left corner cell of the table.
- Press and hold the **SHIFT** key and click in the lower right corner of the table; all the cells in the table will be selected.

	A	B	C	D
1	PART No.	NAME	MATERIAL	QTY
2				
3				
4				

- In the **Table Cell** ribbon, click **Cell Styles > Alignment > Middle Center**; the data in all the cells will appear in the middle center of the cells.

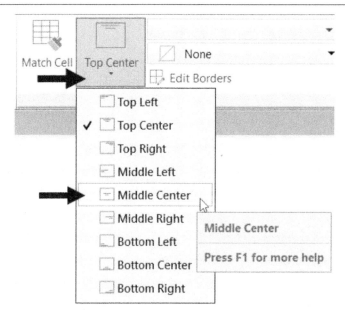

- Double-click in the cell below the **PART No.;** the text editor will be activated.
- Enter the following data in the cells. Use the TAB to navigate between the cells.

PART No.	NAME	MATERIAL	QTY
1	Crank	Forged Steel	1
2	Crank pin	45C	1
3	Nut	MS	1

Questions:

1. Which command is used to create a block?
2. Which tool is used to insert a block?
3. Which tool is used to remove the unused block?
4. Where is **Tool Palettes** button available on the ribbon?
5. Which command is used to insert multiple instances of a block at a time?
6. Which tool is used to create a drawing file from a block or objects?
7. Which tool is used to edit an external reference?
8. Where is **Define Attributes** button available on the ribbon?

Exercise

Exercise 1:

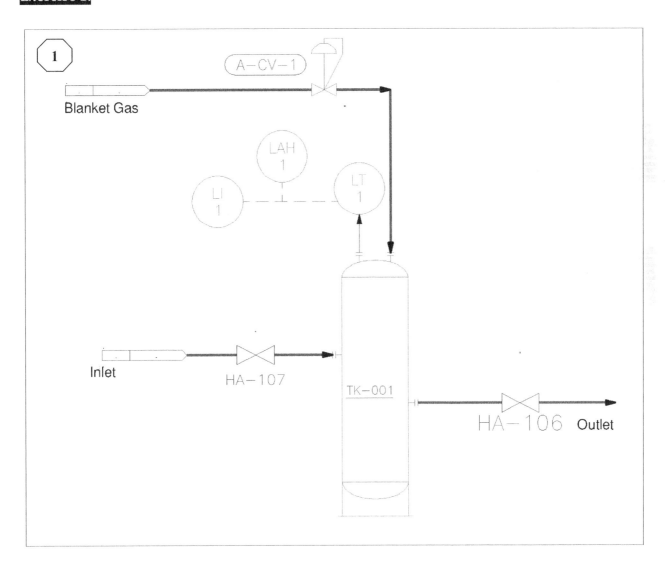

Chapter 10: Layouts & Annotative Objects in AutoCAD

In this chapter, you will learn to do the following:

- ❖ **Create Layouts**

- ❖ **Specify the Paper space settings**

- ❖ **Create Viewports in Paper space**

- ❖ **Change Layer properties in Viewports**

- ❖ **Create Title Block on the layout**

- ❖ **Use Annotative objects in Viewports**

Drawing Layouts

There are two workspaces in AutoCAD: The Model space and the Paper space. In the Model space, you create 2D drawings and 3D models. You can even plot drawings from the model space. However, it is difficult to plot drawings at a scale or if a drawing consists of multiple views arranged at different scales. For this purpose, we use Layouts or paper space. In Layouts or paper space, you can work on notes and annotations and perform the plotting or publishing operations. In Layouts, you can arrange a single view or multiple views of a drawing or multiple drawings by using Viewports. These viewports display drawings at specific scales on layouts. They are mainly rectangular in shape but you can also create circular and polygonal viewports. In this chapter, you will learn about viewports and various annotative objects.

Working with Layouts

Layouts represent the conventional drawing sheet. They are created to plot a drawing on a paper or in electronic form. A drawing can have multiple layouts to print in different sheet formats. By default, there are two layouts available: Layout 1 and Layout 2. You can also create new layouts right-clicking on the layout tab available below the drawing window. Next, select **New layout** from the shortcut menu. Alternatively, you can also create new layouts by clicking the plus (**+**) symbol next to the layout. In the following example, you will create two layouts, one representing the ISO A1 (841 X 594) sheet and another representing the ISO A4 (210 X 297) sheet.

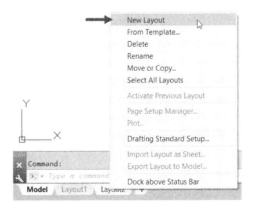

Example:

> ➢ Open a new drawing file.
> ➢ Create layers with the following settings:

Layer	Linetype	Lineweight
Construction	Continuous	Default
Object Lines	Continuous	0.6mm
Hidden Lines	Hidden	0.3 mm
Center Lines	CENTER	Default
Dimensions	Continuous	Default
Section Lines	Continuous	Default
Cutting Plane	Phantom	0.6mm
Title Block	Continuous	1.2mm
Viewport	Continuous	Default

> ➢ Create the drawing as shown below. Do not add dimensions.

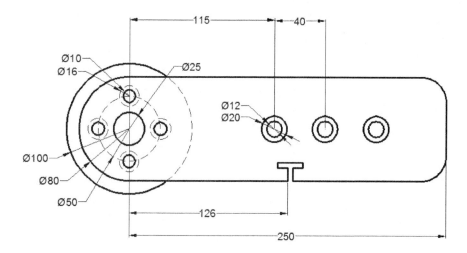

> ➢ Click the **Layout 1** tab at the bottom of the drawing window.

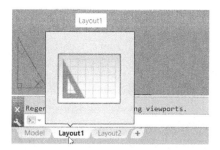

You will notice that a white paper is displayed with automatically created viewport. The components of a layout are shown in figure below.

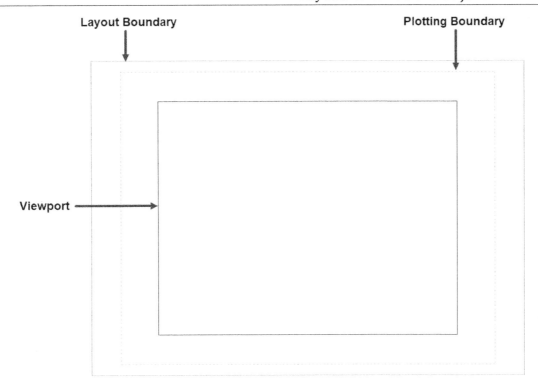

> Click **Output > Plot > Page Setup Manager** on the ribbon; the **Page Setup Manager** dialog box appears.

> In the **Page Setup Manager** dialog box, click the **Modify** button; the **Page Setup –Layout1** dialog box appears.

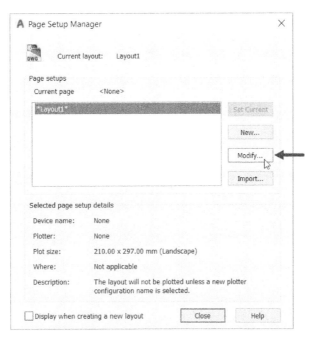

➢ In the **Page Setup** dialog box, select **DWG to PDF.pc3** from the **Name** drop-down under the **Printer/Plotter** group.
➢ Set the **Plot Style table** to **acad.ctb**.
➢ Set the **Paper size** to **ISO A1 (841.00 x 594.00 MM)**. Set the **Plot scale** to **1:1**.

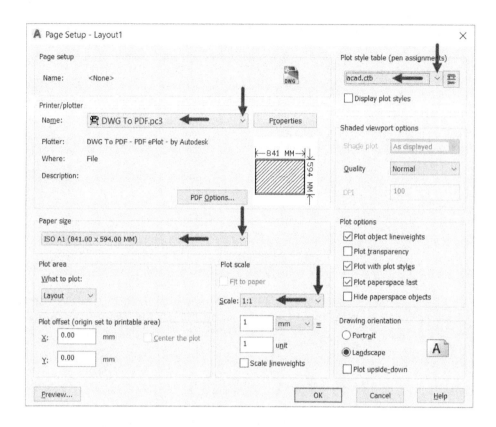

➢ Click **OK**, and then click **Close** on the **Page Setup Manager** dialog box.
➢ Click the **Layout2** tab below the drawing window.
➢ Double-click on the **Layout2** tab and enter **ISO A4**; the **Layout2** will be renamed.
➢ Similarly, rename the **Layout1** to **ISO A1**.
➢ Click **Layout > Layout > Page Setup** on the ribbon; the **Page Setup Manager** dialog box appears.
➢ Select the **ISO A4** from the list.
➢ Click the **Modify** button on the dialog box.
➢ In the **Page Setup** dialog box, select the **DWG to PDF.pc3** plotter and select **acad.ctb** from the **Plot style table** drop-down.
➢ Set the **Paper size** to **ISO A4 (210 x 297 MM)** and **Scale** to **1:1**.
➢ Set **Drawing Orientation** as **Portrait** and click **OK**; you will notice that the size of the Layout is changed to A4 size.
➢ Close the **Page Setup Manager** dialog box.

Creating Viewports in the Paper space

The viewports that exist in the paper space are called floating viewports. This is because you can position them anywhere in the layout and modify their shape size with respect to the layout.

Creating a Viewport in the ISO A4 layout

➢ Open the **ISO A4** layout, if not already open.
➢ Select the default viewport that exists in the **ISO A4** layout.

➤ Press the **DELETE** key; the viewport will be deleted.

➤ Click **Layout > Layout Viewports > Rectangular** on the ribbon.

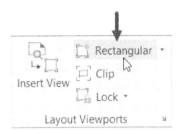

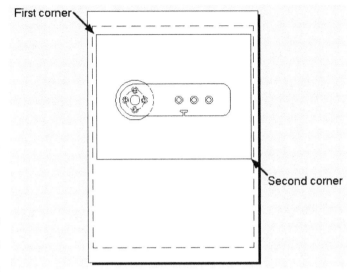

➤ Create the rectangular viewport by picking the first and second corner points, as shown in figure.

➤ Click the **PAPER** button on the status bar; the model space inside the viewport will be activated. Also, the viewport frame will become thicker when you are in model space.

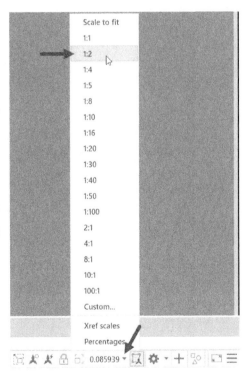

➤ Click the **Viewport Scale** button and select **1:2** from the menu; the drawing will be zoomed out.

➤ Use the **Pan** tool and position the drawing in the center of the viewport.

➤ After fitting the drawing inside the viewport, you can lock the position by clicking the **Lock/Unlock Viewport** button on the status bar.

After locking the viewport, you cannot change the scale or position of the drawing.

➤ Click the **MODEL** button on the status bar to switch back to paper space.

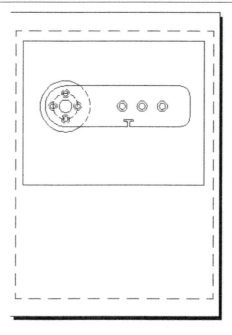

Creating Viewports in the ISO A1 layout

> Click the **ISO A1** tab below the drawing window.

> Select the viewport frame and modify the viewport using the grip, as shown below.

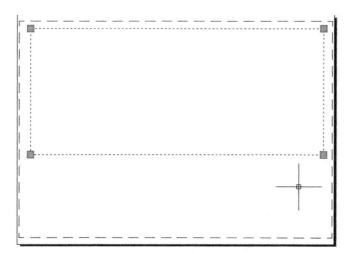

> Double-click inside the viewport to switch to the model space.

> Use the **Zoom** and **Pan** tools and drag the drawing to the center of the viewport.

> Click the **Viewport Scale** button and select the **2:1** from the menu.

> Use the **Pan** tool and position the drawing, as shown in figure.

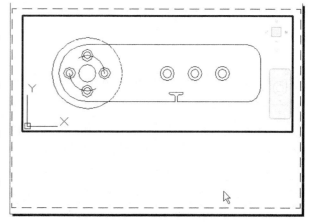

➤ Click the **Lock/Unlock Viewport** button on the status bar.

➤ Double-click outside the viewport to switch to the paper space.

➤ Use the **Circle** tool and create a **180** mm diameter circle on the layout, as shown below.

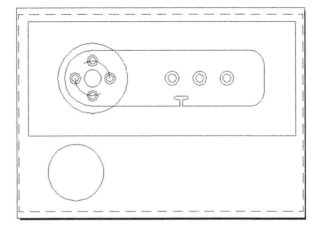

➤ Click **Layout > Layout Viewports > Viewport drop-down > Object** on the ribbon.

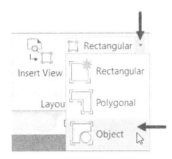

➤ Select the circle from the layout; it will be converted into a viewport.

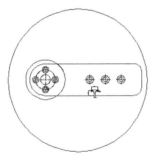

➤ Double-click in the circular viewport to switch to the model space.

➤ Click the **Viewport Scale** button on the status bar and select **4:1** from the menu; the drawing will be zoomed in to its center.

➤ Use the **Pan** tool and adjust the drawing, as shown below.

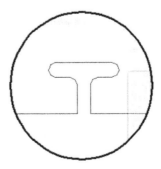

➢ Click the **Lock** button on the **Layout Viewports** panel.
➢ Select the circular viewport and press **ENTER**; the drawing inside the viewport will be locked. Now, you cannot zoom or pan the drawing.

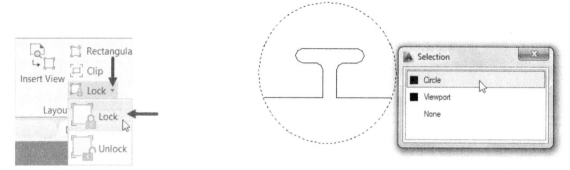

➢ Click **Output > Plot > Preview** on the ribbon; the plot preview will be displayed. You will notice that the viewport frames are also displayed in the preview.

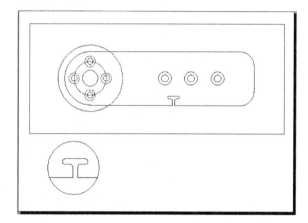

➢ Press ESC to close the preview window.

To hide viewport frames while plotting a drawing, follow the steps given below.

➢ Type **LA** in the command line to open the **Layer Properties Manager**.
➢ In the **Layer Properties Manager**, create a new layer called **Hide Viewports** and make it current.
➢ Deactivate the plotter symbol under the **Plot** column of the **Hide Viewports** layer; the object on this layer will not be plotted.

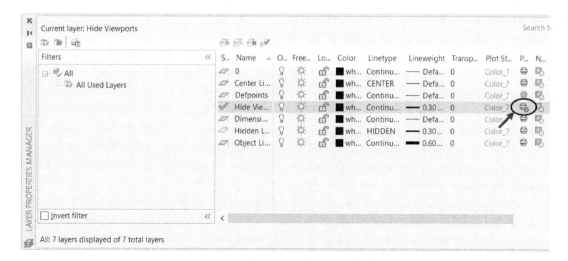

➢ Close the **Layer Properties Manager**.
➢ Click the **Home** tab on the ribbon and expand the **Layers** panel.
➢ Click the **Change to Current Layer** button on the **Layers** panel.

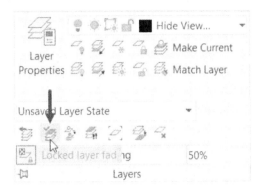

➢ Select the viewports in the **ISO A1** layout and press **ENTER**; the viewport frames will become unplottable. To check this, click the **Preview** button on the **Plot** panel; the plot preview will be displayed as shown below.

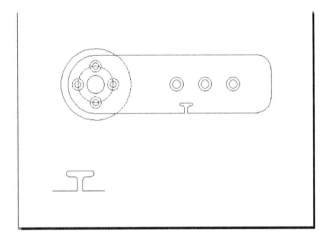

➢ Close the preview window.

Changing the Layer Properties in Viewports

The layer properties in viewports are not related to the layer properties in model space. You can change the layer properties in viewports without any effect in the model space.

➢ Double-click inside the larger viewport to activate the model space.
➢ Type **LA** in the command line to open the **Layer Properties Manager**.
➢ In the **Layer Properties Manager**, click the icon in the **VP Freeze** column of the **Hidden** layer; the hidden lines will disappear in the viewport, as shown below.

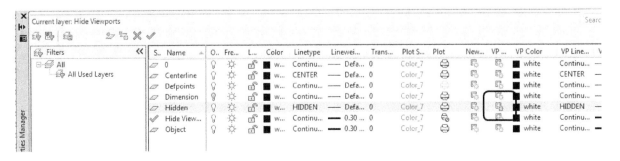

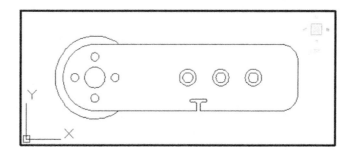

➤ Double-click outside the viewport to switch to paper space.
➤ Click the **Model** tab below the drawing window; you will notice that the hidden lines are retained in the model space.

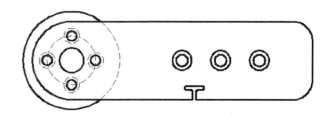

Creating the Title Block on the Layout

You can draw objects on layouts to create title block, borders and viewports. However, it is not recommended to draw the actual drawing on layouts. You can also create dimensions on layouts.

Example1:

➤ Click the **ISO A1** layout tab.
➤ Set the **Title Block** layer as current.
➤ Click the **Rectangle** button on the **Draw** panel.
➤ Pick a point at the lower right corner of the layout.
➤ Select the **Dimensions** option from the command line.
➤ Specify the length of the rectangle as **820** and width as **550**.
➤ Click in the upper area of the layout; a rectangular border will be created.
➤ Create a title block at the lower right corner as shown below.

➤ Create attributes and place inside the title as shown below.

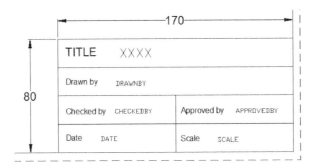

➤ Use the **Create Block** tool and convert it into a block.
➤ Use the **Insert** tool and insert it at the lower right corner of the layout.
➤ Save the drawing file as **Viewports-Example.dwg**.

Working with Annotative Dimensions

In AutoCAD, you create drawings at their actual size. However, when you scale a drawing to fit inside a viewport, the size of the dimensions will not be scaled properly. For example, in the following figure, the viewport on the left is scaled to 1:2 and viewport on the right is scaled to 1:1. The dimensions in the left viewport appear much smaller. You can fix this problem by applying the Annotative property to dimensions.

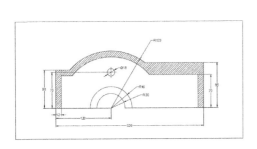

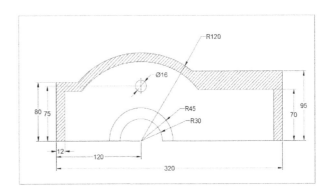

➤ Open the **Viewports-Example.dwg**, if not already opened.
➤ Type **D** in the command line and press **ENTER**.
➤ In the **Dimension Style Manager**, click the **New** button.
➤ In the **Create New Dimension Style** dialog box, enter **New style name** as **Dim_Anno**.
➤ Select the **Annotative** check box and click **Continue**.

- Set the following settings in the **New Dimension Style** dialog box.

  Lines tab: Offset from origin-1.25
  Symbols and Arrows tab: Arrow size -2.5, Center Marks-Line.
  Text tab: Text height – 2.5, Text placement - Vertical-Centered, Text alignment - Horizontal
  Primary Units tab: Units Format – Decimal, Precision – 0, Decimal separator – '.'period

- In the **Fit** tab, ensure that the **Annotative** check box is selected.

- Click **OK** on the **New Dimension Style** dialog box; you will notice that the **Dim_Anno** style is listed in the **Dimension Style Manager**. Also, the annotation symbol is displayed next to it. This indicates that all dimensions created using this style will have annotative property. Click on the **Close** button.

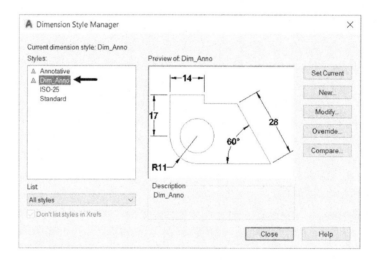

- Use the **Linear** tool and create a linear dimension as shown below.

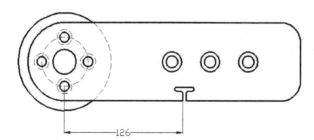

- Click **Add scales to annotative objects when the annotation scale changes** on the status bar.

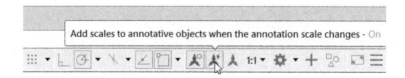

- Set the **Annotation Scale** to **1:2**; the size of the dimension will get automatically increased by two times.

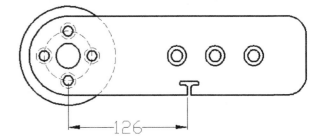

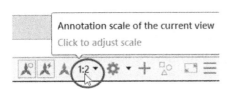

Example 2:

* Ensure that the **Annotation Scale** is set to **1:2** and create another linear dimension as shown in figure.

* Click the **ISO A4** layout in which the viewport scale is set **1:2**; you will notice that the dimensions are scaled with respect to the viewport.

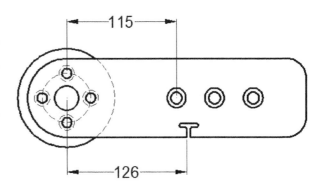

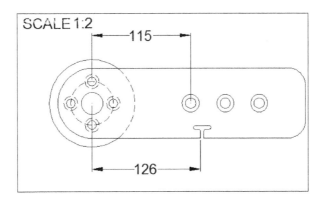

* Click the **ISO A1** layout; you will notice that the dimensions are not displayed in the **2:1** viewport. To display dimensions in the **2:1** viewport, you need to add **2:1** scale to dimensions.

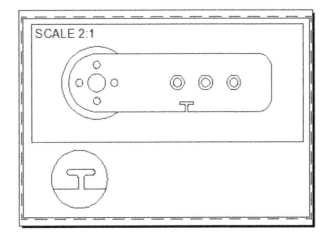

* Click the **Model** tab below the drawing window to switch to the model space.
* Click **Annotate > Annotation Scaling > Add/Delete Scales** on the ribbon.

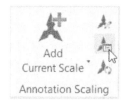

- Select the dimensions from the drawing window and right-click; the **Annotation Object Scale** dialog box appears. In this dialog box, the **Object Scale list** shows the scales applied to selected dimensions. You need to add **2:1** scale to the dimensions so that they will be visible in the **2:1** viewport.

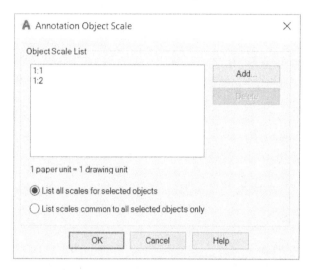

- To add a new scale to the dimensions, click the **Add** button; the **Add Scales to Object** dialog box appears.
- Select the **2:1** scale from the list and click **OK**; the scale will be added to **Object Scale list**.
- Click **OK** on the **Annotation Object Scale** dialog box.
- Click the **ISO A1** layout; the dimensions are displayed in both **2:1** and **1:2** viewports.

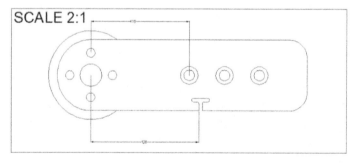

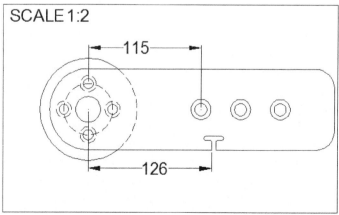

- Similarly, create other dimensions as shown below. Add **2:1** and **1:2** scales to dimensions and check the drawing in two different layouts.

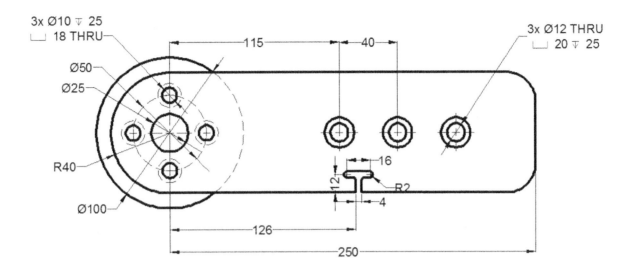

Scaling Hatch relative to Viewports

While working in layouts, you may also need to scale the hatch with respect to the viewport scale. The following figure shows a drawing in two different viewports **1:2** and **1:1**. The hatch in the left viewport is smaller than that in right side viewport. You can correct this problem by **Relative to Paper Space** option.

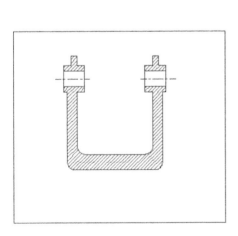

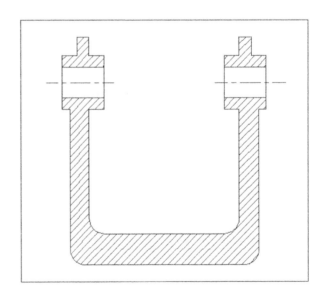

- Double-click inside a viewport; the model space will be activated.
- Select the hatch patterns from the drawing; the **Hatch Editor** tab appears.
- In the **Hatch Editor** tab, expand the **Properties** panel and select the **Relative to Paper Space** button.

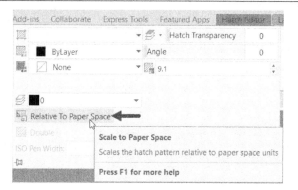

- Click the **Close Hatch Editor** button; you will notice that the hatch will be scaled with respect the viewport scale. Double-click outside the viewport to switch to the paper space.

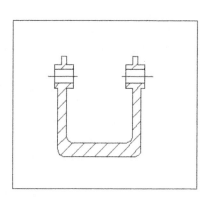

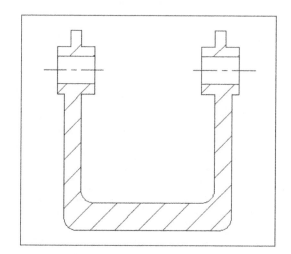

Working with Annotative Text

Annotative property can also be assigned text. The annotative text will be scaled with respect the viewport scale.

➢ Open the **Viewports-Example.dwg**, if not already opened.
➢ Click **Annotate > Text > Text Style** on the ribbon; the **Text Style** dialog box appears.

➢ Click the **New** button on the **Text Style** dialog box; the **New Text Style** dialog box appears.
➢ Enter **Text_Anno** as the **Style name** and click **OK**.

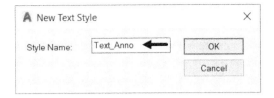

- ➤ Set **Font Name** to **Arial** and select the **Annotative** check box.
- ➤ Set **Paper Text Height** to **2.5** and **Width Factor** to **1**.
- ➤ Click **Apply** and **Close**.
- ➤ Select **1:1** from the **Viewport Scale** menus at the status.
- ➤ Click **Annotate > Text > Multiline Text** on the ribbon.
- ➤ Specify the first corner of the text editor by picking an arbitrary point.
- ➤ Select the **Justify** option from the command line; the command line displays:

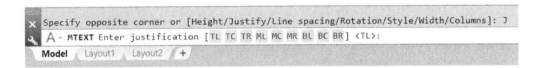

- ➤ Select the **MC** option from the command line.
- ➤ Move the cursor toward right and specify the second corner of the text editor.
- ➤ Type **All dimensions are in mm** and click the **Close Text Editor** button on the **Close** panel.
- ➤ Move the text and place at the bottom left corner of the drawing as shown below.

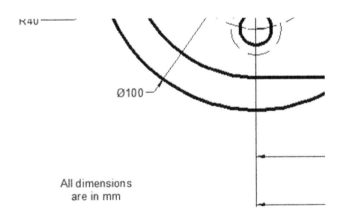

- ➤ View the drawing in the **ISO A4** layout; you will notice that the text is not displayed. This is because the text is set to **1:1** scale.
- ➤ On the status bar, click the **Show annotation objects** button.

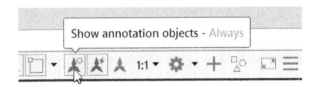

- ➤ Save the drawing as **Layout Example.dwg** and close.

Questions:

1. Which tools is selected to display **Page Setup Manager** dialog box?
2. Where is **PAPER** button available?
3. Which button is selected to lock the position of drawing in Viewport?
4. Which tool is selected to convert a circle into viewport?
5. Which tool is used to convert a title block into a block?

Exercise

Exercise 1:

Create the drawing as shown below. After create the drawing, perform the following tasks:

- Create a layout of A3 size and then create a viewport.

- Set the viewport scale to 1:2.

- Set the scale of the dimensions and hatch lines with respect to the viewport.

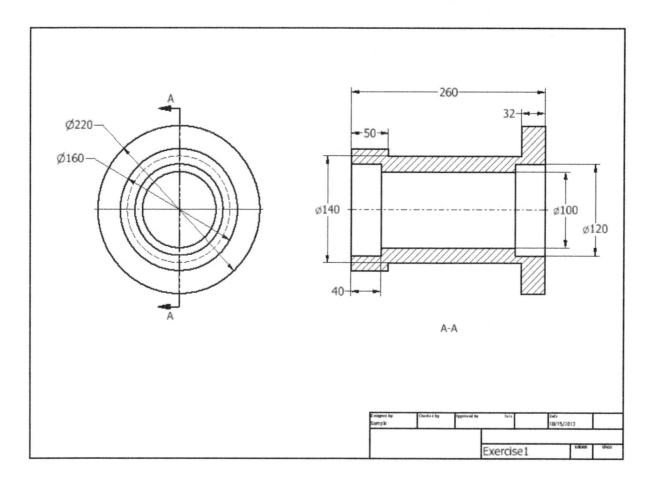

Chapter 11: Templates and Plotting in AutoCAD

In this chapter, you will learn to do the following:

- ❖ **Configure Plotters**
- ❖ **Create Plot Style Tables**
- ❖ **Use Plot styles**
- ❖ **Create Templates**
- ❖ **Plot/Print the drawing**

Plotting Drawings

Plotting is the process of producing a physical copy of the drawing using a printer or plotter. This printer may be directly connected to an AutoCAD workstation or on the network of workstations. Although the process of plotting is very simple, it is important to know how to establish communication between AutoCAD and the plotter. In this chapter, you will learn to connect a plotter with AutoCAD, define plotting style, and produce professional prints of drawings. You will also learn to print and publish drawings in digital format.

Configuring Plotters

It is assumed that you have connected plotter to your workstation and installed the drivers related to it. Even after doing so, you need to set a connection between the plotter and AutoCAD. You can establish this connection by using the Add-plotter wizard. The following example explains the procedure to connect a plotter to AutoCAD.

Example:

- Start AutoCAD 2020.
- Click **Application Menu > Print > Manage Plotters** or type **PLOTTERMANAGER** in the command line; the **Plotters** folder will be opened, as shown below. All the configured plotters are displayed in this folder.

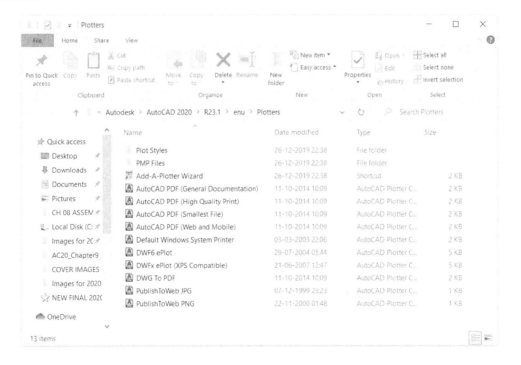

- In the **Plotters** folder, double-click on the **Add-A-Plotter Wizard** icon; the **Add Plotter – Introduction** page appears.
- Click the **Next** button; the **Add Plotter – Begin** page appears. In this page, there are three options that allow you to setup a plotter: **My Computer**, **Network Plotter Server**, and **System Printer**. These options are explained on the dialog box itself, as shown below.
- Select the **System Printer** option and click **Next**; the **System Printer** page appears. A list of printers installed on your workstation is displayed, as shown below.

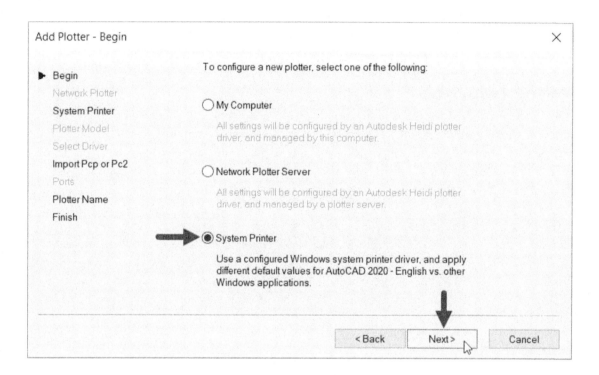

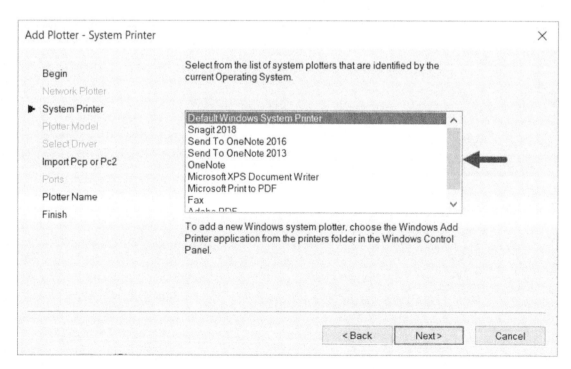

- From the list, select the required printer and click **Next**; the **Import** page appears.

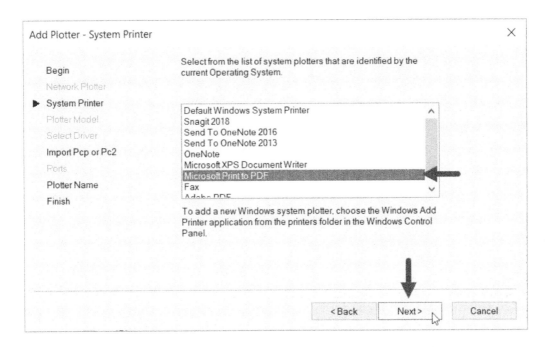

- As you are configuring the plotter for first time, click the **Next** button; the **Plotter Name** page appears.

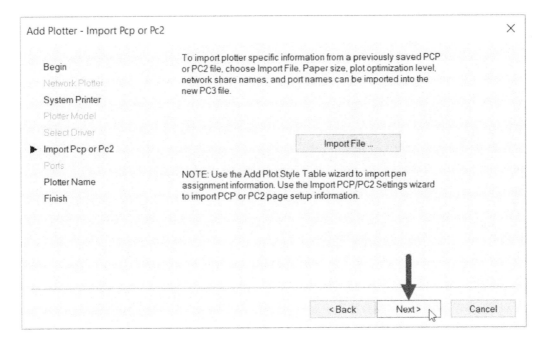

- Type name of the plotter in the **Plotter Name** box and click **Next**; the **Finish** page appears. You can edit the configuration of the plotter by using the **Edit Configuration** button.

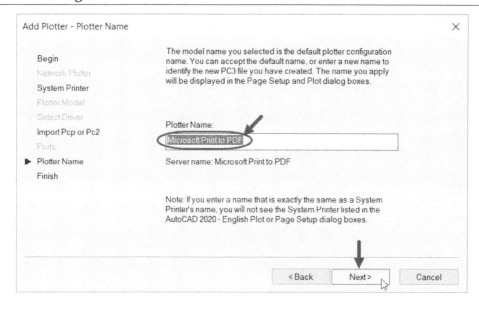

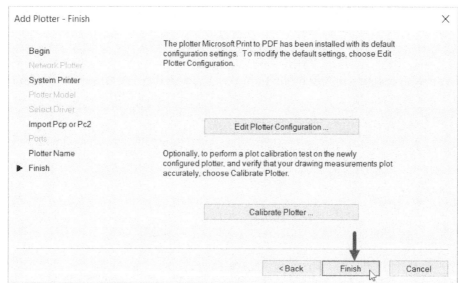

If you click the **Edit Plotter Configuration** button, the **Plotter Configuration Editor** dialog box appears. In this dialog box, you can modify the default settings of the plotter. The **Calibrate Plotter** button is used to test the plotter.

- Click the **Finish** button; a new plotter will be added to the **Plotters** folder.

Creating Plot Style Tables

Plot styles determine the final look of the plotted drawing. They are used to override the layer properties such as color, linetype, lineweight and so on when the drawing is printed. After configuring a plotter, you need to create a plot style. Basically, there are two types of the plot styles: **Color-dependent** and **Named** plot style. The **Color-dependent** plot styles are assigned based on the object color, whereas the **Named** plot styles are assigned based on layer or by object.

- On the **Application Menu**, click **Print > Manage Plot styles** or type **STYLESMANAGER** in the command line; the **Plot Styles** folder appears.

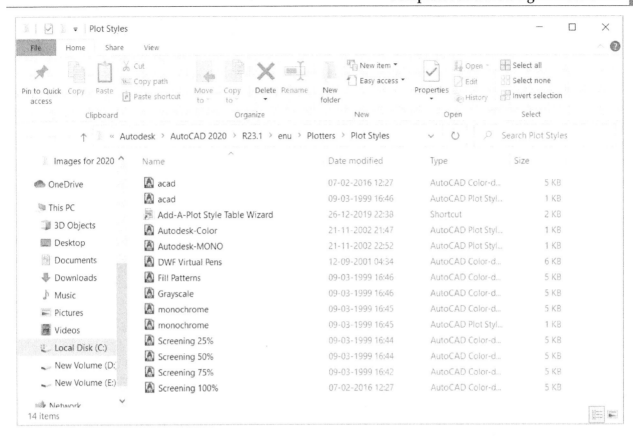

- Double-click on the **Add-A-Plot Style Table Wizard** icon; the **Add Plot Style Table** dialog box appears. Read the information on this dialog box and click **Next**.

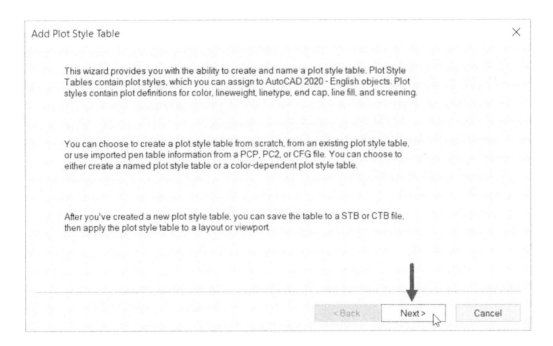

- Select the **Start from Scratch** option and click **Next**.

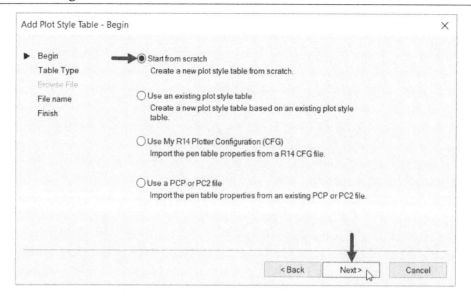

- Select the **Named Plot Style Table** option and click **Next**.

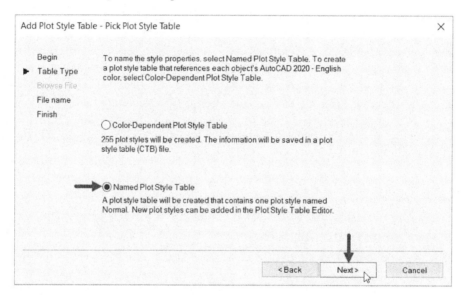

- Enter **Sample** in the **File name** box and click N**ext**; the **Finish** page appears.

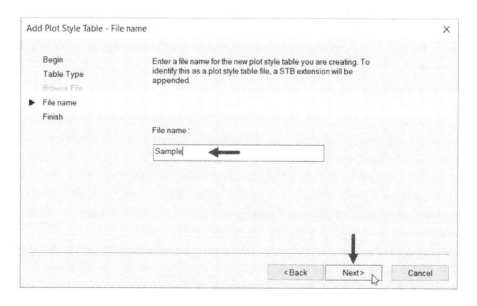

- Click the **Plot Style Table Editor** button; the **Plot Style Table Editor** dialog box appears.

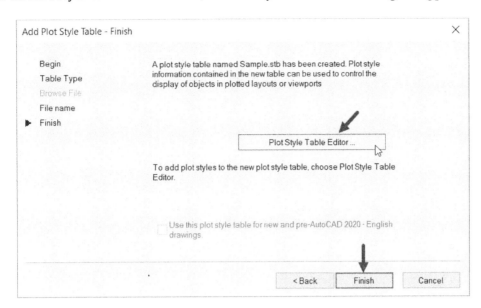

- Click the **Add Style** button available at the bottom left of the dialog box; a new style named **Style 1** will be added.

- Enter **PS1** in the **Name** box.
- Select **Black** from the **Color** drop-down.
- Set the **Screening** value to **70**. The screening factor will fade objects in the printed output. A **20%** screening factor will result in more fading of objects than a **50%** screening factor.

- Click **Save & Close** to the **Plot Style Table Editor** dialog box.
- Click **Finish** to close the **Add Plot Style Table** dialog box; the **Sample** plot style will be added to the **Plot Style** folder.

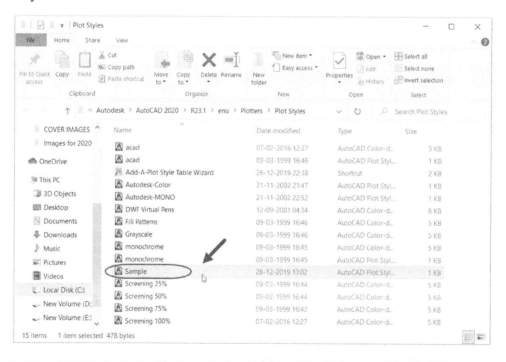

Using Plot Styles

In AutoCAD, the Color-Dependent Plot style is used by default. In order to use the newly created plot style, you need to specify a setting in the **Options** dialog box.

- Right-click in the drawing window and select **Options**; the **Options** dialog box appears.
- Select the **Plot and Publish** tab in the **Options** dialog box and click the **Plot Style Table Settings** button; the **Plot Style Table settings** dialog box appears.

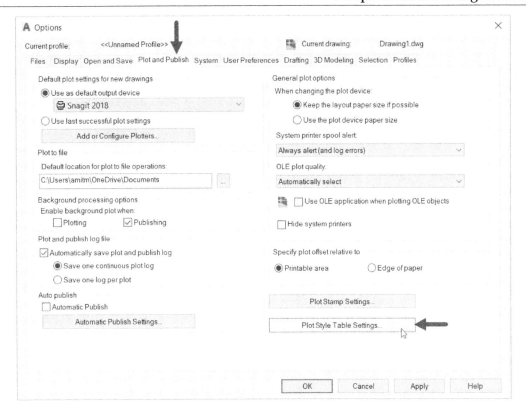

- Select the **Use named plot styles** option from the dialog box, as shown.
- Select **Sample.stb** from the **Default plot style table** drop-down.
- Select **PS1** from the **Default plot style for layer 0** drop-down.
- Set the **Default plot style for objects** to **ByLayer**.

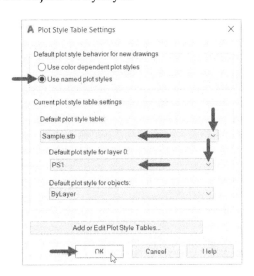

- Click **OK** twice to close both dialog boxes.
- Close the drawing file by clicking the **Close** button located at the top-right corner of the drawing area.
- Click **NO** on the **AutoCAD** alert message.
- Click the **New** button on the **Quick Access Toolbar**; the **Select Template** dialog box appears.
- Select **Open > Open with no Template – Metric** from the bottom right corner of the dialog box; a drawing file will be opened.

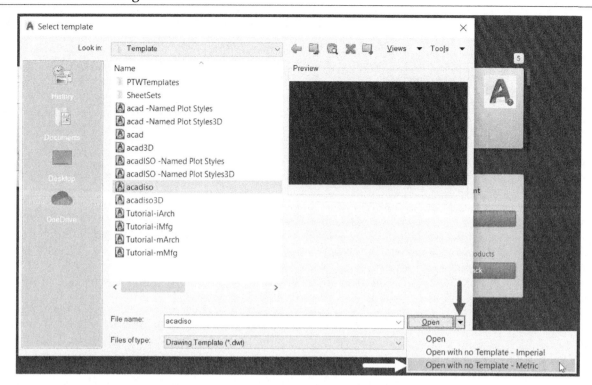

- Open the **Layers Properties Manager** and create the layers contained in the table below:

Layer	Linetype	Lineweight	Plot Style
Construction	Continuous	Default	PS1
Object	Continuous	0.7 mm	PS1
Hidden Lines	Hidden	0.3 mm	PS1
Center Lines	CENTER	0.25 mm	PS1
Dimensions	Continuous	0.25 mm	PS1
Section Lines	Continuous	0.5 mm	PS1
Cutting Plane	Phantom	0.6mm	PS1
Title Block	Continuous	1mm	PS1
Viewport	Continuous	0.25 mm	PS1
Text	Continuous	Default	PS1
Title block text	Continuous	Default	PS1

- Click the **Layout 1** tab to activate the paper space.
- Click **Output > Plot > Page setup Manager** on the ribbon; the **Page Setup Manager** dialog box appears.
- Click **Modify** on the **Page Setup** Manager; the **Page Setup** dialog box appears.
- Under the **Printer/plotter** group, select the plotter that you have configured to your workstation.

- Set the **Paper Size** to **A3** and **Drawing Orientation** to **Landscape**.
- Click **OK** and **Close** to exit both the dialog boxes.
- Draw a title block in the paper space as shown below.

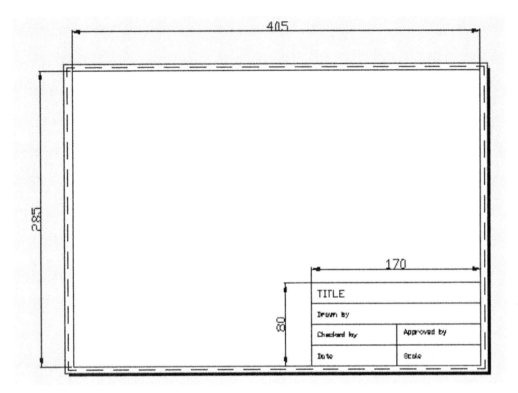

- Create a viewport inside the title block.

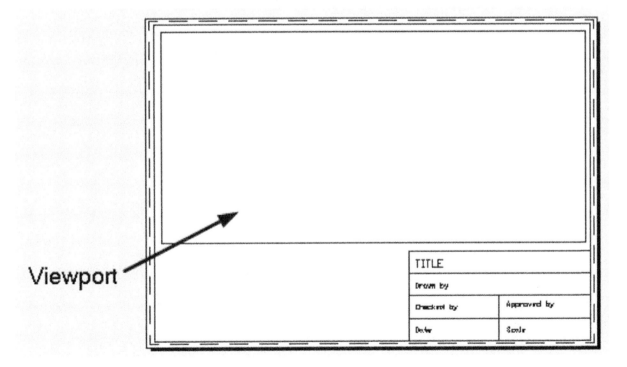

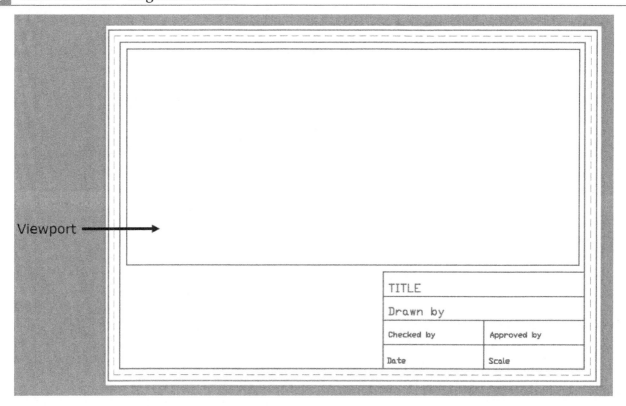

Viewport

TITLE

Drawn by

Checked by | Approved by

Date | Scale

Creating Templates

After specifying the required settings in a drawing file, you can save those settings for the future use. You can do so by creating a template. Template files have settings such as units, limits, and layers already created, which will increase your productivity. In previous sections, you have configured various settings, such as layers, colors, linetypes and plotting settings. Now, you will create a template file containing all of these settings and the title block that you have created.

- On the **Quick Access toolbar**, click the **Save** button; the **Save Drawing As** dialog box appears.
- In the **Save Drawing As** dialog box, set **Files of type** to **AutoCAD Drawing Template (*.dwt).**
- Enter **ISOA3** in the **File name** box and click **Save**.

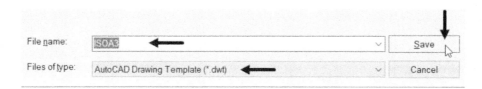

- In the **Template Options** dialog box, enter **ISO-A3 Horizontal layout with title block** in the **Description** box.

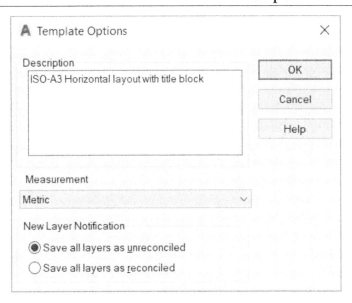

- Click **OK** to close the dialog box and save the template files.

Plotting/Printing the drawing

- Click on the **Start** tab.
- Select **Get Started** > **Templates** > **ISOA3.dwt**. A new drawing will start with the selected template.

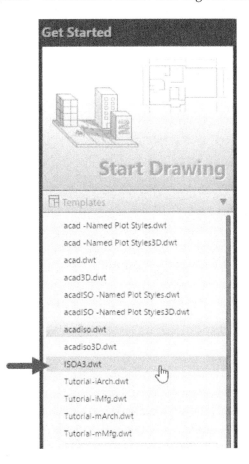

- Open the **Layer Properties Manager**; you will notice that the layers saved in the template file are loaded automatically.

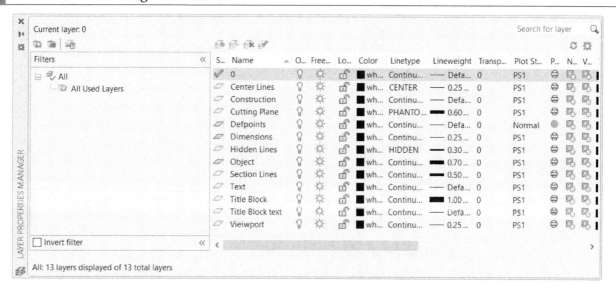

- Close the **Layer Properties Manager**.
- Create a drawing as shown below.

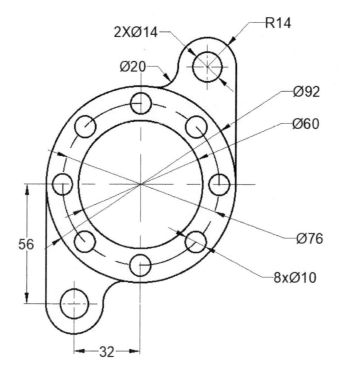

- Click the **Layout 1** tab to activate the paper space.
- Double-click inside the viewport to activate the model space.
- Set the **Viewport Scale** to 1:1 on the status bar.
- Use the **Pan** tool and position the drawing in the center of the view port.
- Double-click outside the viewport to activate the paper space.
- Hide the viewport frame by freezing the **Viewport** layer, as shown.

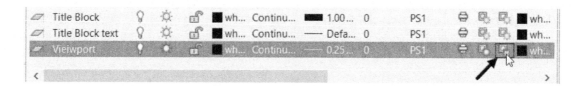

- Click the **Plot** button on the **Quick Access Toolbar**; the **Plot** dialog box appears.

- Make sure that the options in this dialog box are same as that you specified while creating the template.
- Click the **Preview** button located at the bottom left corner; the preview window appears.
- Click the **Zoom Original** button to fit the drawing to the window.

- Examine print preview for the desired output and click the **Plot** button; the drawing will be plotted.

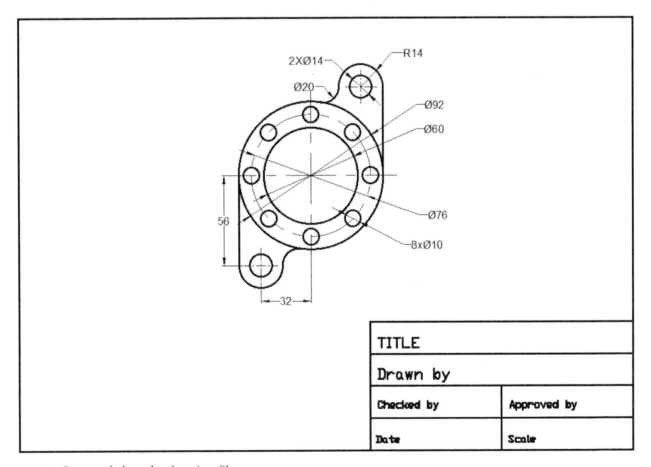

- Save and close the drawing file.

Questions:

1. Which option is selected to display the **Plotters** folder?
2. Which option is selected to display the **Plot Styles** folder?
3. Where is **Page setup Manager** button available in the Ribbon?
4. Which button is selected to display the **Select template** dialog box?
5. Which button is selected to display the **Plots Style Table settings** dialog box?

Exercise

Exercise 1:

Create and plot the drawing as shown in figure.

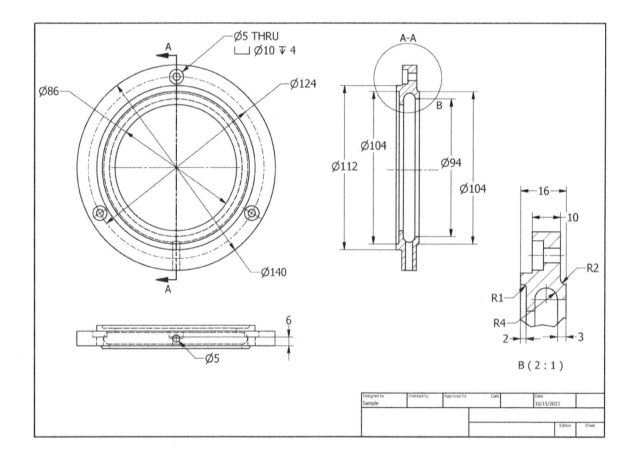

Chapter 12: 3D Modeling Basics in AutoCAD

In this chapter, you will learn to do the following:

- ❖ **Create boxes, cylinders, wedges, cones, pyramids, spheres, and torus**

- ❖ **Create User Coordinate Systems**

- ❖ **Work with Dynamic UCS**

- ❖ **Change the View Style of objects**

- ❖ **Create Viewports in model space**

- ❖ **Create walls using the Polysolid tool**

- ❖ **Change the view orientation**

- ❖ **Create extruded, revolved, swept, lofted, and press-pulled objects**

- ❖ **Perform Boolean operations**

- ❖ **Align objects**

- ❖ **Create spiral and helical curves**

Introduction

In AutoCAD, you can create three types of 3D models: surfaces, solids, and meshes. Solids are used to create 3D models of engineering components and assemblies, surfaces are used to create complex shapes such as plastic parts, and meshes are used for games and movies. Solids are three-dimensional models of actual objects that possess physical properties such as mass properties, center of gravity, surface area, moments of inertia, and so on. Surfaces are construction features without any thickness. They do not possess any physical properties. Meshes are similar to solids without mass and volume properties. In this chapter, you will learn the basics of 3D modeling such as creating, navigating and visualizing solid models.

3D Modeling Workspaces in AutoCAD

In AutoCAD, there are separate workspaces created to work on 3D models. In these workspaces, the tools are organized into ribbon tabs, menus, toolbars, and palettes to perform a specific task in 3D modeling. You can invoke these workspaces by using the **Workspace** drop-down located on the **Quick Access Toolbar**, or by using the **Workspace Switching** menu on the status bar. You can also directly start an AutoCAD session in 3D Modeling using the **acad3D.dwt**, **acadiso3D.dwt**, **acad -Named Plot Styles3D**, or **acadISO-Named Plot Styles3D** templates.

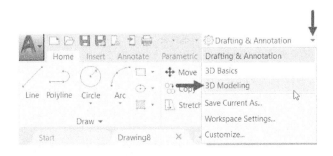

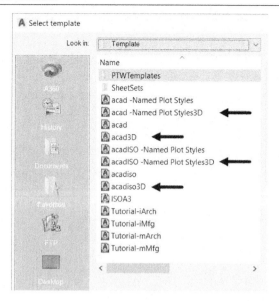

There are two workspaces of 3D modeling: **3D Basics** and **3D Modeling**. The **3D Basics** workspace has commonly used tools, whereas the **3D Modeling** workspace includes all the tools required for creating 3D models.

The 3D Modeling Workspace

Invoking the **3D Modeling** workspace either by using the template or from the **Workspace** drop-down displays the screen as shown below. It contains the ribbon and tools related to 3D modeling. By default, the **Home** tab is activated in the ribbon. From this tab, you can access the tools for creating and editing solids and meshes, modifying the model display, working with coordinate systems, sectioning 3D models and so on.

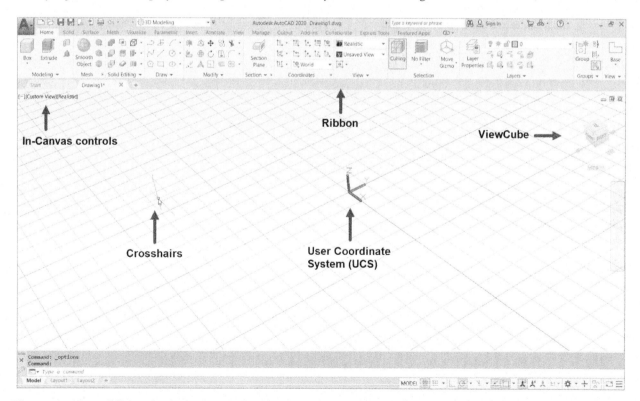

There are some additional tabs such as **Solid, Surface, Mesh**, and **Render**. The **Solid** tab contains tools to create solid models; the **Surface** and **Mesh** tabs are used to create surface models and complex shapes; the **Visualize** tab is used for creating realistic images of solid and surface models.

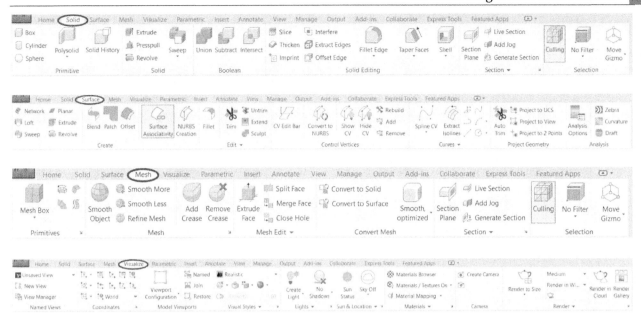

The **ViewCube** can be used to modify the view of the model quickly and easily. It is located at the top right corner of the drawing window. Using the ViewCube, you can switch between the standard and isometric views, rotate the model, switch to the **Home** view of the model, and create a new user coordinate system, and so on. You can also change the way the ViewCube functions by using the **ViewCube Settings** dialog box. Right-click on the ViewCube, and then select the **ViewCube Settings** option; the **ViewCube Settings** dialog box will be opened.

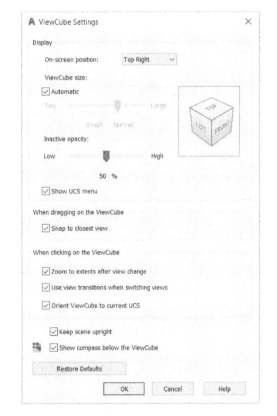

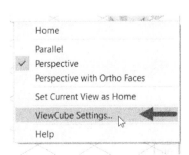

You can also modify the model view by using the In-canvas controls. In addition to that, you also change the view style of the model and control the display of other tools in the drawing window using the In-canvas controls.

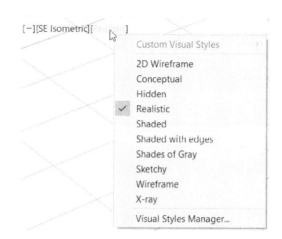

Now, you will create 3D models using the tools available in AutoCAD.

The Box tool

The **Box** tool is used to create boxes having six rectangular or square faces. It is most commonly used tool as many 3D objects are made of boxes.

- Click the **AutoCAD 2020** icon on your desktop.
- On the welcome screen, click **Get Started > Templates > acadiso3D.dwt**. A new file will be started in the **3D Modeling** workspace.

    Alternatively, click on the **New** icon from the **Quick Access toolbar** and then click on the **acadiso3D** from the **Select template** dialog box. A new file will be started in the **3D Modeling** workspace.

- Click **Home > Modeling > Box** on the ribbon or type **BOX** in the command line; the message, "**Specify the first corner**" appears in the command line.
- Pick an arbitrary point in the drawing window; the message, "**Specify the other corner**" appears in the command line.
- Ensure that the **Dynamic Input** is active on the status bar. You will notice that two value boxes are displayed to specify the length and width of the box.
- Type **120** in the length box and press the **TAB** key.
- Type **80** in the width box and press **ENTER**.
- Move the cursor upward, type **70** as height and press **ENTER**; the box will be created as shown below.

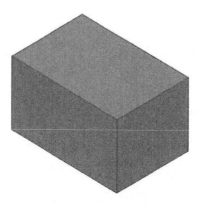

Creating the User Coordinate System

User Coordinate Systems assist you while creating 3D models. They are used to create construction planes on which you can add additional features to the models. Various methods to create User coordinate systems are discussed next.

Example :

- Deactivate the **Dynamic UCS** option on the status bar. You will learn about this option later in this chapter.

- Click **Home > Coordinates > UCS** on the ribbon; the UCS is attached to the cursor and the message, "Specify the origin of UCS" appears.

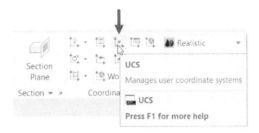

- Ensure that **3D Object Snap** is activated on the status bar.

- Select the vertex point on the top left corner of the box as shown below; the message, "**Specify point on X-axis or <accept>:**" appears in the command line.
- Press **ENTER** to accept the orientation of the **UCS** as shown below.

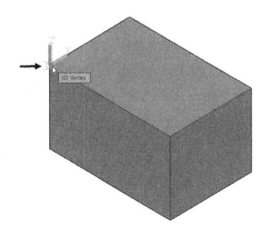 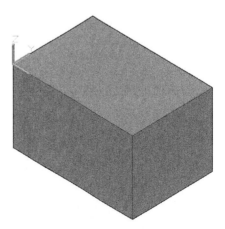

Note: If you find any icon/button missing on the status bar then, click on the **Customization** button to display the menu and select the required option from it, to make it visible on the status bar, as shown.

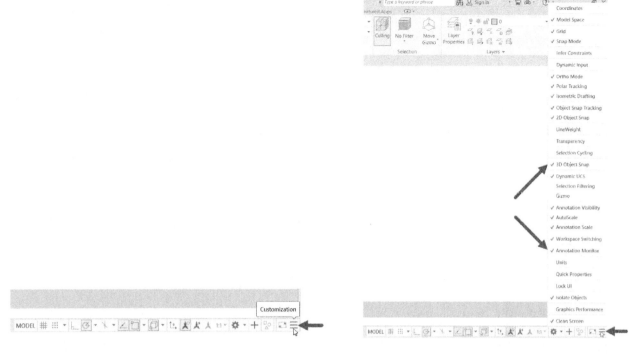

Creating a Wedge

When you slice a box diagonally, it results in a wedge. A wedge has five faces, three rectangular and two triangular.

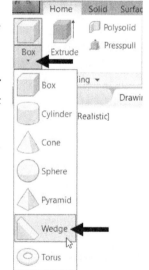

- Click **Home > Modeling > Primitives drop-down > Wedge** on the ribbon or type **WE** in the command line and press **ENTER**; the message, "**Specify first corner or [Center]**" appears in the command line.

- Select the endpoint of the top face of the box as shown in figure; the message, "Specify other corner or [Cube Length]:" appears in the command line.

- Select the midpoint of the front edge of the box as shown below.

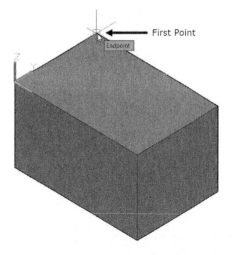

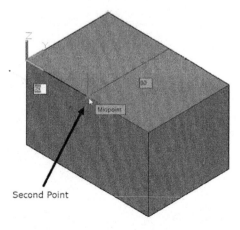

- Move the cursor upward and enter 30 as the height; the wedge will be created, as shown below.

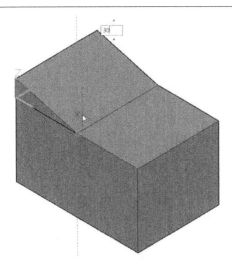

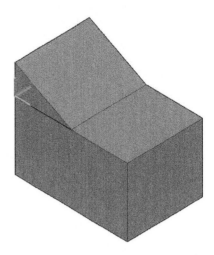

Example : (Creating UCS by selecting 3-points)

You can create a UCS by selecting three points. The first point will be the origin of the UCS, the second point will define the X axis, and the third point defines the Y-axis.

- Click **Home > Coordinates > 3 Point** on the ribbon; the UCS is attached to the cursor and the message, "**Specify new origin point <0,0,0>:**" appears.
- Select the lower endpoint of the wedge as shown in figure.
- Move the cursor toward right and select the other endpoint of the bottom edge of the wedge, as shown in figure.

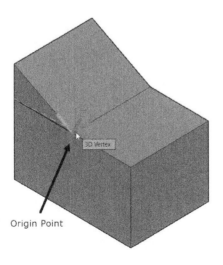

Origin Point

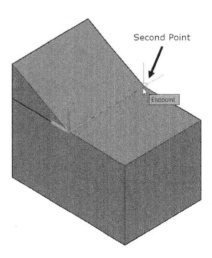

Second Point

- Move the cursor along the diagonal edge of the wedge and select the endpoint on the top edge as shown below; the UCS will be created and aligned to the inclined face of the wedge.

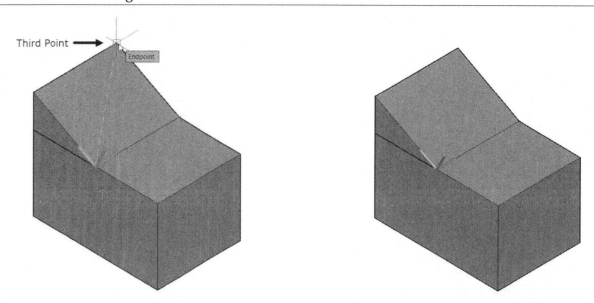

Creating a Cylinder

Cylinders are commonly used features after boxes. In AutoCAD, you can create cylinders easily by using the **Cylinder** tool. You can create a circular or elliptical cylinder by using this tool.

- Click **Home > View > View Style drop-down > Wireframe** on the ribbon; the view style of the model will be changed wireframe.

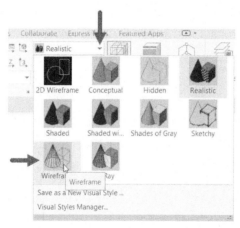

- Also, change the model view from **SE Isometric** to **NE Isometric** from **In-canvas Controls**.

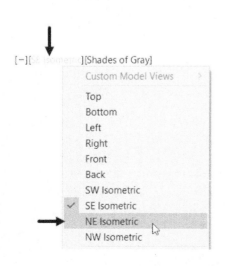

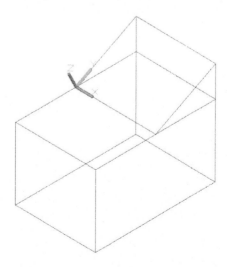

- Deactivate the **3D Object Snap** on the status bar and ensure that the **Object Snap** in turned on.

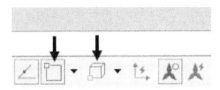

- Click **Home > Modeling > Primitives drop-down > Cylinder** on the ribbon or type **CYL** in the command line.
- Specify the center point of the cylinder on the inclined face of the wedge. You can use the tracelines from the midpoints of the vertical and horizontal edges of the face.
- Type the base radius as **18** and press **ENTER**.

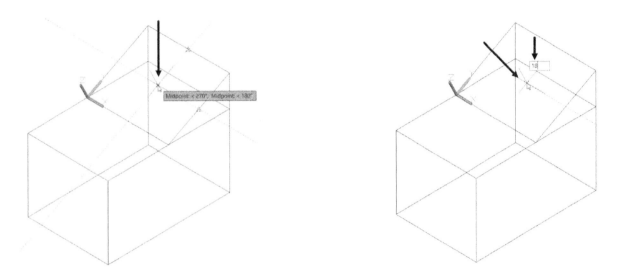

- Move the cursor upward; you will notice that the cursor moves along the Z-axis of the UCS.
- Type **24** as height and press **ENTER**; the cylinder will be created as shown below.

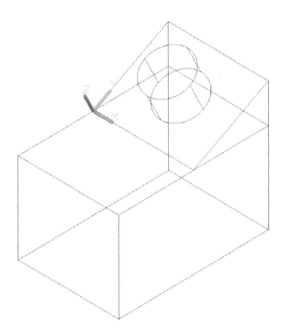

Example : (Returning to previous position of the UCS)

- Click **Home > Coordinates > UCS, Previous** on the ribbon; the UCS will return to its previous position.

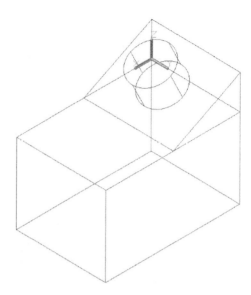

- If you change the model view from **NE Isometric** to **SE Isometric** from **In-canvas Controls**, the object looks.

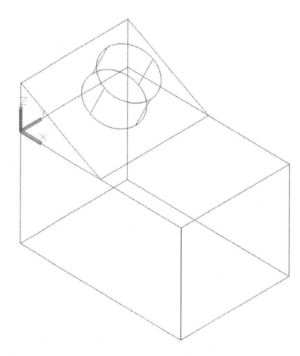

Example : (Creating a UCS by specifying its origin)

- Click **Home > Coordinates > Origin** on the ribbon; the UCS will be attached to the cursor.
- Select the lower left corner point of the box; the UCS will be placed at that point. Note that the orientation will not change.

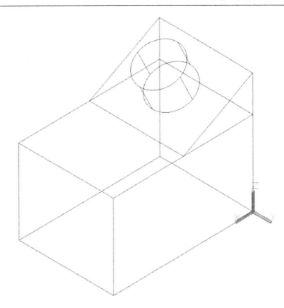

Example: (Rotating the UCS about X, Y, and Z axes)

You can rotate a UCS about X, Y, or Z axes by using the drop-down available in the **Coordinates** panel, as shown below.

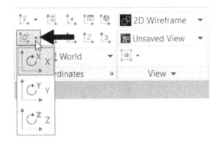

- Click the **X** option from the drop-down shown in the above figure; the message, "**Specify rotation angle about X axis <90>:**" appears in the command line. Also, a rubber band line originating from the Y axis is attached to the cursor.
- Rotate the cursor and pick a point to specify the rotation angle. You can also type-in the rotation angle in the dynamic input or command line.
- Similarly, you can rotate the UCS about the Y and Z axes using the respective options from the drop-down.

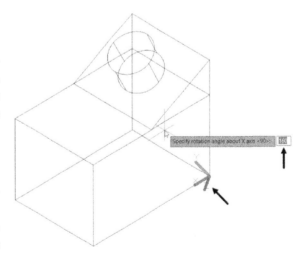

Example: (Creating the UCS by specifying the Z-axis)

Using the **Z-Axis Vector** tool, you can create a UCS by specifying its Z-axis.

- Click **Home > Coordinates > Z-Axis Vector** on the ribbon.
- Select the bottom right endpoint as the origin; the message, "**Specify point on positive portion of Z-axis:**" appears in the command line. Also, a rubber band line originating from the Z-axis is attached to the cursor. Now, as you move the cursor, you will notice that the Z-axis also moves.
- Move the cursor and select the right endpoint of the bottom right edge as shown below; the Z-axis will be aligned to the bottom edge.

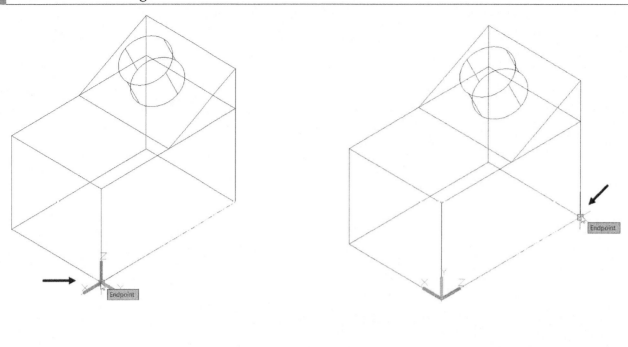

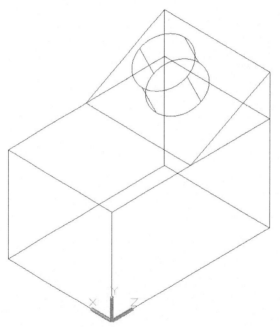

Example: (Creating UCS parallel to the screen)

Using the **View** tool in the **Coordinates** panel, you can create a UCS which is parallel to the screen.

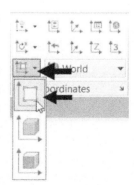

- Click **Home > Coordinates > View drop-down > View** ⌶ on the ribbon; the XY plane of the UCS will become parallel to the screen. The UCS origin will not change. This option is useful if you want to use the current view and add a title block, or any other annotation.

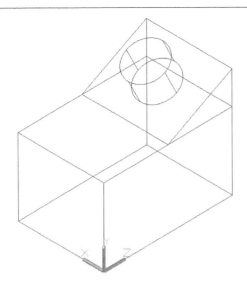
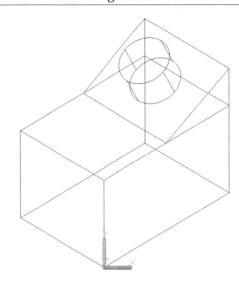

Example: (Creating UCS aligned to an object)

You can create a UCS aligned to an object. The origin of the UCS will be aligned to the nearest endpoint of the object.

- Click **Home > Coordinates > View drop-down > Object** on the ribbon; the message, "**Select object to align UCS:**" appears in the command line.
- Select the cylindrical object from the model; the UCS will be aligned to it.

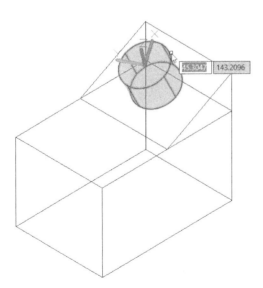
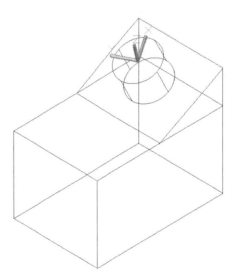

Example: (Creating UCS aligned to face)

You can align a UCS to a planar or curved face of a model using the **Face** tool.

- Click **Home > Coordinates > View drop-down > Face** on the ribbon; the message, "**Select face of solid, surface, or mesh:**" appears in the command line.
- Move the cursor over the front faces of the model; you will notice that the UCS is displayed on the faces.

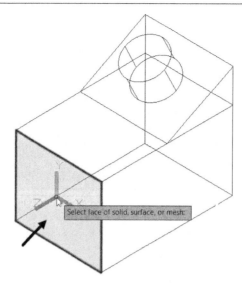

- Now, click on the selected face of the box; the message, "**Enter an option [Next Xflip Yflip]** **<accept>:**" appears in the command line.

  If you select the **Next** option, the adjacent face will be highlighted. The **Xflip** option is used to rotate the UCS **180** degrees about the X axis. The **Yflip** option is used to rotate the UCS **180** degrees about the Y axis.

- Press **ENTER** to accept; the UCS will be aligned to the selected face.

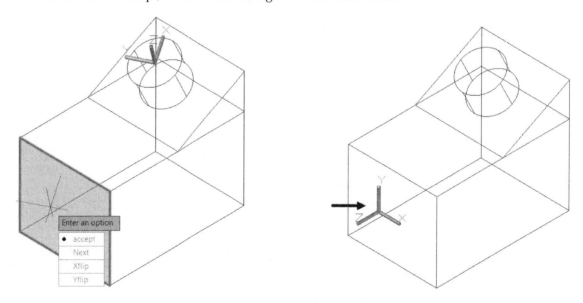

Using Dynamic User Coordinate System

In the previous section, you have learned to create various types of static user coordinate systems. They are active until you define another user coordinate system. You can also create dynamic user coordinate systems. A Dynamic User Coordinate System is a temporary UCS that appears automatically when you place your cursor over the face of a 3D solid object. Note that the Dynamic User Coordinate appears only when you use tools which create objects directly (For example, drawing tools and primitive tools). In order to create a Dynamic UCS, you need to activate the **Dynamic UCS** option on the status bar.

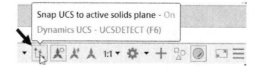

- Click the **Cylinder** button from the **Modeling** panel.
- Ensure that the **Dynamic UCS** button is active on the status bar.
- Move the cursor over the side face of the model; it will get highlighted, as shown.
- Click on the side face of the box and create the cylinder as shown.

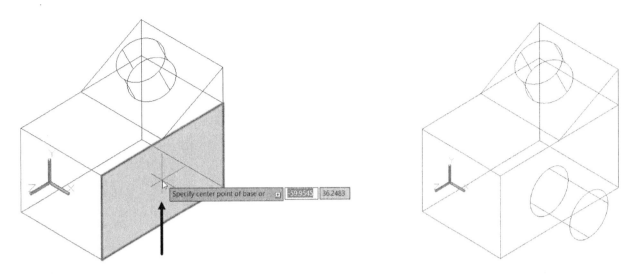

Model Space Viewports For 3D Modeling

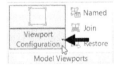

While creating 3D models, it is useful to have a look at your model from several different orientations at the same time. For this purpose, you need to create different viewports in modelspace. You can create multiple viewports in modelspace using the **Viewport Configuration** drop-down available in the **Model Viewports** panel of the **Visualize** tab. This can also be done by using the **Viewports** dialog box. To load this dialog box, click **Visualize > Model Viewport > Named** [Named] to display the **Viewports** dialog box. In the dialog box, select the **New Viewports** tab and then select **Four: Equal** from the **Standard viewports** list. Next, select **3D** from the **Setup** drop-down. Click the **OK** button; four tiled view-ports are displayed in the screen. You can notice that each viewport has a different view and a different UCS. Click inside any viewport to activate it and perform any operation. To return to single viewport, click the **Restore Viewports** [Restore] button on the **Model Viewports** panel; the currently active viewport will fill the screen area.

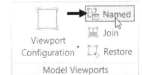

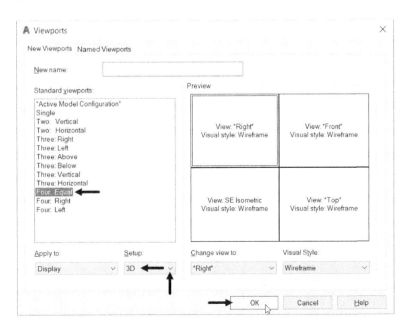

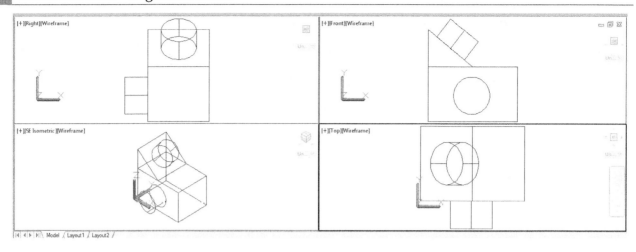

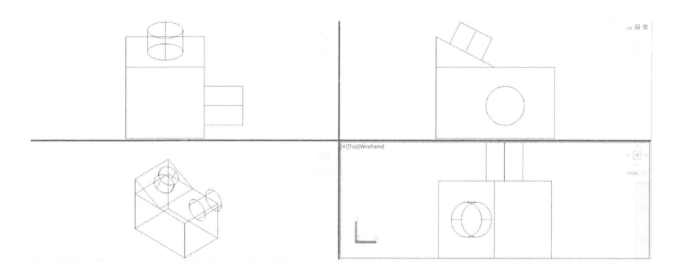

Creating Other Primitive Shapes

In AutoCAD, there are set of tools to create basic geometric shapes. In earlier sections, you have learned to create boxes, wedges, and cylinders. Now, you will learn to create other primitive shapes.

Creating Cones

Creating a cone is similar to creating a cylinder. It has a similar shape compared to a cylinder; but it is tapered on one side.

Example:

- To create a cone, click **Home > Modeling > Primitives drop-down > Cone** on the ribbon; the message, "**Specify center point of base or [3P 2P Ttr Elliptical]:**" appears in the command line.
- Pick an arbitrary point from the drawing window; the message, "**Specify base radius or [Diameter]:**" appears.
- Type a radius value in the command line and press **ENTER**. You can also select the **Diameter** option to specify the diameter of the base.
- Move the cursor in vertical direction and pick a point to specify the height of the cone. You can also type-in the height value in the command line and press **ENTER**; the cone will be created.

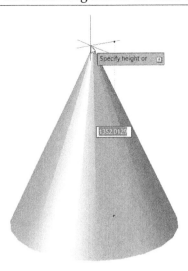

Example:

- Type **CONE** in the command line and press **ENTER**.
- Select the **Elliptical** option from the command line; the message, "**Specify endpoint of first axis or [Center]:**" appears in the command line.
- Pick a point to specify the end point of the first axis.
- Move the cursor and click specify the other end point of the first axis. You can also type-in the length of the first axis and press **ENTER**; the message, "**Specify endpoint of second axis:**" appears.
- Pick a point or type-in the radius value to specify the second axis.
- Move the cursor upward and pick a point to specify the height. You can also enter the value of height in the command line or **Dynamic Input** box.

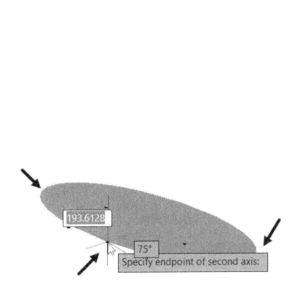

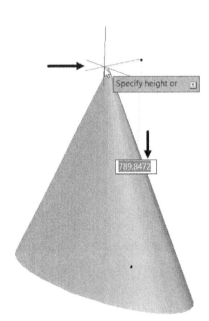

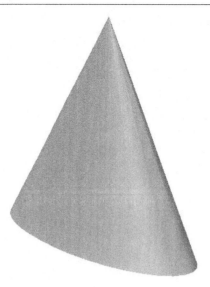

Example:

- Click **Solid > Primitive > Primitive drop-down > Cone** on the ribbon.
- Select the center point and specify the base radius as **200**; the message, "**Specify height or [2Point Axis endpoint Top radius]**" appears in the command line.
- Select the **Top radius** option from the command line; the message, "**Specify top radius:**" appears.
- Type **100** as the top radius value and press **ENTER**.
- Move the cursor upward and enter **400** as the height.

Creating a Sphere

- Click **Home > Modeling > Primitives drop-down > Sphere** on the ribbon.
- Specify the center point of the sphere.
- Move the cursor outward and enter the radius value. You can also select the **Diameter** option to specify the diameter of the sphere.

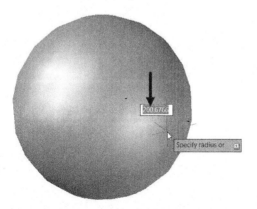

Creating a Pyramid

Pyramids are similar to cones except that the base of the pyramid is not circular in shape.

- To create a pyramid, click **Home > Modeling > Primitives drop-down > Pyramid** on the ribbon or type **PYR** in the command line and press **ENTER**.

- Specify the center point of the base. The base of pyramid is a polygon. The method to create a polygon is already discussed in Chapter 2.
- After creating the base, move the cursor in vertical direction and pick a point to specify the height of the pyramid. You can also type the value of the height and press **ENTER**; the pyramid will be created.

  The other options displayed in the command line while creating the pyramid are same as in the **Cone** tool.

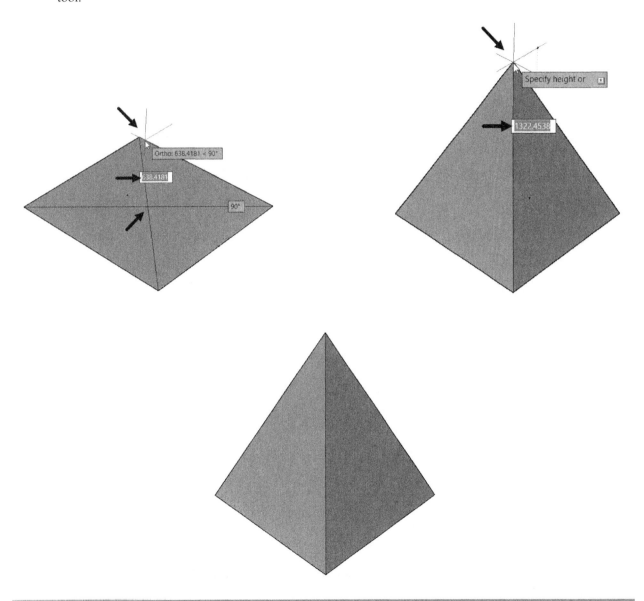

Creating a Torus

Torus is a donut shaped solid primitive. To create a torus, you need to specify center of the torus, radius or diameter of torus, and radius or diameter of the tube.

- Click **Home > Modeling > Primitives drop-down >Torus** 🔘 Torus on the ribbon or type **TOR** in the command line and press **ENTER**.
- Specify the center point of the torus.
- Move the cursor outward and enter the radius of the torus. You can also select the **Diameter** option to specify the diameter of the torus.
- Type the tube radius and press **ENTER**; the torus will be created.

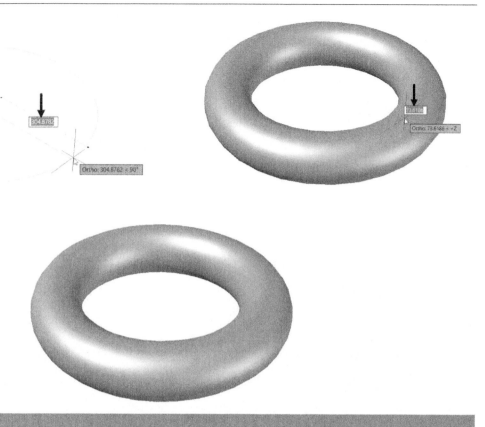

Creating a Wedge

Wedge is used to create a 3D solid wedge with taper in one end. The direction of the taper is always in the X + direction of the UCS. To create a torus, you need to specify start point, end point, and height.

- Click **Home > Modeling > Primitives drop-down > Wedge** on the ribbon or type **WE** in the command line and press **ENTER**.
- Specify the start point as first corner of the wedge.
- Move the cursor outward and enter **100** in both **Dynamic Input** boxes as length in both directions. Now press **ENTER**.

  Alternatively, you can simply enter **100, 100** in the command line.

- Move the cursor in upwards direction and enter **90** as height of wedge and press **ENTER**; the wedge will be created.

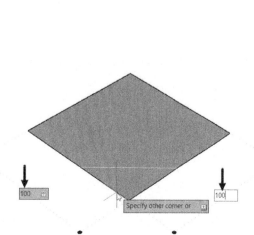

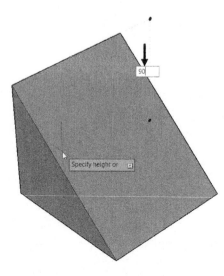

Using the Polysolid tool

The **Polysolid** [Polysolid] tool is used to create a 3D wall. It can also be used to convert a line, polyline, arc,or a circleto a wall. The **Polysolid** tool is similar to **Polyline** tool except that you create a rectangular shaped wall that has a pre-defined height and width.

- Click **Home > Modeling > Polysolid** [Polysolid] on the ribbon; the message, "**Specify start point or [Object Height Width Justify] <Object>:**" appears in the command line.
- Activate the **Ortho Mode** on the status bar.
- Pick an arbitrary point in the drawing window and move the cursor in the X-direction.
- Type **150** in the command line and press **ENTER**; a 3D wall of 150 length is created.
- Select the **Arc** option from the command line and move the cursor in the Y-direction.
- Type **100** as the arc diameter and press **ENTER**.
- Select the **Line** option from the command line and move the cursor in the –X-direction.
- Type **50** and press **ENTER**.
- Move the cursor in the Y-direction and enter **100** as the wall length.
- Move the cursor in –X-direction and enter **100** as the wall length.
- Select the **Close** option from the command line; the wall will be closed.

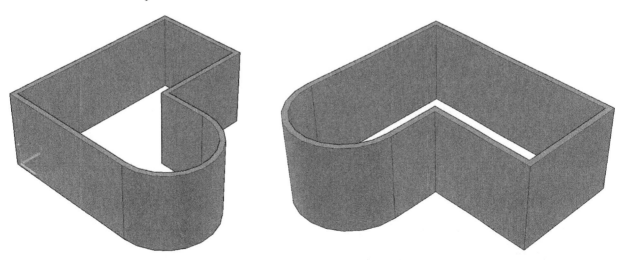

Using the Extrude tool

The **Extrude** [Extrude] tool is used to add a third dimension (height) to an existing 2D shape. If you extrude a closed shape such as circle and closed polylines, a solid is created. If you extrude an open sketch such as lines and arcs, a surface is created.

- Start a new AutoCAD file in **3D Modeling** workspace.
- Click **Home > View > 3D Navigation > Front** on the ribbon; the front view will become parallel to the screen.
- Click **Home > Draw > Polyline** on the ribbon and create the sketch as shown below.

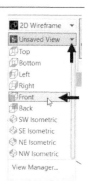

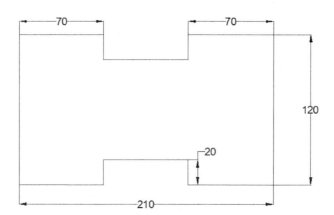

- Select **SE Isometric** from the **In-canvas controls**; the view orientation will be changed **SE Isometric** (South East Isometric).

- Click **Home > Modeling > Extrude.**
- Select the polyline sketch and move the cursor toward right.
- Type **200** in the command line or **Dynamic Input** box and press **ENTER**; the polyline sketch will be extruded.

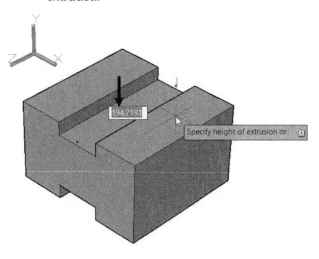

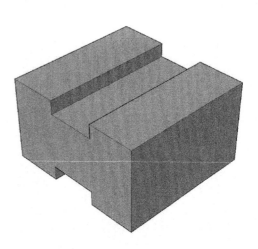

Example:

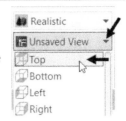

- Open a new AutoCAD file in **3D Modeling** Workspace.
- Click **Home > View > 3D Navigation > Top** on the ribbon; the view will become parallel to the screen.
- Click **Home > Draw > Line** on the ribbon and create the sketch as shown below.

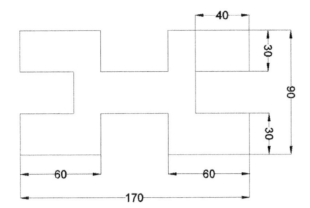

- Click **Home > View > 3D Navigation >SW Isometric** on the ribbon; the view orientation will be changed to south west Isometric.

- Expand the **Draw** panel of the **Home** tab and click the **Region** button.

  Alternatively, enter **REG** in the command line to activate the **Region** tool.

- Press and drag a window and select all the objects of the sketch.
- Press **ENTER**; the sketch will be converted into a region. Now, you can extrude the region to create a solid. If you try to extrude the lines without creating a region, it will result in a surface.

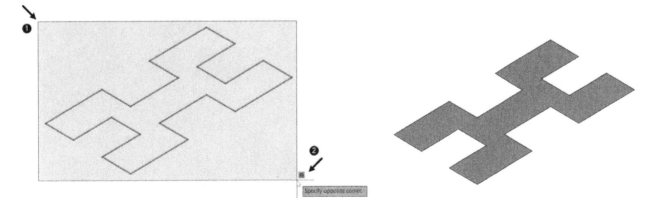

- Click **Solid > Solid > Extrude** [Extrude] on the ribbon.
- Select the region and press **ENTER**; the message, "**Specify height of extrusion or [Direction Path Taper angle Expression]:**" appears in the command line.
- Select the **Tape angle** option from the command line.
- Type **15** as the taper angle and press **ENTER**.
- Move the cursor upward, type **20** in the command line and press **ENTER**; the extruded solid will be created with a taper.

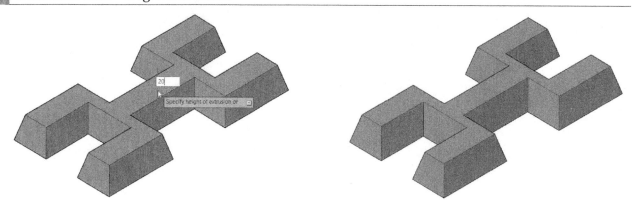

Example:

- Click **Home > View > 3D Navigation > SE Isometric** on the ribbon; the view orientation will be changed to south east Isometric.
- Type **EXT** in the command line and press **ENTER** to activate the **Extrude** tool.
- Press and hold the **CTRL** key and select the top face of the model.
- Press **ENTER** and move the cursor upward.
- Type **20** as the extrusion height and press **ENTER**; the extruded solid will be created.

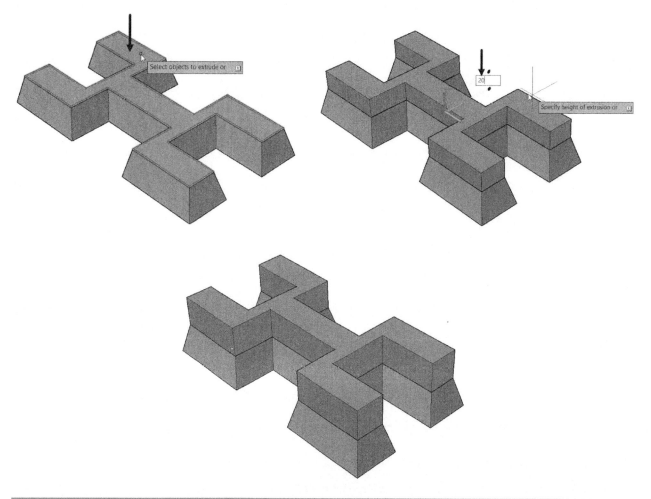

Using the Loft tool

Using the **Loft** [Loft] tool, you can create a solid or surface by selecting a series of cross sections. The selected cross sections will define the shape of the lofted solid.

Example:

Create three circles as shown below. The diameters and center point locations are given in the table.

Circle Center points (Absolute Coordinates)	Circle Diameters
0,0,0	Ø60
0,0,80	Ø120
0,0,160	Ø60

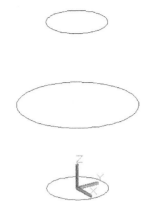

- Click **Home > Modeling > Solids drop-down > Loft** on the ribbon or type **LOFT** in the command line and press **ENTER**.

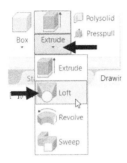

- Select the cross-sections one by one; the preview of the lofted solid appears.
- Press **ENTER** to accept the selection; the message, "**Enter an option [Guides Path Cross sections only Settings] <Cross sections only>:**" appears in the command line.
- Select the **Settings** option from the command line; the **Loft Settings** dialog box appears. In this dialog box, the **Smooth Fit** option is selected by default. As a result, a smooth connection is created between the cross-sections. If you select the **Ruled** option, the lofted solid or surface has sharp edges.

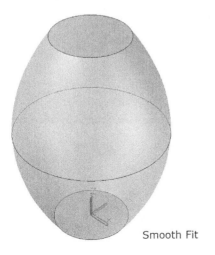

Smooth Fit

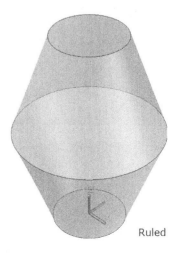

Ruled

The **Normal to** option creates a solid or surface normal to the cross-section. You can select the loft solid or surface to be normal to **Start Cross Section**, or **End Cross Section**, or **Start and End Cross Sections**, or **All cross sections**.

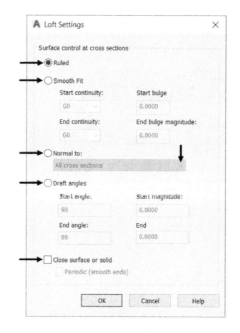

Start cross section   **End cross section**   **All cross section**

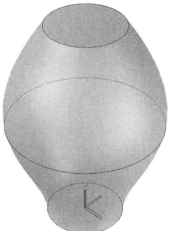 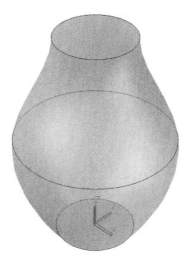 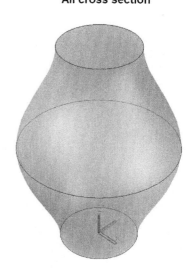

The **Draft angles** option is used to specify the draft angle and magnitude at start and end cross sections. The draft angle is the beginning direction of the loft surface. If you set the draft angle to **90** degrees, the loft surface starts vertically from the cross section and the **0** degrees draft angle starts loft surface horizontally. The Magnitude is the relative distance upto which the loft surface will follow the draft angle before it bends.

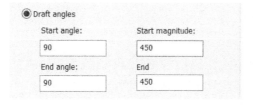

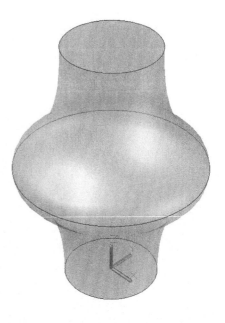

The **Close surface or solid** option connects the start and end section of the lofted object. Note that this option is available only for **Ruled** and **Smooth Fit** surfaces.

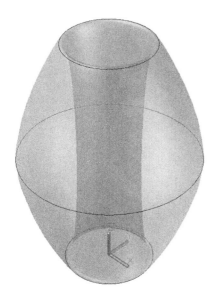 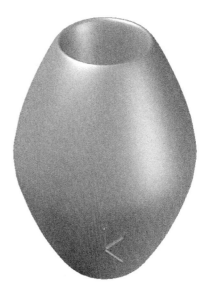

- Select the **Normal to** option and select **All cross sections**. Click **OK**; the loft solid will be created as shown below.

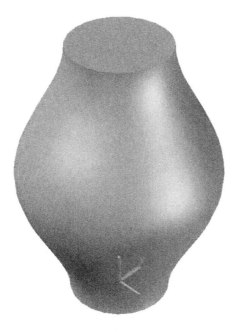

Using the Revolve tool

The **Revolve** [Revolve] tool is used to revolve an open or closed 2D sketch about a selected axis. If you revolve a closed profile such as a polyline sketch, polygon, circle, or a sketch region, a solid object is created. An open profile results in a surface. The sketch is deleted after revolving it. If you want to retain the sketch, you need set the **DELOBJ** system variable to 0.

- Open a new file in **3D Modeling** workspace.
- Set the view orientation to front and create the sketch using the **Line** tool.

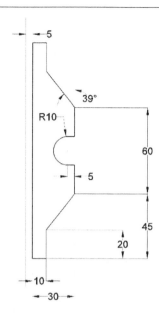

- Convert the sketch into region using the **Region** tool.

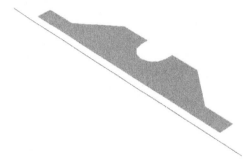

- Click **Solid > Solid > Revolve** on the ribbon or type REV in the command line.
- Select the sketch region and press **ENTER**; the message, "**Specify axis start point or define axis by [Object X Y Z] <Object>:**" appears in the command line.
- Select the **Object** option from the command line and select the vertical line created at an offset; the message, "**Specify angle of revolution or [STart angle Reverse EXpression] <360>:**" appears.
- Press **ENTER** to specify **360** as the revolution angle.

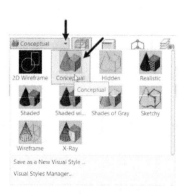

You can also revolve the sketch at a required angle by enter the required value for angle of revolution. Below is the model, revolved at an angle of **270** degrees. For better visibility, we have shown model in Conceptual view also, by selecting the **Conceptual** option from the **Visual Styles** drop-down, as shown.

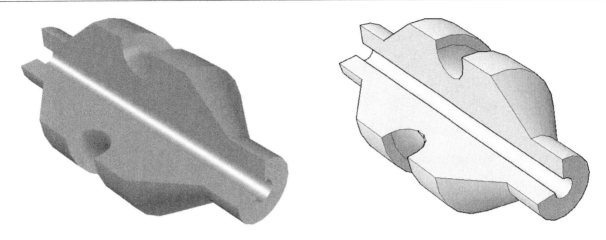

Using the Sweep tool

The **Sweep** [Sweep] tool is used to create a new solid or surface by sweeping a closed or open planar profile along an open or closed 2D or 3D path. The procedure to create a solid by using the **Sweep** tool is discussed next.

Example:

- Open a new file in **3D Modeling** workspace.
- Set the view orientation to **Front** and create the sketch using the **Polyline** tool.

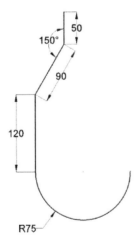

Use the **Fillet** tool and apply fillets of **40** mm radius.

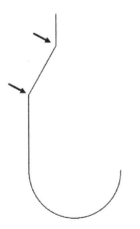

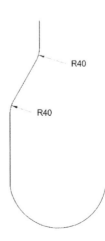

- Change the view orientation to **SE Isometric**.
- Click **Home > Coordinates > Z-Axis Vector** 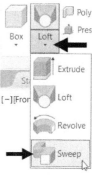 on the ribbon.
- Select the endpoint of the top vertical line as the UCS origin and align the Z-axis to it.

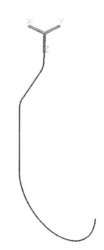

- Click the **Circle** button on the **Draw** panel.
- Select the end point of the vertical line to specify the center point of the circle. Specify **20** mm as radius of the circle.
- Click the **UCS, World** button on the **Coordinates** panel; the User Coordinate System will be set to World Coordinate System (0,0,0).
- Click **Home > Modeling > Solids drop-down > Sweep** on the ribbon.
- Select the circle as the profile and press **ENTER**; the message, "**Select sweep path or [Alignment Base point Scale Twist]:**" appears in the command line.
- Select the path to create the swept solid object.

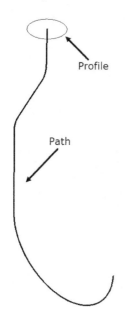

> ➤ The **Alignment** option is used to align the profile perpendicular to the direction of the sweep path. By default, the profile is aligned to the path.

> ➤ The **Base point** option is used to specify the base point of the profile. By, default, the center of the profile is used as the base point. You can select any other point the profile to define the base point.

➢ The **Scale** option is used to scale the profile along the path.

➢ The **Twist** option is used to twist the profile as it is swept along the length of the path.

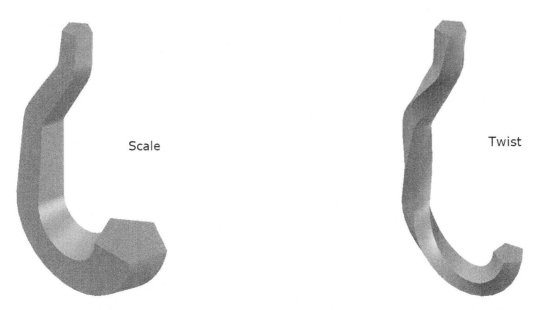

Scale   Twist

Using the Presspull tool

The **Presspull** [Presspull] tool is used to create and modify solid models with a greater ease and speed. It can be used to accomplish two types of operations: extruding closed 2D shapes and add or remove material from a solid object based on whether you "pull" or "push" the extrusion.

- Start a new file.
- Create two layers called **Sketch** and **Solid**. Make the **Sketch** layer are current.
- Set the view orientation to **Right** and draw the sketch as shown below.

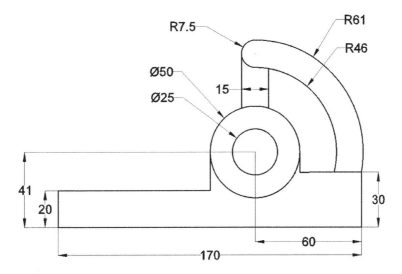

- Change the view orientation to **SE Isometric**.
- Ensure that the **Dynamic Input** is activate
- Set the **Solid** layer are current.
- Click **Home > Modeling > Presspull** on the ribbon.
- Click inside the bottom region of the sketch and move the cursor backwards. Type **80** in the Dynamic input box and press **ENTER**; the extruded feature will be created.

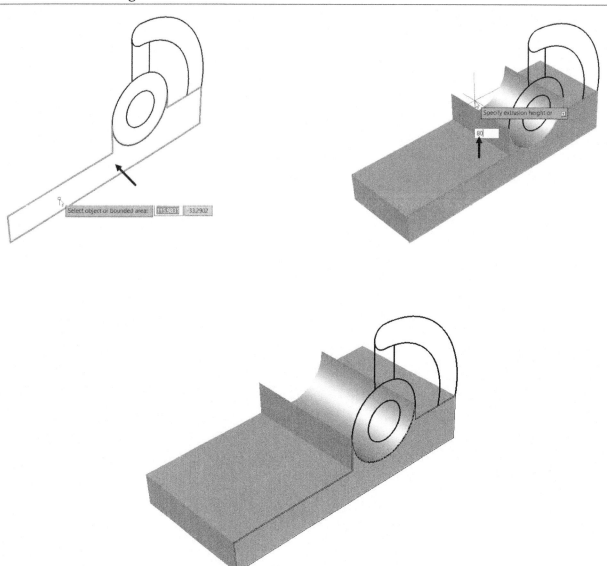

- Click in the region enclosed by the larger circle and extrude it upto **85** mm distance.

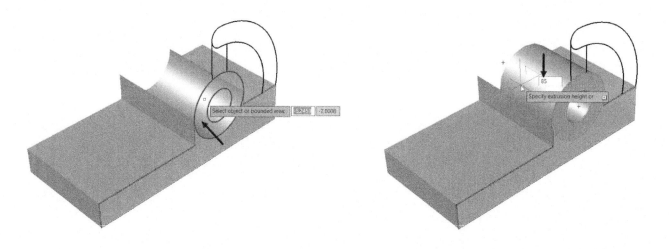

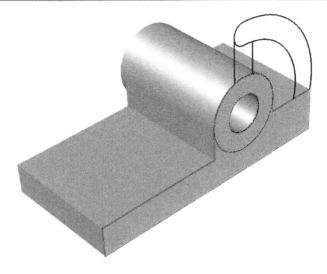

- Press and hold the **CTRL** key and select the front face of the cylindrical object. Move the cursor forward. Type **5** in the dynamic input box and press **ENTER**.

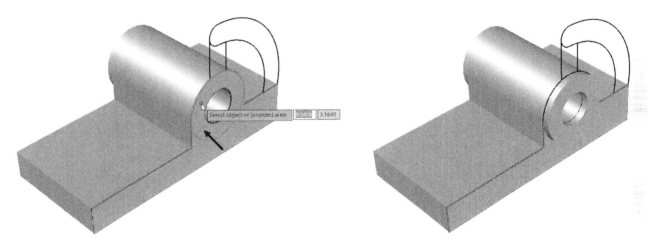

- Click in the curved slot region and move the cursor backward; the message, "**Specify extrusion height or [Multiple]:**" appears in the command line.
- Select the **Multiple** option from the command line and click in the region enclosed by the two vertical lines.
- Right-click and move the cursor backwards. Type **14** in the dynamic input box and press **ENTER**.

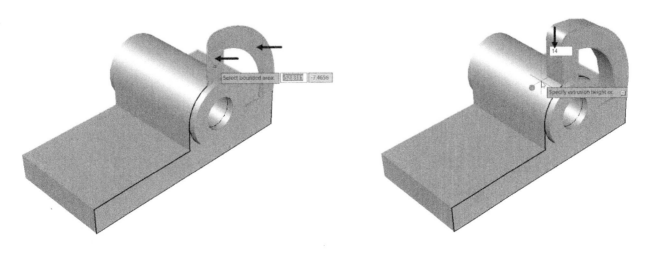

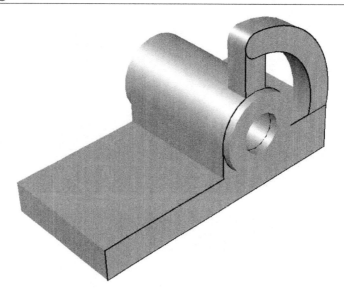

- Press and hold the **CTRL** key and select the front face of the slot and move the cursor forward. Type **5** in the dynamic input box and press **ENTER**.

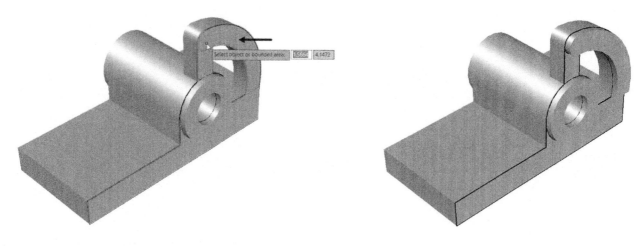

- Set the **Sketch** layer as current.
- Click the **Circle** button on the **Draw** panel.
- Press and hold the **SHIFT** key. Right-click and select the **Center** option from the shortcut menu.
- Select the center point of the slot end cap and create a circle of **5** mm radius.

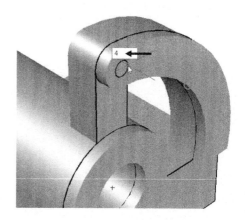

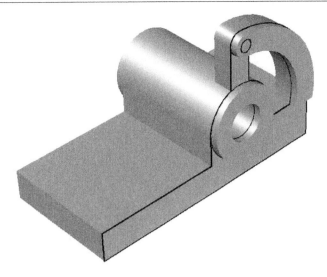

- Click **Home > Modify > Array drop-down > Polar Array** on the ribbon
- Select the recently created circle and press **ENTER**.
- Select the arc as the path curve; the preview of the path array is displayed.

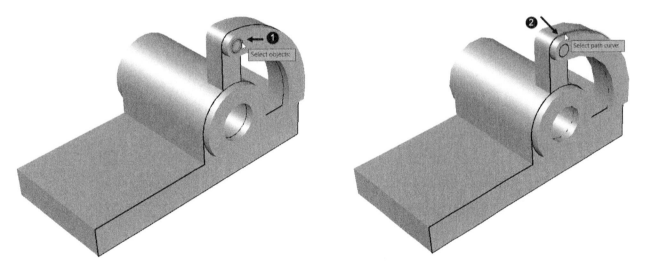

- In the **Array Creation** tab, set the **Between** value to **24**; the item count is automatically adjusted.
- Click the **Close Array** button on the ribbon; the polar array is created.

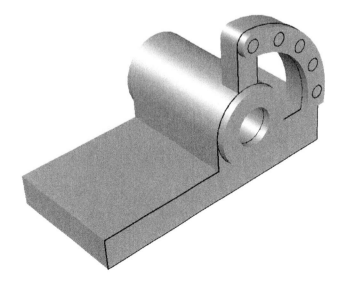

- Activate the **Presspull** tool.
- Click in any one of the circles and select the **Multiple** option from the command line.
- Click inside rest of the circles of the polar array. Right-click to accept.

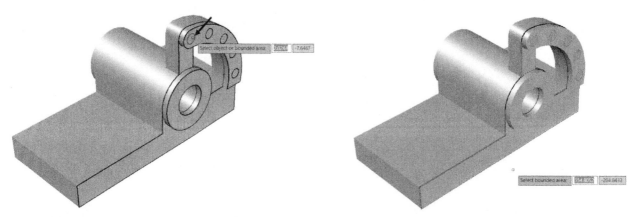

- Move the cursor backward and click; holes will be created as shown in figure.

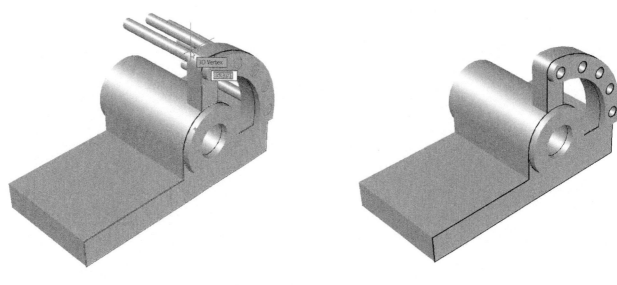

- Turn Off the **Sketch** layer; the sketches will be hidden.
- Click the **Orbit** button on the **Navigation Bar**.
- Press and drag the left mouse button to rotate the model.

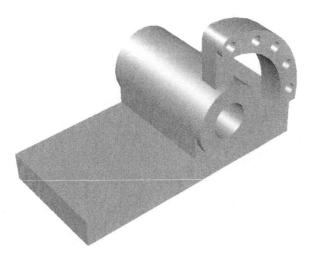
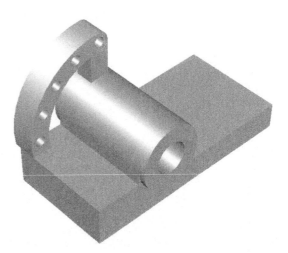

Performing Boolean Operations

Boolean operations are performed to add two or more solids together, subtract a single solid or group of solids from another, or form a common portion when two solids are combined. You need to have at least two solids in order to perform a boolean operation. There are three tools available to perform Boolean Operations- **Union**, **Subtract**, and **Intersect**. These tools are discussed next.

The Union tool

The **Union** tool is used to join two or more solids together into a single solid. For example, when you try to select the complete model, its individual objects are selected. But, after performing the Union operation, all the solid objects are combined together and act as one object.

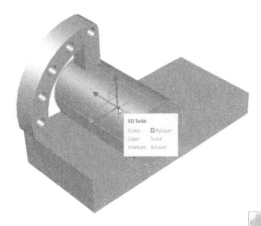

- To perform the Union operation, click **Solids > Boolean > Union** on the ribbon.
- Press and hold the left mouse button and drag a selection window across the model; all the objects of the model will be selected.
- Press **ENTER**; all the solid objects of the model will be combined.

  Now, when you select an individual object, the complete model will be selected.

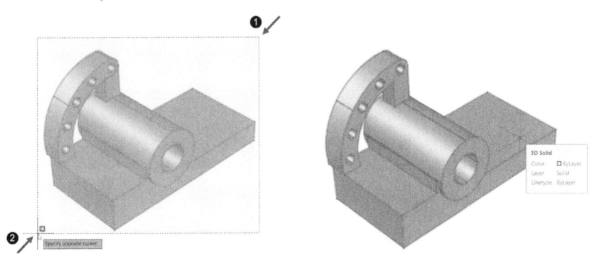

The Subtract tool

The **Subtract** tool is used to subtract one or more solid objects from another object.

- Create two concentric circles of **200** and **180** mm diameter.
- Use the **Presspull** tool and extrude upto 220 mm distance.

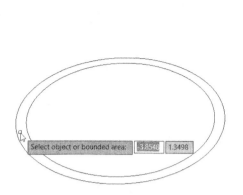

- Set the view orientation to **Right** and create a cylinder of **80** mm diameter and **240** mm length.

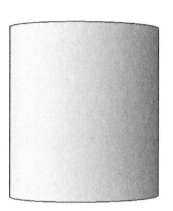

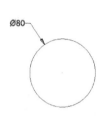

Ø80

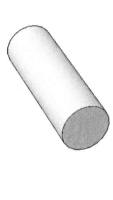

- Expand the **Modify** panel and click the **Align** button.
- Select the horizontal cylinder press **ENTER**; the message, "**Specify first source point:**" appears in the command line.
- Press and hold the **SHIFT** key. Right-click and select the **Center** option.
- Select the center point of the front face of the horizontal cylinder; the message, "**Specify first destination point:**" appears in the command line.
- Press and hold the **SHIFT** key. Right-click and select the **Quadrant** option.
- Select the quadrant point of the outer circle on the top face of the hollow cylinder.
- Press **ENTER**; the horizontal cylinder will be aligned with hollow cylinder.

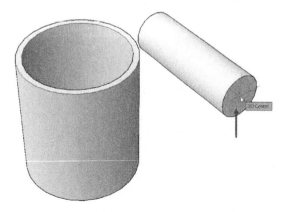

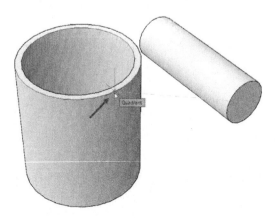

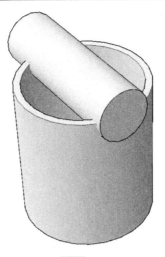

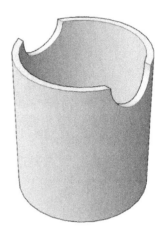

- Click **Solid > Boolean > Subtract** [Subtract] on the ribbon; the message, "**Select solids, surfaces, and regions to subtract from**" appears above the command line.
- Select the hollow cylinder and press **ENTER**; the message, "**Select solids, surfaces, and regions to subtract**" appears above the command line.
- Select the horizontal cylinder and press **ENTER**; it will be subtracted from the hollow cylinder as shown below.

The Intersect tool

The **Intersect** [Intersect] tool is used to create a composite solid by finding common volume shared by the selected objects.

- Start a new file.
- Set the view orientation to **Front** and create the sketch as shown below.

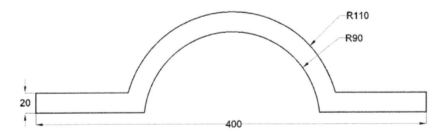

- Use the **Presspull** tool and extrude the sketch upto 150 mm distance.

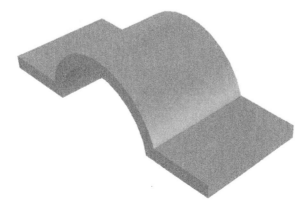

- Set the view orientation to Top and create the sketch as shown below.

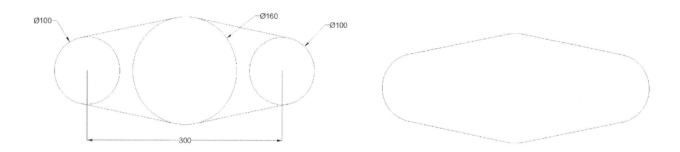

- Use the **Presspull** tool and extrude the view upto **200** mm height as shown below.

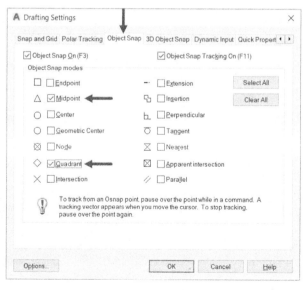

- Change the View style to **Wireframe**.
- Deactivate the **3D Object Snap** option on the status bar, as showns.

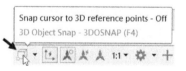

- Type **DS** in the command line and press **ENTER**; the **Drafting Settings** dialog box appears.
- Click the **Object Snap** tab and **Clear All** the **Object Snap** modes.
- Now, select the **Quadrant** and **Midpoint** options, as shown. Click **OK**.
- Type **AL** in the command line and press **ENTER**.
- Select the second extrusion and press **ENTER**; the message, "**Specify first source point:**" appears.
- Select the point on the source object as shown below; the message, "**Specify first destination point:**" appears.
- Select the point on the destination object as shown below; the message, "**Specify second source point:**" appears.

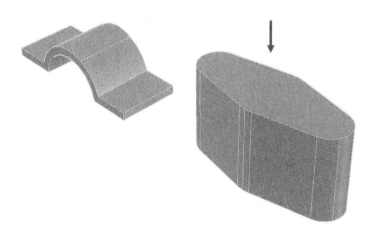

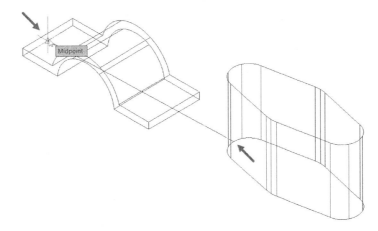

- Select another point on the source object, as shown below; the message, "Specify second destination point:" appears.
- Select another point on the destination object, as shown below; the message, "Specify third source point or <continue>:" appears.
- Press **ENTER** to continue; the message, "Scale objects based on alignment points? [Yes No] <N>:" appears.
- Select the **NO** option; the two objects will be aligned.

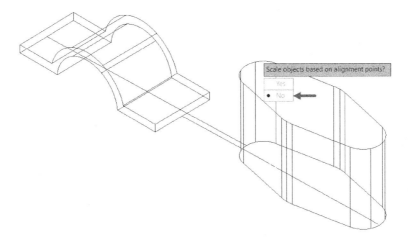

- Change the **View style** to **Shade of Gray**.

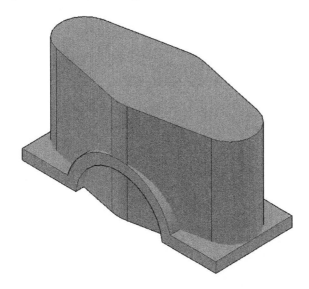

- Click **Solid > Boolean > Intersect** on the ribbon.
- Select the two objects and press **ENTER**; the intersection object will get created as shown below.

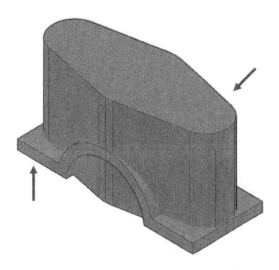
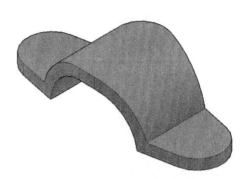

Using the Helix tool

The **Helix** tool is used to create a spiral or helix object. You can use this helix object as a path for a swept solid object.

Example:

- Start a new file.
- Expand the **Draw** panel in the **Home** tab and click the **Helix** button.
- Type **0, 0** as the center point of the helix and press **ENTER**; the message, "**Specify base radius or [Diameter]:**" appears in the command line.
- Type **60** and press **ENTER**; the message, "**Specify top radius or [Diameter] <50.0000>:**" appears.
- Type **0** and press **ENTER**; the message, "**Specify helix height or [Axis endpoint Turns turn Height tWist] <1.0000>:**" appears.
- Select the **Turns** option from the command line.
- Type **10** as number of turns and press **ENTER**; the message, "**Specify helix height or [Axis endpoint Turns turn Height tWist] <1.0000>:**" appears.
- Type **0** as the height and press **ENTER**; the spiral curve will be created as shown in figure.

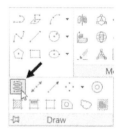

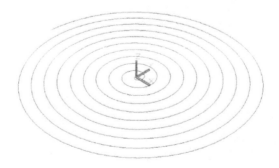

Example:

- Start a new file.
- Type **HELIX** in the command line and press **ENTER**.
- Type **0,0** as the center point of the helix.

- Type **60** as the base radius and press **ENTER**.
- Press **ENTER** to accept **60** as the top radius.
- Select the **turn Height** option from the command line.
- Type **30** as the turn height (pitch) and press **ENTER**.
- Type **300** as the total height of the helix and press **ENTER**; the helix will be created as shown in figure.

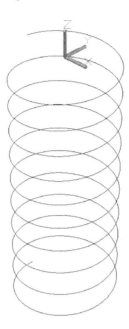

Questions:

1. Which tool is used to create a 3D wall?
2. Where is **Presspull** tool available on the Ribbon?
3. Which tool is used to join two or more solids together into a single solid?
4. Which tool is used to subtract one or more solid objects from another object
5. Which tool is used to create a composite solid by finding common volume shared by the selected objects?

Exercises

Exercise 1:

Create 3D models using the drawing views and dimensions.

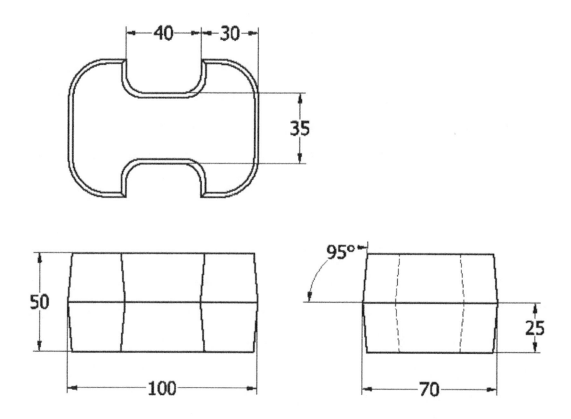

Exercise 2:

Create 3D models using the drawing views and dimensions.

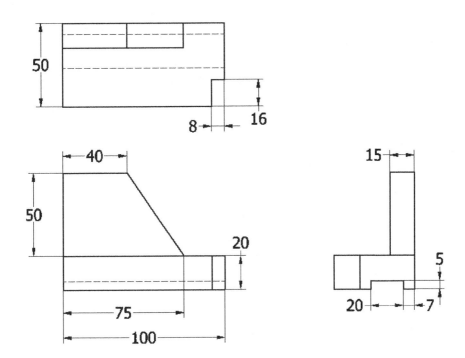

Exercise 3:

Create 3D models using the drawing views and dimensions.

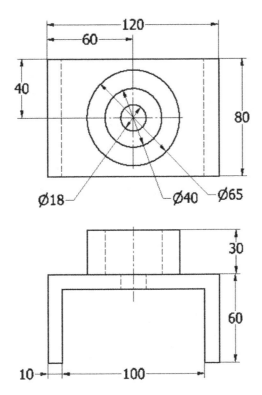

Chapter 13: Solid Editing & Generating 2D Views

In this chapter, you will learn to do the following:

- ❖ **Move objects**
- ❖ **Create 3D Arrays**
- ❖ **Mirror objects in 3D spaces**
- ❖ **Fillet edges**
- ❖ **Taper faces of the solid object**
- ❖ **Offset faces**
- ❖ **Rotate objects**
- ❖ **Create 3D Polylines**
- ❖ **Shell objects**
- ❖ **Chamfer edges**
- ❖ **Create Live sections**
- ❖ **Generate 2D views of a 3D model**
- ❖ **Create section and detailed views**

Introduction

In the previous chapter, you have learnt to create simple solid objects. Now, you will learn to use solid editing tools to create complex models. You will also learn to generate orthographic views of 3D models.

Using the Move tool

The **Move** tool that you used in 2D drawings can also be used in 3D modeling. You can change the position of an object using the **Move** tool. The application of this tool in 3D modeling is discussed next.

Example:
- Start a new file in the **3D Modeling** workspace.
- Select **Front** from the **3D Navigation** drop-down of the **View** panel.
- Create the sketch on the front view and presspull it upto 120 mm distance.

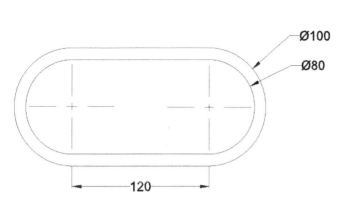

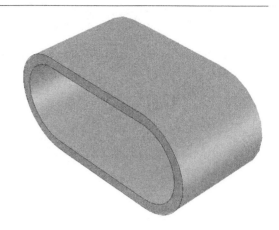

- Create a cylinder of **30** mm diameter and **30** mm height.

- Type **M** in the command line and press **ENTER**; the **Move** tool is invoked.
- Select the cylinder and press **ENTER**.
- Select the center point of the cylinder to define the base point, as shown.
- Select the end point of the base object; the cylinder will be aligned to it, as shown.

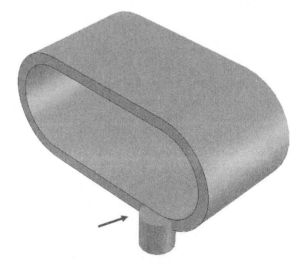

Using the 3D Move tool

The **3D Move** tool is similar to the **Move** tool. You can use this tool to move objects in 3D space. By default, the **3D Move** tool is activated and the **Move gizmo** is displayed when you select an object. You can use the **Move gizmo** to move the object along a particular axis.

- Select the cylinder, the **Move gizmo** will be displayed on it.
- Select the X-axis (Red arrow) of the gizmo and move the cursor backwards.
- Type **20** and press **ENTER**; the cylinder will be moved through **20** mm distance along the X-axis.

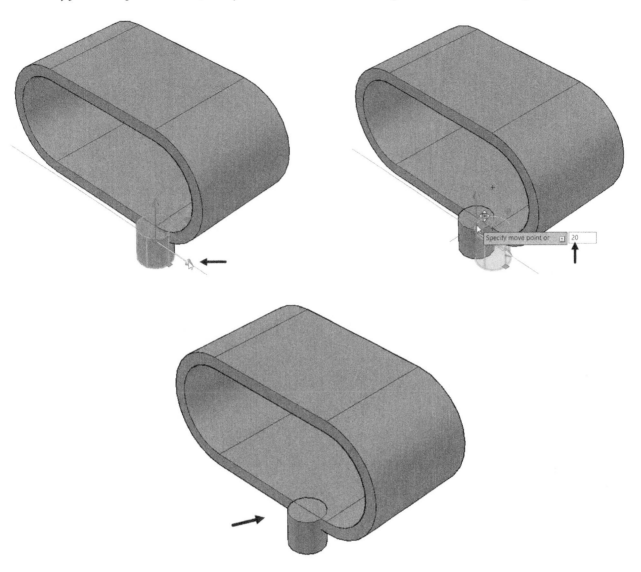

- Similarly, select the Y-axis (Green arrow) of the gizmo and move the cursor toward right.
- Type **20** and press **ENTER**; the cylinder will be moved through **20** mm distance along the Y-axis.

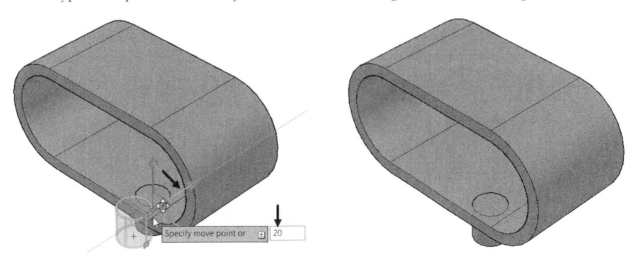

Using the 3D Array tool

The **3D Array** tool is used to create Rectangular and polar arrays. You can create a rectangular array by specifying the item count and distance along the X, Y and Z directions. For creating the 3D polar array, you need to select any 3D axis to rotate about.

Example 1 (Rectangular Array)

- Type **3DARRAY** in the command line and press **ENTER**.
- Select the cylinder from the model and press **ENTER**; the message, "**Enter the type of array [Rectangular Polar] <R>:**" appears in the command line.
- Select the **Rectangular** option from the command line; the message, "**Enter the number of rows (---) <1>:**" appears.
- Type **2** and press **ENTER**; the message, "**Enter the number of columns (| | |) <1>:**" appears.
- Type **2** and press **ENTER**; the message, "**Enter the number of levels (...) <1>:**" appears.
- Type **2** and press **ENTER**; the message, "**Specify the distance between rows (---):**" appears.
- Type **60** and press **ENTER**; the message, "**Specify the distance between columns (| | |):**" appears.
- Type **-80** and press **ENTER**; the message, "**Specify the distance between levels (...):**" appears.
- Type **90** and press **ENTER**; the rectangular array will be created as shown below.

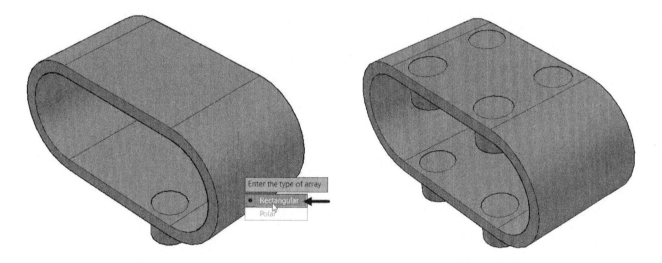

For better visibility, rotate the model, as shown.

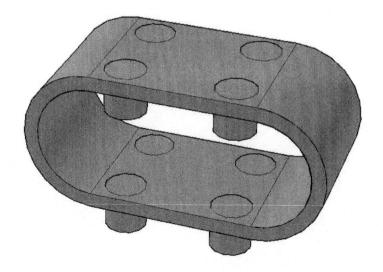

- Type **SU** in the command line and press **ENTER**; the **Subtract** tool will be invoked.
- Select the base object and press **ENTER**; the message, "**Select solids, surfaces, and regions to subtract**" appears.
- All the cylinders and press **ENTER**; holes will be created on the model.

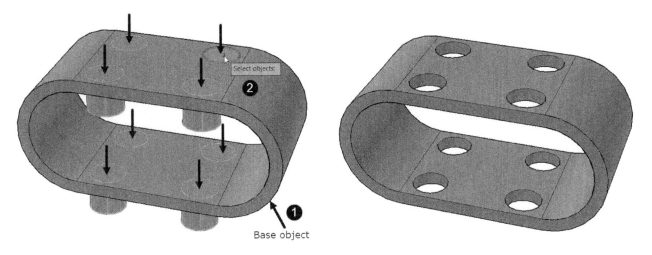

Base object

Using the 3D Align tool

The **3D Align** tool is used to align one solid with another. It translates and rotates the object to align with the destination object. You need to select three points on the source object and destination object to align them together. An example of **3D Align** tool is given next.

Example:

- Start AutoCAD in **3D Modeling** workspace.
- Select **Front** from the **3D Navigation** drop-down in the **View** panel. Create the solid object as shown below. The extrusion distance is **50** mm.

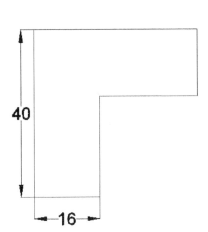

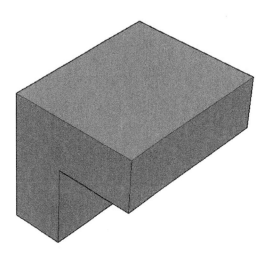

- Select **Front** from the **3D Navigation** drop-down in the **View** panel. Draw the sketch as shown below and extrude it upto **16** mm using the **Presspull** tool.

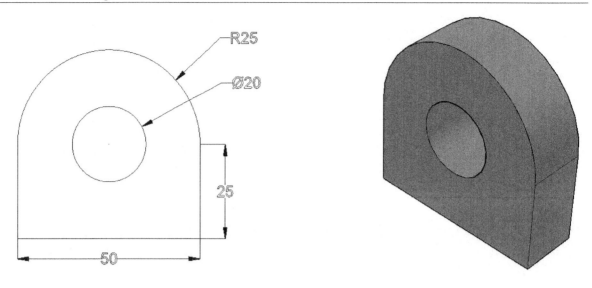

- Deactivate the **3D Object Snap** button on the status bar.
- Type **DS** in the command line and press **ENTER**; the **Drafting Settings** dialog box appears.
- Click the **Object Snap** tab and **Clear All** the **Object Snap** modes.
- Now, select the **Endpoint** checkbox and click **OK**.

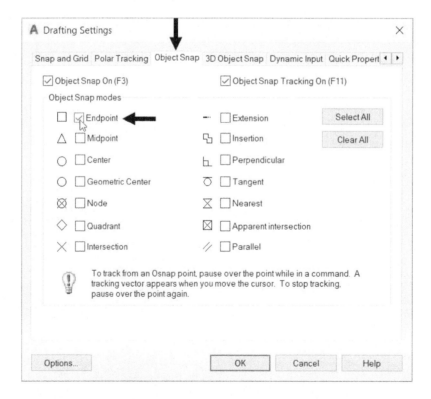

Alternatively, you can activate the **OSNAP** (Object Snap) from the status bar, as shown. And, you can select/deselect the required **Object Snap** modes from the shortcut menu displayed after clicking on the down-arrow with it, as shown.

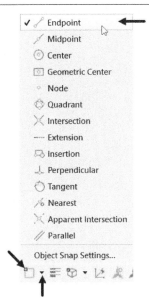

- Click **Home > Modify > 3D Align** on the ribbon.

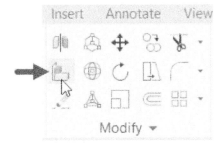

- Select the second solid object from the drawing window and press **ENTER**; the message, "**Specify base point or [Copy]:**" appears in the command line.
- Select the **Copy** option from the command line.
- Select three end points on the source object as shown below.

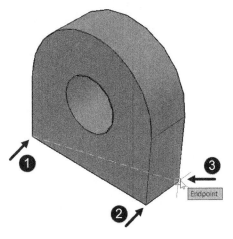

After selecting three end points, the copy of the selected object gets attached with the cursor.

- Select three end points on the destination object as shown below; a copy of the source object will be aligned to the destination object.

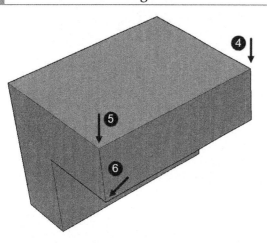

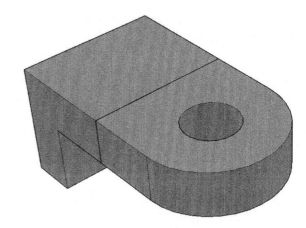

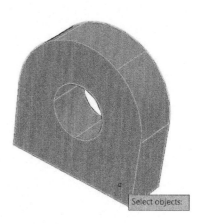

- Activate the **Ortho Mode** button on the status bar.
- Type **3DALIGN** in the command line and press **ENTER**.
- Select the object which you have copied and aligned in the previous step. Press **ENTER** to accept the selection.
- Select the base point on the object as shown below; the message, "**Specify second point or [Continue] <C>:**" appears in the command line.
- Select the **Continue** option from the command line; the message, "**Specify first destination point:**" appears in the command line.
- Select the endpoint on the destination object as shown below.

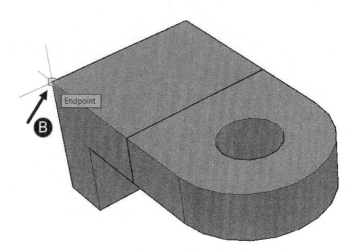

- Move the cursor along the X-direction and select the endpoint as shown in figure; the message, "**Specify third destination point or [eXit] <X>:**" appears in the command line.
- Select the **eXit** option from the command line; the source object will be aligned as shown below.

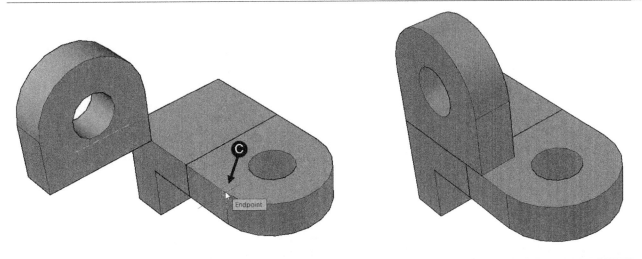

Using the 3D Mirror tool

The **3D Mirror** ![icon] tool is similar to the **Mirror** tool. Using the **Mirror** tool, you can create mirrored replica of an object in a 2D drawing. The objects are mirrored about an axis lying on the XY plane. But, with the **3D Mirror** tool, you need to define a plane about which the object will be mirrored. The **3D Mirror** tool provides many options to define the mirror plane.

- Click **Home > Modify > 3D Mirror** on the ribbon.

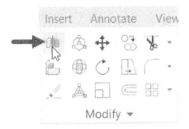

- Select the object to be mirror from the model and press **ENTER**; the message, "**Specify first point of mirror plane (3 points)**" appears above the command line.

  The **3points** option is selected by default to create the mirror plane. You need to specify three points to create the mirror plane. The mirror plane will pass through the selected points.

- Select the first and second point of the mirror plane as shown below.

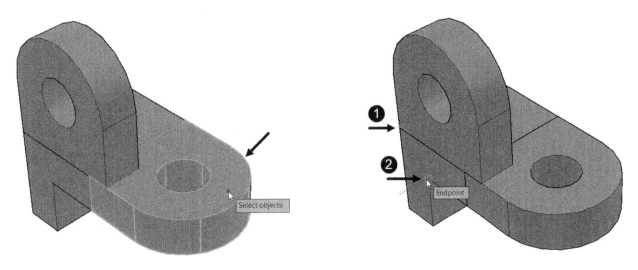

- Click the **Orbit** button on the **Navigation Bar** and rotate the model as shown below.

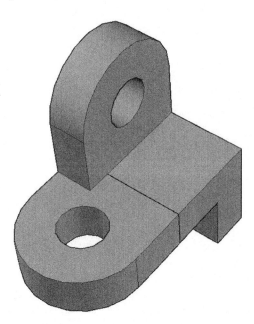

- Right-click and select **Exit** from the shortcut menu.
- Select the third point to define the mirror plane; the message, "**Delete source objects? [Yes No] <N>:**" appears in the command line.
- Select the **No** option from the command line; the object will be mirrored.

  Alternatively, you can select the **No** option from the shortcut menu displayed after selecting the third point, as shown.

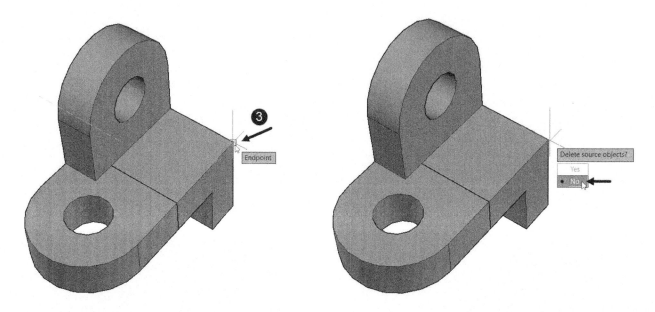

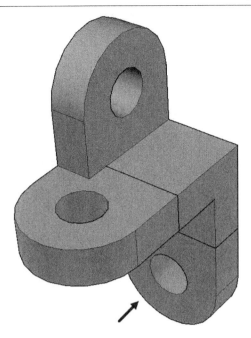

- Type **3DMIRROR** in the command line and press **ENTER**.
- Select the object to be mirror from the model and press **ENTER**.
- Select the **XY** option from the command line; the message, "**Specify point on XY plane <0,0,0>:**" appears in the command line.

  The **XY** option creates plane parallel to the XY plane. You need to specify a point at which the plane parallel to the XY plane will be created.

- Select the center point of the horizontal hole to define the mirror plane; the message, "**Delete source objects? [Yes No] <N>:**" appears in the command line.

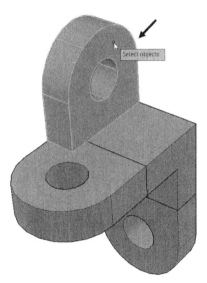

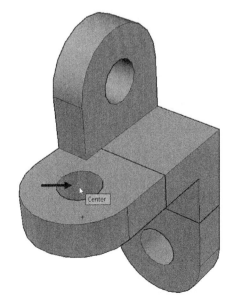

- Select the **No** option; the object will be mirrored as shown below.

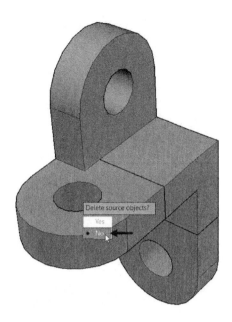
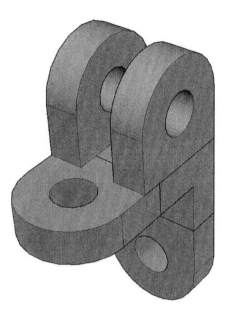

- Click the **Union** button on the **Solid Editing** panel and select all the object of the model.
- Press **ENTER**; the objects will be combined into a single object, as shown.
- Change the view to **SE Isometric**.

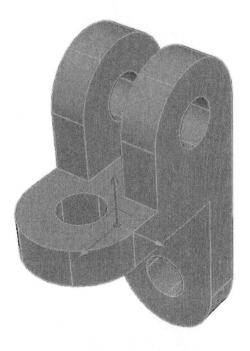
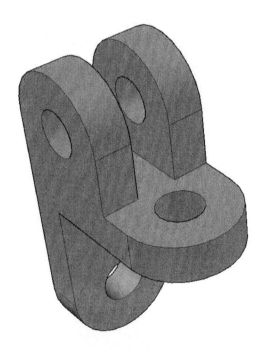

Using the Fillet Edge tool

The **Fillet Edge** tool is used to create rounds (convex corners) or fillets (concave corners) on solid objects, just as in 2D drawings. When you create a fillet or round, a cylinder is created automatically and the Boolean operation is performed to subtract or add it to the solid object.

- Click **Solid > Solid Editing > Fillet Edge** on the ribbon (or) type **FILLETEDGE** in the command line and press ENTER; the message, "Select an edge or [Chain Loop Radius]:"

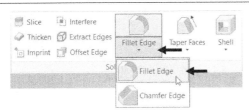

- Select the **Chain** option from the command line; the message, "**Select an edge chain or [Edge Radius]:**" appears.
- Select the edges from the model, as shown below; you will notice that a chain of edges is selected.

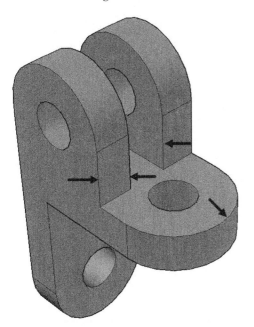

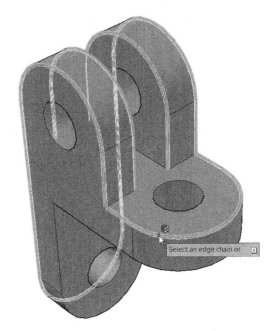

- Select the **Radius** option from the command line; the message, "**Enter fillet radius or [Expression] <1.0000>:**" appears.
- Type **2** in the command line and press **ENTER**.
- Press **ENTER**; the message, "**Press Enter to accept the fillet or [Radius]:**" appears. Also, a grip displayed on the fillets. You can use this grip to dynamically change the fillet radius.

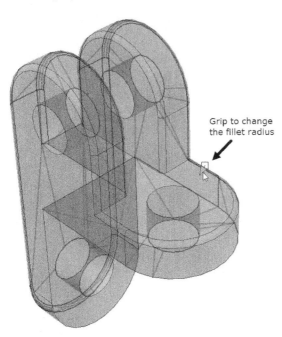

Grip to change the fillet radius

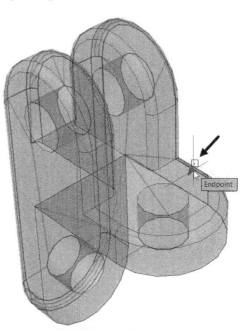

Endpoint

- Press **ENTER** to create rounds as shown in figure.

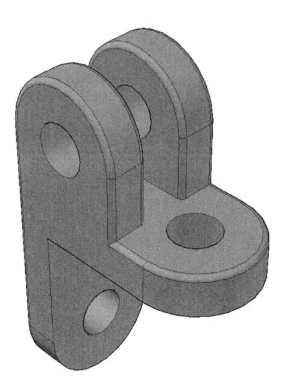

- Click the **Fillet Edge** button from the **Solid Editing** panel.
- Select the **Loop** option from the command line and select the edge from the model, as shown in figure; the edges on the front face of the model are highlighted. Also, the message, "**Enter an option [Accept Next] <Accept>:**" appears in the command line.
- Select the **Next** option from the command line; the edges on the side face will be highlighted.

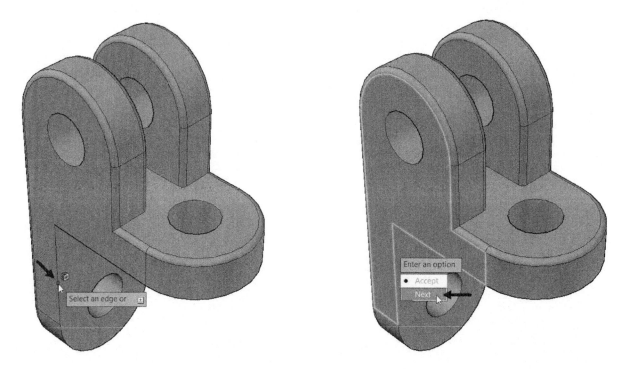

- Select the **Accept** button; rounds and fillets are displayed on the side face.

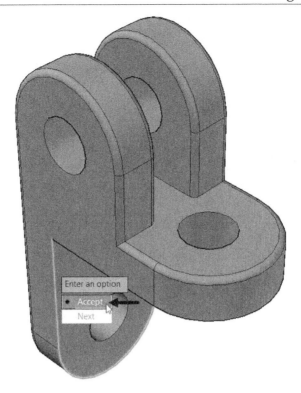

- Similarly, select the round edge as shown in figure and select the **Next** option from the command line; the edges on the bottom face of the model will be highlighted.
- Click the **Orbit** button on the **Navigation Bar** and rotate the model.
- Select the **Accept** option to view rounds and fillets on the bottom face.

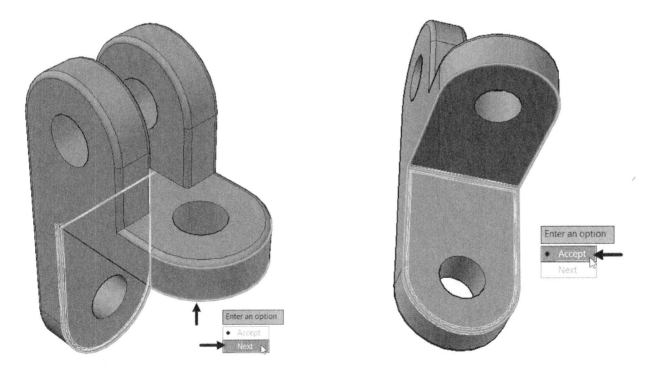

- Select the **Radius** option and type **2**. Press **ENTER** to accept.
- Press **ENTER** twice to create rounds as shown in figure.

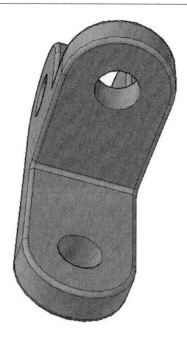

- Similarly, create fillets on remaining edges by using the **Chain** option.

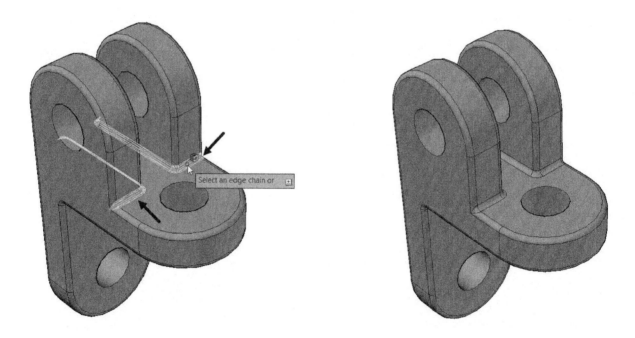

- Save and close the file.

Using the Taper Faces tool

The **Taper Faces** tool is used to taper faces. You can use this tool to change the angle of planar or curved faces.

Example:

In this example, you will create a polysolid and taper the outer face.

- Start a new AutoCAD file.
- Select **Front** from the **3D Navigation** drop-down on the **Views** panel.

- Create a solid model with the dimensions as shown with model.
- Click **Solid > Solid Editing > Taper Faces** on the ribbon.

- Select the outer cylindrical face of the polysolid and press **ENTER** to accept; the message, "**Specify the base point:**" appears in the command line.
- Press and hold the **SHIFT** key and right-click to display the shortcut menu. Select the **Center** option from the shortcut menu.

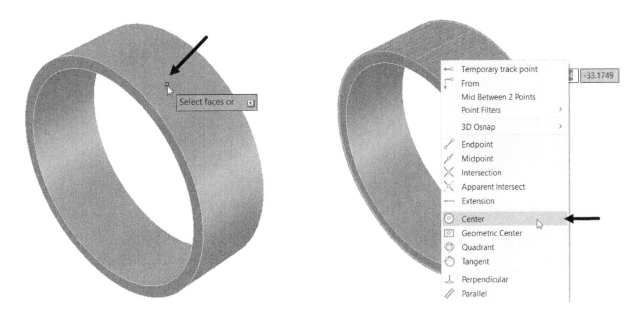

- Move the cursor over the circular edge on the front face; the center point of the circular edge will be highlighted.
- Select the center point of the circular edge.
- Move the cursor along the Z-direction and click to specify the axis of the taper; the message, "**Specify the taper angle:**" appears in the command line.

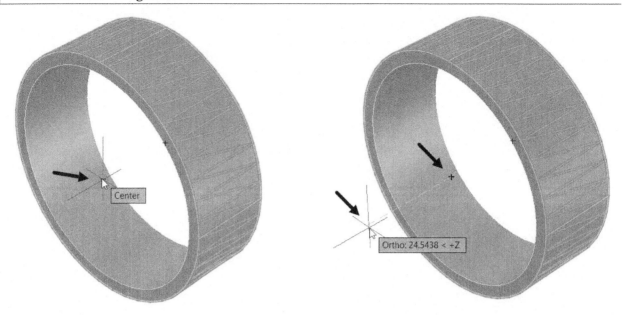

- Type **15** as the taper angle and press **ENTER**; the outer cylindrical face of the polysolid will be tapered as shown in figure.

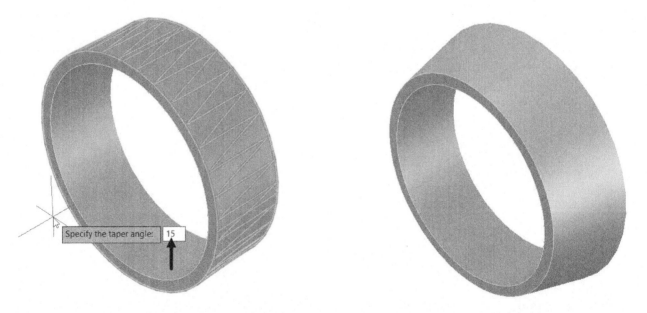

Using the Offset Faces tool

The **Offset Faces** tool is used to make parallel copy of faces of a 3D object.

- Click **Solid > Solid Editing > Faces drop-down > Offset Faces** on the ribbon.

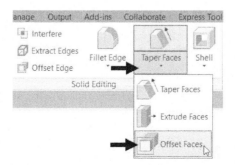

- Select the front face of the model and press **ENTER**; the message, "**Specify the offset distance:**" appears in the command line.
- Type **-10** in the command line and press **ENTER**; the face will be offset.

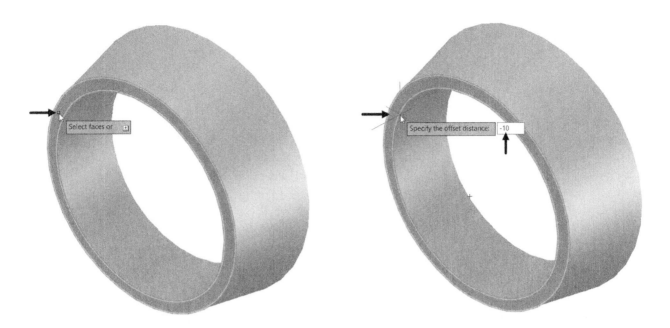

Press the **Esc** button to exit the "**Enter a face editing option**" shortcut menu displayed. For better visibility, delete the sketch lines.

- Create a cylinder of **12** mm diameter and **10** mm length at the center of the polysolid, as shown.

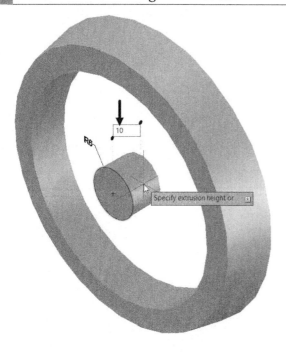

- Create a truncated cone with the following dimensions.

    Base radius: **4** mm

    Top radius: **2** mm

    Height: **30** mm

Using the 3D Rotate tool

The **3D Rotate** tool is used to rotate objects about an axis. You can define the axis of rotation by using the **Rotate Gizmo** tool. The **Rotate Gizmo** tool will be displayed when you invoke the **3D Rotate** tool and select an object.

- Click **Home > Modify > 3D Rotate** on the ribbon.

- Select the recently created truncated cone and press **ENTER**; the **Rotate Gizmo** tool will be displayed.
- Select the center point of the front face as the base point; the **Rotate Gizmo** tool will be moved to the selected point.

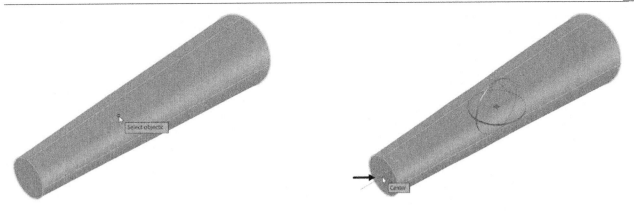

- Select the **Z**-axis (Blue ring) of the **Rotate Gizmo**; an axis line is displayed along the **Z**-axis.
- Type **270** as the rotation angle and press **ENTER**; the cone will be rotated by **270** degrees.

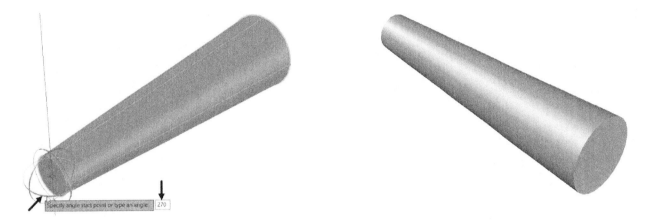

- Click the **Move** button on the **Modify** panel and select the cone. Press **ENTER** to accept.
- Select the base point and the destination point as shown below; the cone will be placed at the destination point.

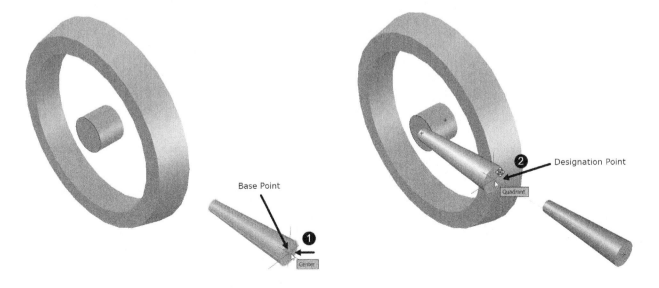

- Select the cone; the **Move Gizmo** tool will be displayed on it.
- Select the **Y**-axis (Green arrow) of the **Move Gizmo** tool and move the cursor toward right.
- Type **5** in the command line and press **ENTER**; the cone will be moved through **5** mm.

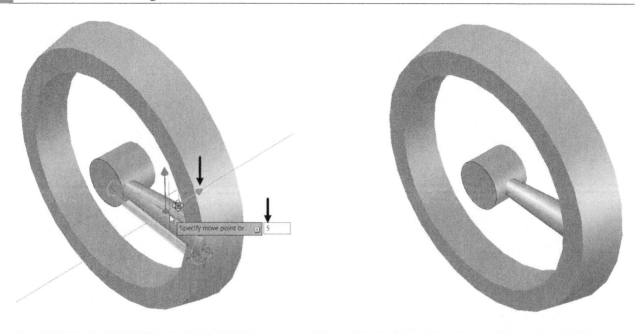

Using the 3D Polyline tool

The **3D Polyline** 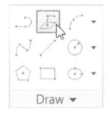 tool is similar to the **Polyline** tool, except that you can create a polyline by specifying coordinate points in three dimensions. Also, you can only create straight lines using this tool.

- Change the **Visual Style** of the model to **Wireframe**.
- Click **Home > Draw > 3D Polyline** 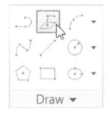 on the ribbon.

- Select the center point on the front face on the cylindrical object.
- Move the cursor toward right and select the center point on the back face of the cylindrical object.
- Press **ENTER**; the 3D polyline will be created.

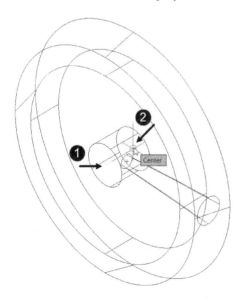

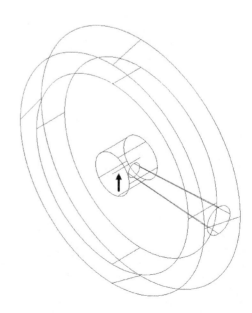

Creating a 3D Polar Array

You can create a 3D polar array by using the **Polar** option of the **3DARRAY** command. This option is similar to the 2D **Polar Array** tool. The only difference between these two tools is that you need to specify an axis of rotation in 3D polar array, whereas in 2D Polar array you need to specify an axis point. The axis of rotation in 3D polar array can be specified by selecting two points. This allows you to create a 3D polar array about any axis in the 3D workspace.

- Type **3A** in the command line and press **ENTER**.
- Select the truncated cone from the model and press **ENTER**.
- Select the **Polar** option from the "**Enter the type of array**" shortcut menu displayed; the message, "**Enter the number of items in the array:**" appears.
  You can also select the **Polar** option from the command line

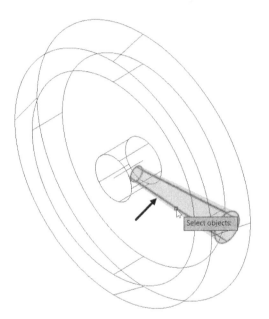
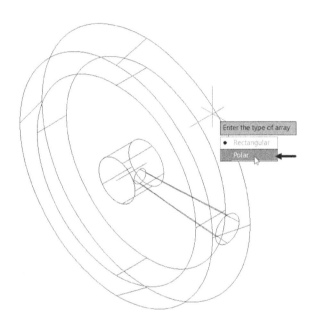

- Type **6** in the command line and press **ENTER**; the message, "**Specify the angle to fill (+=ccw, -=cw) <360>:**" appears in the command line.

> **Note**: You need to type **+** with the angle value to create the polar array in counter clockwise direction and type **–** with the angle value to create it in the clockwise direction.

- Press **ENTER** to accept **360** as the fill angle; the message, "**Rotate arrayed objects? [Yes No] <Y>:**" appears in the command line.
- Select the **Yes** option from the command line; the message, "**Specify center point of array:**" appears.
- Select the first and second points of the axis as shown in figure; the polar will be created.

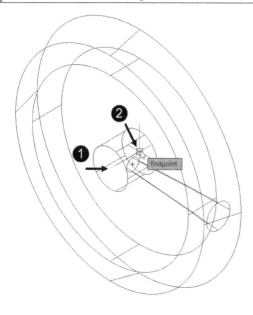
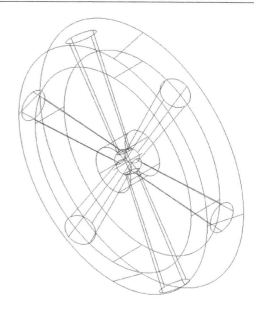

- Change the **Visual Style** to the **Shades of Grey**.
- Perform the **Union** operation to combine all the objects.

Using the Shell tool

The **Shell** [icon] tool is used to convert a solid object into a thin walled hollow object. You need to first select the object to be shelled, and then select the faces to be removed and enter the thickness of the walls.

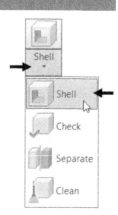

- Click **Solid > Solid Editing > Shell** [icon] on the ribbon.
- Select the solid model; the message, "**Remove faces or [Undo Add ALL]:**" appears.
- Select the front face of the cylindrical object.
- Press and hold the **SHIFT** key, and then press the middle mouse button on drag; the model will be rotated.
- Select the back face of the cylindrical object.

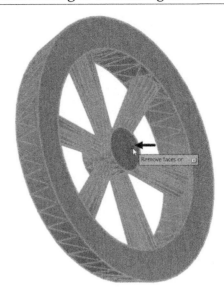

- Press **ENTER**; the message, "**Enter the shell offset distance:**" appears.
- Type **4** in the command line and press **ENTER**; the cylindrical object will be shelled.
- Select the **eXit** option from the command line.

Using the Chamfer Edge tool

The **Chamfer Edge** tool is used to bevel sharp edges of a solid object. When you chamfer an edge, a wedge is created automatically and the Boolean operation is performed to subtract it from the solid object.

- Click **Solid > Solid Editing > Chamfer Edge** on the ribbon, as shown.

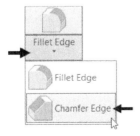

- Select the outer circular edge of the cylindrical object.

- Select the **Distance** option from the command line; the message, "**Specify Distance1 or [Expression] <1.0000>:**" appears.
- Type **2** in the command line and press **ENTER**; you will notice that preview of the chamfer changes. Also, the message, "**Specify Distance2 or [Expression] <1.0000>:**" appears in the command line.
- Type **1** in the command line and press **ENTER**.
- Press **ENTER** twice to the chamfer as shown in figure.

Using the Section Plane tool

The **Section Plane** tool is used to create a translucent cutting plane passing through a solid object to show the inside portion of it. This tool is very useful when the inside portion of the solid is not visible. You can move this cutting plane dynamically to view the inside portion at different locations of the solid.

- To create a section plane, click **Solid > Section > Section Plane** on the ribbon; the message, "**Select face or any point to locate section line or [Draw section Orthographic Type]:**" appears.
- Select the **Orthographic** option from the command line.
- Now select the **Right** option from the "**Align section to**" shortcut menu displayed to display the object with solid plane, as shown.

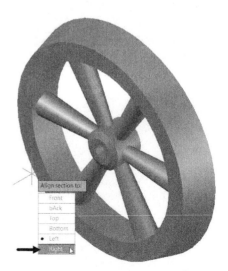

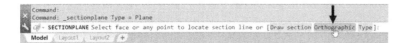

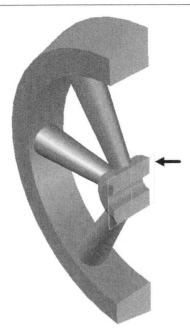

You can also create the section plane at a required angle by selecting the center point and defining   the second point at the required location, as shown.

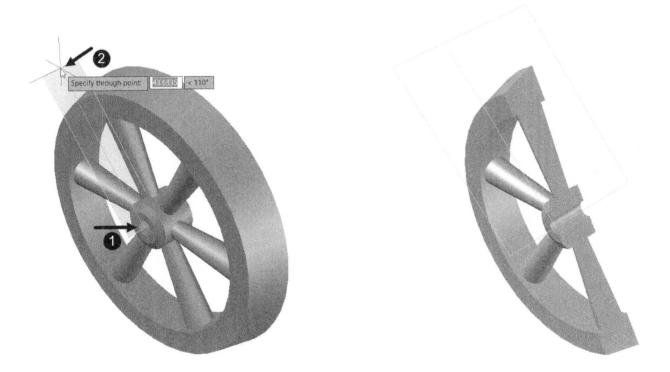

Using the Live Section tool

The **Live Section** [🗗 Live Section] tool is used to make one side of the section plane invisible. When you create a section plane by selecting plane, one side of the section plane will be invisible automatically. However, when you create a section plane by selecting points, you need to use the **Live Section** tool to make the one side invisible.

• Click **Solid > Section > Live Section** on the ribbon. Next, select the section plane; one side of the section plane will be hidden as shown in figure.

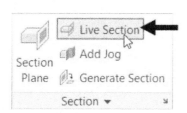

- Again, click the **Live Section** button from the **Section** panel and select the section plane; the hidden side will be retained.

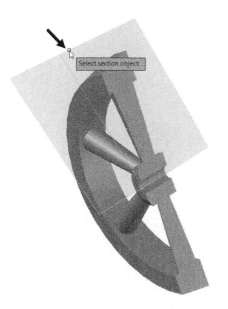

- Save the file as Example 3.

Creating Drawing Views

In Chapter 5, you have learned to create multi view drawings using the standard projection techniques. Now, you will learn to automatically generate views of a 3D model. The tools to generate drawing views are available in the **Layout** tab of the ribbon.

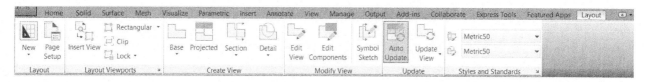

Setting the Drafting Standard

Before you start generating the drawing views of 3D model, you need to specify the 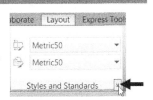 drafting standard. This defines the way the views will be generated. To specify the drafting standard, click **Layout > Styles and Standards > Drafting Standard (inclined arrow)** on the ribbon; the **Drafting Standard** dialog box appears.

- In the **Drafting Standard** dialog box, set the **Projection type** to **Third angle.**

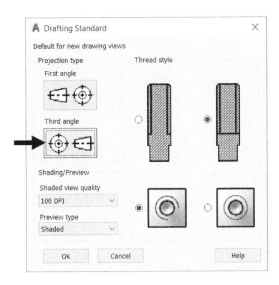

- Examine the other options in the dialog box, as they are self-explanatory.
- Click the **OK** button.

Creating a Base View

Base view will be the first view of the drawing. It can be any view (front, top, right, left, bottom, back) of the model. But commonly, the front or top views of the model are generated first.

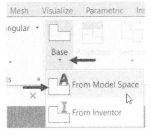

- Open the **Example 3.dwg**, if it is not already opened.
- To generate the base view of the model, click **Home > View > Base > From Model Space** on the ribbon; the message, "**Select objects or [Entire model] <Entire model>:**" appears in the command line.
- Select the **Entire model** option from the command line; the model in the model space will be selected and the message, "**Enter new or existing layout name to make current or [?] <Layout1>:**" appears in the command line.
- Press ENTER to select **Layout 1**; the base view will be attached to the cursor and the message, "**Specify location of base view or [Type sElect Orientation Hidden lines Scale Visibility] <Type>:**" appears in the command line. Also, the **Drawing View Creation** tab appears in the ribbon.
- Specify the location of the view in the paper space, as shown below.
- In the **Drawing View Creation** tab, set the **Orientation** to **Front**.
- Select the **Visible Lines** option from the **Hidden Lines** drop-down.
- Set the **Scale** in the **Appearance** panel to **1:40**.
- Click the **OK** button on the **Create** panel to create the base view; a projected view will be attached to the cursor and you will be asked to specify its location. You will learn to create projected views in the next section.

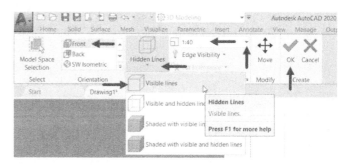

- Press **ENTER** to exit the command line.

Creating a Projected View

A projected view can be created from an existing view. It can be an orthographic view or isometric view generated by projecting from a base view or any other existing view.

- To create a projected view, click **Layout > Create View > Projected** on the ribbon, and then select the base view from the **Layout 1**; the projected view will be attached to the cursor.
- Move the cursor downward and specify the location of the projected view as shown below.

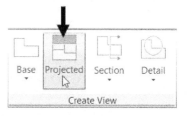

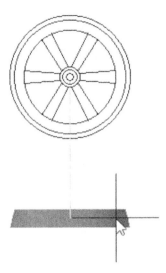

- Move the cursor diagonally toward top-right corner and place the isometric view as shown below.

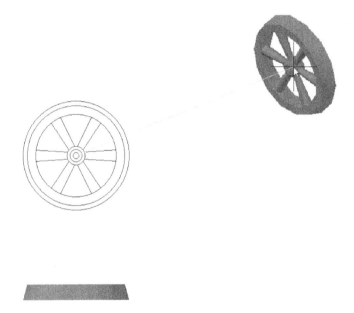

- Select the **eXit** option from the command line to exit the command.

Creating Section Views

In Chapter 8, you have learned to create section views manually. Now, you will learn to generate section views automatically from a 3D model. You can create different types of section views using the tools available in the **Section** drop-down in the **Create Views** panel.

Creating the Section View Style

Section View Style defines the display of the section view and the cutting plane. To create a section view style, click **Layout > Styles and Standards > Section View Style** on the ribbon; the **Section View Style Manager** dialog box appears. Click the **New** button in the **Section View Style Manager** dialog box; the **Create New Section View Style** dialog box appears. Type **Example** in the **New Style Name** box and click **Continue**; the **New Section View Style** dialog box appears. In this dialog box, click the **Cutting Plane** tab and select the **Show cutting plane lines** option, if it is not selected.

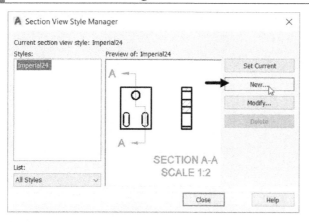

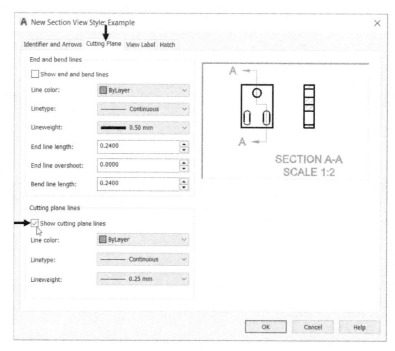

Click the **Hatch** tab and set the **Hatch Scale** to **0.5** and click **OK**. Click the **Set current** button on the **Section View Style Manager** dialog box and click **Close**.

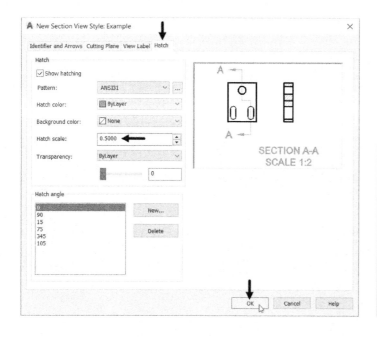

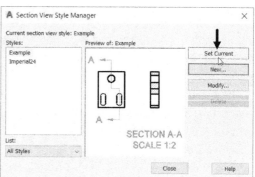

Creating a Full Section View

To create a full section view, click **Layout > Create Views > Section > Full** on the ribbon. Next, select the base view from the layout. After selecting the base view, you need to specify the start and end points of the cutting plane. Select the start point of the cutting plane by as shown below. Move the cursor vertically upward and specify the end point of the cutting plane.

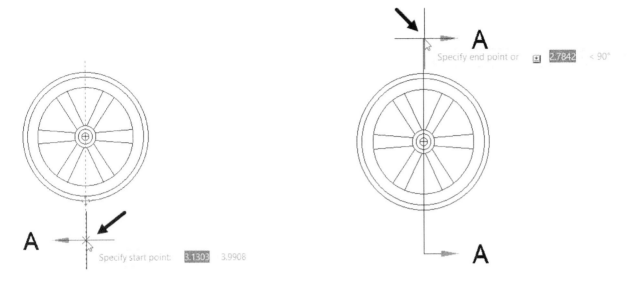

Move the cursor toward right and click to specify the location of the section view. Select the **eXit** option to create the section view.

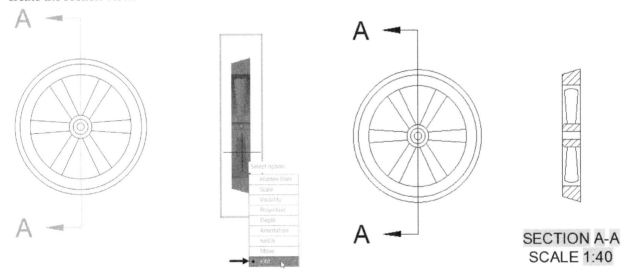

Creating a Detailed View

A detailed view is created to enlarge and view small portions of a drawing.

- To create a detailed view, click **Layout > Create Views > Detail > Circular** on the ribbon; the message, "**Select parent view**" appears in the command line.
- Select the section view from the layout; the message, "**Specify center point or [Hidden lines Scale Visibility Boundary model Edge Annotation] <Boundary>:**" appears in the command line.

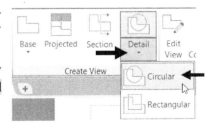

- Select a point on the section view, as shown below; the message, "**Specify size of boundary or [Rectangular Undo]:**" appears in the command line.
- Draw a circle similar to the one shown below.

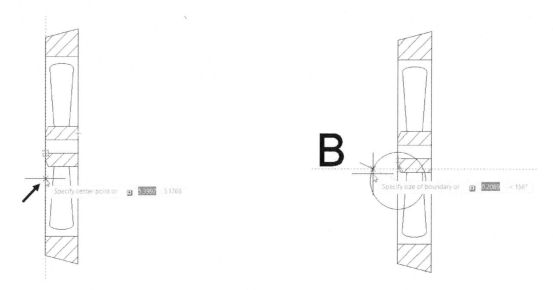

- Next, place the detail view on the lower right corner of the layout, as shown.

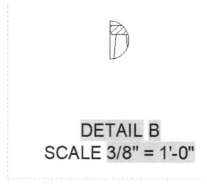

DETAIL B
SCALE 3/8" = 1'-0"

- Select the **Smooth with border** button on the **Model Edge** panel of the **Detail View Editor** tab.

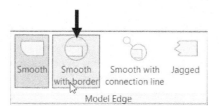

- Click **Detail View Editor > Edit > OK** on the ribbon; the detail view will be created.

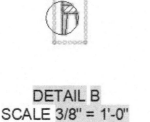

DETAIL B
SCALE 3/8" = 1'-0"

DETAIL B
SCALE 3/8" = 1'-0"

Questions:

1. Which tools is used to model a object in 3D space?
2. Which tool is used to align one solid with another?
3. Which tool is used to create fillets or rounds on the solid object?
4. Which tool is used to make parallel copy of faces of a 3D object
5. Which tool is used to convert a solid object into a thin walled hollow object.
6. Which tool is used to make one side of the section plane invisible.

Exercises

Exercise 1:

Create 3D models using the drawing views and dimensions.

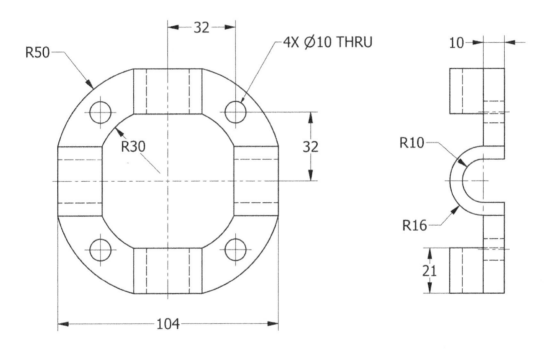

Exercise 2:

Create 3D models using the drawing views and dimensions.

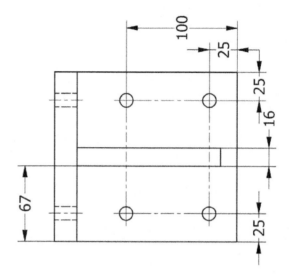

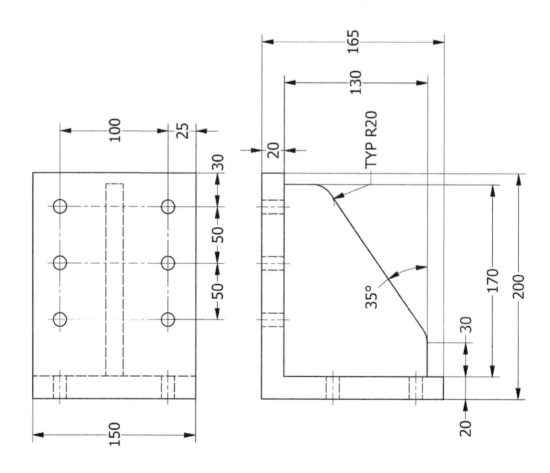

Exercise 3:

Create 3D models using the drawing views and dimensions.

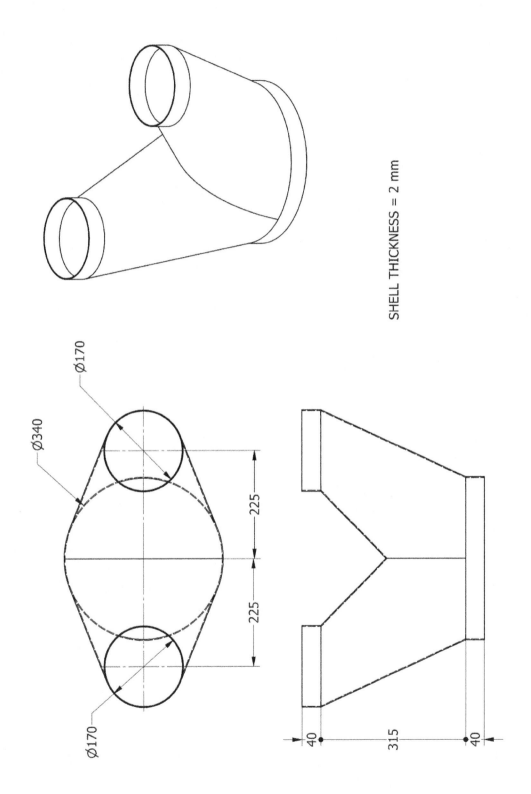

SHELL THICKNESS = 2 mm

Ø170

Ø340

Ø170

225

225

40

315

40

Exercise 4:

Create 3D models using the drawing views and dimensions.

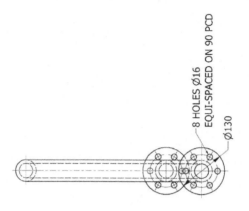

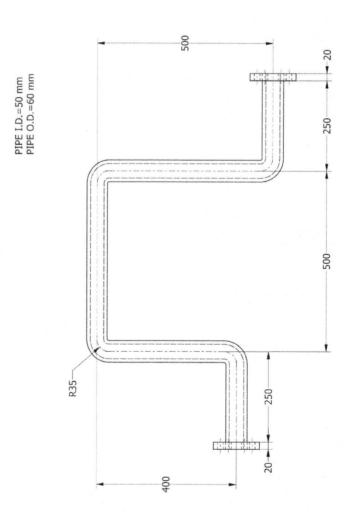

Index

Printed in Great Britain
by Amazon